A Guide to the Reading Workshop, Intermediate Grades

Lucy Calkins

Photography by Peter Cunningham

HEINEMANN ◆ PORTSMOUTH, NH

To Mary Ann Mustac, who makes my world go round, with thanks for grace under pressure, for the wisdom and power to say no to me, and for helping colleagues, students, and friends have access to me.

Heinemann
361 Hanover Street
Portsmouth, NH 03801–3912
www.heinemann.com

Offices and agents throughout the world

The author and publisher wish to thank those who have generously given permission to reprint borrowed material:

Charlotte's Web, by E.B. White. Copyright 1952 by E.B. White. Text copyright renewed 1980 by E.B. White. Used by permission of HarperCollins Publishers and ICM Partners. All rights reserved.

Cataloging-in-Publication data is on file with the Library of Congress.

ISBN-13: 978-0-325-09210-2

Series editorial team: Anna Gratz Cockerille, Karen Kawaguchi, Tracy Wells, Felicia O'Brien, Debra Doorack, Jean Lawler, Marielle Palombo, and Sue Paro
Production: Elizabeth Valway, David Stirling, and Abigail Heim
Cover and interior designs: Jenny Jensen Greenleaf
Photography: Peter Cunningham
Composition: Publishers' Design and Production Services, Inc.
Manufacturing: Steve Bernier

Printed in the United States of America on acid-free paper
21 20 19 18 17   EBM   1 2 3 4 5

Contents

Acknowledgments

THIS IS THE LAST Acknowledgements that I'll be writing for this series—this book goes to press just under the wire—and so it is fitting that I thank my parents, Evan and Virginia Calkins, for all that I am. At the ages of 94 and 92, Mom and Dad continue to lead our clan of 9 kids and 36 grandchildren. They have just bought a new rooster for their flock and hosted a barn dance for the community, and their days continue to be filled with efforts to help neighbors in need, to steer the Buffalo medical establishment toward more community involvement, to remind the extended family of all that matters most: music, politics, dogs, service, friends, adventures, and each other.

I'm grateful also to my husband, John Skorpen, who couldn't do more to make my life possible. Having him at the center makes all the rest possible and happy. Miles and Evan Skorpen, my two sons, have grown up to be optimistic, energetic, gracious, productive young men, and my pride in them knows no bounds.

At the Project, my closest colleagues include the other leaders at the Project: Kathleen Tolan, Laurie Pessah, Mary Ehrenworth, and Amanda Hartman. They're at the heart of it all, and the Project bears their signature. They, and Mary Ann Mustac, make it all possible. I'm also grateful to my colleagues in the Literacy Specialist Program—to Marjorie Siegel, Maria Paula Ghiso, Ellen Ellis, and Rebecca Bellingham. What a fabulous gift it is to support our students together.

All that I know about writing has been influenced by a few mentors who will always mean the world to me. I am forever grateful, especially, to Pulitzer Prize–winning writer Don Murray and to Kate Montgomery, who was my editor for years, and led the effort to create the units of study line of work.

Finally, thanks to the entire Heinemann team, and especially to Abby Heim who is at the helm of it all.

A Note to My Readers

IN A MOMENT, I'm going to ask that you step with me into this series, into this effort to give young people the richest possible education as readers. I couldn't be more delighted to be sharing this work and the sister effort to support units of study in writing. The two series—Units of Study for Teaching Reading and Units of Study in Opinion, Information, and Narrative Writing—represent the culmination of decades of research and collaboration. They grow from think tanks, pilot teaching, and staff development. The effort represents the work of dedicated colleagues and of countless skilled teachers and visionary school leaders from around the world. I know that as you dive into these resources, you'll find that they help you teach with greater efficiency and power.

Nonetheless, I want to ask you to stop for a moment before you read on. Before you turn to the ins and outs of curriculum, to the anchor charts and the comprehension strategies and the stories of young people, pause for a moment to picture the face of a young person you teach. Someone you know well. When you see her, stopping by your classroom, sitting backward on a chair, leaning in to talk, does it make you smile? When you picture him, walking slowly away with his backpack slumped over his shoulder, do you want to reach out, maybe call him back? And when you think of all of them, their quirky, tousled, grubby, intent faces looking up at you, I know you feel the tug in your chest, that tug of feeling so responsible for them all, for how they'll succeed in school and beyond. We feel it deeply. And this is what I want to say: *that* is the core of all that matters in teaching. Without that core, the greatest curriculum in the world is only paper and a little dry ink.

My hope is that these resources in Units of Study for Teaching Reading save you hundreds of hours of planning. I hope that the time you save can be spent studying student work and working with individuals and small groups of kids—and with your colleagues. I hope that you'll find that with less planning time, you are still able to be *better* planned—prepared for the arc of the whole workshop, not just the minilesson, prepared for assessment-based small groups and conferences, as well as whole-class units. I hope that you'll find that the teaching tools—the rubrics and exemplars, the anchor charts, the performance assessments, the progressions—function like a big toolkit, the kind a plumber or a carpenter brings to any job, the sort of toolkit that allows you to know that everything is there inside, ready to be pulled out at a moment's notice.

I do have some suggestions for how to get started. I suggest that rather than trying to read the first unit of study book cover to cover, you read just the "An Orientation to the Unit" portion of that unit book—it is just a few pages—and the first session. Then glance at a learning progression in *Reading Pathways: Grades 3–5*. Because your first unit will be a fiction unit, look at the Narrative Reading Learning Progression (knowing the informational one parallels it). For now, read just one strand (perhaps "Inferring About Characters and Other Story Elements" or "Determining Themes/Cohesion"). Read it from grade 2 on up and think about the journey that your students will be traveling. Then glance at the *If . . . Then . . . Curriculum: Assessment-Based Instruction, Grades 3–5* book, and note the overview section written for teachers at your grade level. If you are uneasy about something, chances are good that I address that area of unease in that section. For example, if your kids are behind, if colleagues the year before didn't teach the preparatory units, if you worry about this or that high-stakes test, you'll see that I address those worries in the *If . . . Then . . .* chapter written for your grade level. Take a quick look at the Online Resources so that you don't reinvent the wheel. Then I recommend that you skim a few chapters of this book, *A Guide to the Reading Workshop*. If you are new to both a reading and a writing workshop, you'll want to read at least Chapter 4 (The Big Picture of a Reading Workshop), Chapter 5 (The Architecture [and the Principles] that Inform Minilessons), and Chapter 6 (Management Systems) before getting started. If you have read and taught *A Guide to the Common Core Writing Workshop*, you can rely on your knowledge of workshop teaching in general and turn directly to Chapter 8 (Small-Group Work: Developing a Richer Repertoire of Methods). This guide will illuminate generic methods more than grade-specific curriculum, but I promise you that when you pay attention to your methods, you'll find that you are more efficient and prepared, and your students' learning will accelerate.

Teaching is hard work, and this series makes no bones about that. People often say to me, "Your Units of Study series is sure not for the weak of heart— but yes, it absolutely yields dramatic results." The beautiful thing is that those results are so gratifying that they tap an incredible energy source in you and your colleagues. Chances are good that you'll feel a new lift to your step, a new sense of collegiality across your grade level, a new ambitiousness to your teaching.

Chapter 1

The Need for This Series

TO KNOW WHAT YOU NEED TO TEACH, you need to picture what you want for your readers. My hunch is that you want your children to become flexible, resilient readers who read for pleasure as well as for academic purposes. You want them to know when they are having difficulty and to have a toolkit of strategies for dealing with difficulty. You want them to be knowledgeable on a range of subjects from their nonfiction reading and empathetic and nuanced in their interactions with others from their reading of literature. You want them to read broadly and deeply, alert to the intricacies of texts and to the power of language. You want them to carry with them, for their entire lives, the invisible knapsack of privilege that is literacy. You want the choices they make—for which courses to take in college, for which careers to pursue—not to be mitigated by their reading levels, but for them to feel confident that they can tackle any reading task with vigor and expertise.

Yet when your children come to you at the start of the school year, they don't necessarily come cherishing written language. You see this in the books strewn under the coatrack, grimy with footprints, and in those snarled into the darkest recesses of children's desks. You see this in the child who tells you, "I read sixty-two pages last night." Impressed, you ask, "What happened in the story?" and he scrunches up his face and looks up at the ceiling, saying "Uhhhh . . ." as he wracks his mind for some recollection of what he has read. Nothing surfaces, but he hastens to reassure you, "I read the whole thing—honest! I just can't remember it, that's all." He's not your only Teflon® reader. You watch one child reach the final page of *Number the Stars*, and you're ready for her to look up, eyes brimming; you know the passage by heart and know how impossibly hard it is to take in. You watch her eyes move down the page to the last paragraph, then the last line. Your eyes well, just thinking about what she will find there. She reads. For a second, she pauses. Then she snaps the book shut, slings it toward you, and says, "I'm done. What should I do now?"

How do you say to her, "You should live differently for the rest of your life because you've read that book"?

How do we teach reading—the soul-searching kind of reading, the reading that makes you feel as if you are breathing some new kind of air? How do we teach the kind of reading that makes you walk through the world differently because a lightbulb is no longer just a lightbulb—it's filaments and electricity and the Industrial Revolution and all the rest that tumbles around that? How do we teach the power of reading—the way it allows us to see under the words, between the words, beyond words? How do we teach the intimacy of reading—of belonging to a community that has a shared vocabulary, shared stories, shared petitions and projects?

The irony is that often when it comes to teaching reading, we convince ourselves that the subject is so important that we outsource it to large for-profit companies that don't know us, don't know our kids, and don't necessarily even know how to teach well. Because we're sure that teaching children to read is the single most important thing we do, we want someone else to make the decisions about how our teaching will go. "Tell me what to do, and I'll do it," we say. And then, when the core reading program channels 19,000 little things toward us, we don't stop long enough to think, "Does this match what I know from my own experiences learning to read? Does this reflect what the research shows kids need? Does this draw upon what I've learned from all my years of teaching?" We're too intent on racing through those 19,000 steps, on doling out, checking off, drilling, monitoring, and on and on.

We need to catch our breath and to pause long enough to think, to remember, to research, and to make informed choices. Racing faster and covering more is not the answer. Years ago, when I wrote the first chapter of *The Art of Teaching Writing*, I wrote some words that have become foundational to everything I do.

> If our teaching is going to be an art, we need to remember that artistry does not come from the sheer quantity of red and yellow paint or from the amount of clay or marble, but from the organizing vision that shapes the use of those materials. It's not the number of good ideas that will turn our teaching into something significant and beautiful, but the selection, balance, coherence, and design of those ideas. (Calkins 1994)

Perhaps the place to start is by thinking about our own lives as readers for a minute. (Don't worry—it will take just a minute.) Think for just a minute about the times in your life when reading was the pits, and then think about times when reading was the best thing in the world. What were the conditions that made reading so bad? What made it so good?

I'm pretty sure that you are saying that reading works for you when you choose books that matter to you, when you have lots of time to actually eyes-on-print read, and when you can finish one chapter and, instead of answering twenty questions, read the next chapter. If you've had the exquisite pleasure of sharing reading—in a book club, a Bible study group, a women's group, a writing group, or in a friendship that includes books—then the social fabric of reading will be part of what makes reading work for you. And I'm pretty sure that when reading has been the pits for you, someone else told you what to read, what to think about, and what to do when you finished reading. You probably felt as if your every move was monitored and judged, making reading a performance for someone else.

How can it be that thousands and thousands of teachers, principals, and reading researchers are clear about the conditions that have made reading be the pits—the worst thing in the world, for us—and yet we allow a big publishing company to establish a gigantic system around the teaching of reading that results in us teaching in ways that exactly replicate the worst of what has been done to us? How can it be that half the teachers in America have been convinced to teach in ways that directly counter what we know kids need? Above all, how can this system perpetuate itself when it clearly hasn't worked, as Richard Allington predicted in *Big Brother and the National Reading Curriculum* (2002a)? The average college graduate in this country reads one book a year. The longer kids stay in school, the less they like to read.

These are important times in the teaching of reading, though. There's been a gigantic crack in the system. Judgment is no longer pending. The verdict is in. Not one of those core reading programs mandated under No Child Left Behind has been shown to work reliably. After reviewing the evidence that supports even programs that regularly proclaim themselves to be "research based," Richard Allington wrote, "There is a long-standing federal enthusiasm for packaged reading reform. Unfortunately, we have fifty years of research showing that packaged reading reforms simply do not seem reliable to improve student achievement" (2011, 16). He continues, saying, "None of the proven programs that generated so much excitement a decade ago has withstood the independent research review. None of the commercial reading series has either."

Meanwhile, there is an increasing sense of urgency in the air. Today's information age requires that young people develop literacy skills that are significantly higher than any that have ever been required of them—and this education needs to be for all students, not just for the elite. Consider this statistic—and it is but one of many that can take a person's breath away. Between 1997 and 2002, the amount of new information produced in the world was equal to the amount produced over the entire previous history of the world (Darling-Hammond et al. 2008). The amount of new technical information is being produced at such a rapidly increasing rate that it is predicted soon to double every seventy-two hours (Jukes and McCain 2002). Clearly, this is a time for ambitious reform.

As this nation wakes up to the fact that the education that millions of Americans received in the past simply isn't adequate for today, more and more school systems are taking a good look at the expensive core reading programs of the past, and they're thinking, "Could it be that the emperor has no clothes on?"

Study after study shows that globalization and new information technologies have made it especially urgent for schools to chart a new mission. In their important book, *Breakthrough*, Michael Fullan, Peter Hill, and Carmel Crévola (2006) point out that the old mission for schools was to provide universal access to basic education and then to provide a small elite with access to university education. The world has changed, however; whereas twenty years ago 95% of jobs were low-skilled, today those jobs constitute only 10% of our entire economy (Darling-Hammond et al. 2008). Children who leave the school system without strong literacy skills will no longer find a job waiting for them. "The new mission is to get all students to meet high standards of education and to provide them with a lifelong education that does not have built-in obsolescence of so much old-style curriculum but that equips them to be lifelong learners." Those words form the prelude of the book *Breakthrough* (Fullan et al. 2006), and they could be the prelude to this series as well. There's been a crack in the system, and light is shining through.

The problem and the opportunity coalesce. Now is the time for a new vision for reading instruction.

THE RELATIONSHIP BETWEEN THIS SERIES, THE COMMON CORE STATE STANDARDS, AND OTHER GLOBAL STANDARDS AND ASSESSMENTS

This curriculum does everything possible to ultimately bring kids to global standards, including International Baccalaureate, Advanced Placement, and the Common Core. We conceive of the curriculum as one which will send kids into AP and IB classes. It includes, though it is not limited to, skills that will be assessed on the high-stakes exams kids may take, such as the Partnership for Assessment of Readiness for College and Careers (PARCC) and the Smarter Balanced Assessment Consortium (SBAC).

As the series goes to press, we look beyond the Common Core for a few reasons. One is that the Common Core State Standards (CCSS) are not a curriculum. They are a series of benchmarks, and they don't include all the reading skills that children need to be engaged or successful. Another reason is that we've found that when you use an initiative such as the Common Core as the driving force for doing better work, that work might falter when the initiative itself is attacked. I've often said that if you are going to embrace the standards, embrace them as a mission, not as a mandate. That is, whether or not your state has adopted the CCSS, you will not want your teaching to be nothing more than a curriculum of preparation for those standards; you will want to teach toward something bigger and deeper and more personal. And yes, whether or not your state or country has adopted the CCSS, those standards will probably inform the vision that you and your colleagues value. But I urge you and your colleagues to clarify your own values, so you teach in such a way that your students will not only reach but also exceed standards.

Attacks on the Common Core usually do not question the rigor of the standards. Instead, those attacks question the politics of the standards, the over-zealous interpretations of them, and the punitive nature of their rollout. The standards have often been caged in judgment, fear, shame, and panic; in talk of compliance and of ratings; and in pressure to make reading myopic and teacher-controlled, with test-like questions masquerading as text-based questions. In all too many places, kids now spend their entire reading time inching through teacher-selected, testlike passages, answering swarms of little questions with sentences of "evidence" copied from the text. Many educators now look in dismay at these developments, asking, "Is this what has become of the standards that filled us with ambition and resolve? Is this the way to create state-of-the-art schools—places where teachers, principals, and kids innovate, invent, problem solve, take risks, create, dream, and achieve?"

Countries and states are responding differently. Some places have rejected the Common Core State Standards altogether, replacing them with other standards, most of which are similar. Other places, like New York City, have called for a reset on the Common Core to achieve new pathways of implementation.

This series does not take a stand on questioning the Common Core but does aim to interpret those and other iterations of global standards in ways that build vibrant, sustainable learning communities among teachers and students. Units of Study for Teaching Reading aims to achieve balance. On the one hand, the impetus for the standards remains. There continues to be an intense need for heightened expectations and for fresh approaches to teaching reading and writing. The Common Core's call for students to be able to read more closely, rather than simply glossing over texts and reducing complex texts to bare-bones plot summaries, is a critically important one. The new emphasis on reading argument texts, being able to note and to evaluate the evidence and to differentiate an author's opinion from facts, is critical. The emphasis on reading fiction and nonfiction alike interpretively, gleaning themes and main ideas, whether they are explicit or implicit, is important. And no one is questioning that students need to read in ways that allow them to handle progressively more complex texts. Educators who ignore the expectations in the standards do so at their peril.

This series provides you with the tools to move your students expeditiously toward what are now the new grade level expectations, while also supporting students' self-concepts as readers and their enthusiasm, tenacity, and sense of personal agency and power.

On a related point, however, the series does take a stand. There are some who have interpreted the Common Core to mean that young readers should spend reading time persevering in an effort to read grade level complex texts, even in instances when those texts are well beyond that child's reach. Everything we know about reading development tells us that when working with children who need to make rapid progress as readers, teachers have a choice: either we work expeditiously to make every moment count in an effort to move students forward so they can read the most complex texts possible, or we scaffold them so they participate in class work without actually being able to read anything with independence. Our choice is clearly toward a curriculum that differentiates, so that all children are working with texts that are at the upper end of what they can handle, applying rigorous grade level skills to texts that are at each student's instructional level.

The fact that the standards are in contention brings home the important point that no school should reform its reading curriculum solely because of any one initiative. Ultimately, a school needs to choose its priorities. So reform your curriculum because you believe that in today's world, people need to be more critical, thoughtful readers. Reform your curriculum because you believe it matters that students can read across texts, synthesizing those texts. Reform your curriculum because you believe that analytic thinking can be taught and that if students think analytically about texts, they'll learn to think

analytically about anything and everything. But don't reform your curriculum simply because of the Common Core or a state test or any other iteration of global standards.

If you are teaching in a state where your children will take Common Core–aligned reading assessments (such as PARCC, SBAC, and most of the state exams coauthored by Pearson), you'll be wondering how these units of study set kids up to be successful on those assessments. Be aware that while we in no way intended or wanted to create a curriculum of test prep, we did study those assessments closely and have been careful to develop the skills children will be assessed on across these units. Knowing that fifth-graders, for instance, not only need to discern more than one idea within nonfiction texts, but also need to be able to rank those ideas for which are best supported and rank the details that best support each idea, we made sure to teach those skills and give children a variety of authentic experiences practicing those skills. Knowing that third-graders will be asked about character's traits, changes, and what causes them to change, we made sure the third-grade unit of study on character gives children extensive training in that work. We also looked to the text-based writing tasks, knowing that much of children's success as writers on these assessments will hinge on their ability to read, analyze, and glean text evidence and to compare and contrast authors' ideas, themes, and points of view.

All of these tests, of course, not only assess kids' analytical skills, but they also assess their reading levels. At their heart, they are reading tests. In studying the children who piloted these tests, we found that classrooms where kids read at and above grade level, with no specific test prep, did well overall. Classes where kids read below grade level didn't. The spreadsheets that teachers got back, noting that so-and-so struggled with the main idea, or supporting ideas with evidence, could all actually be deciphered as "so-and-so couldn't read texts above level x." So within these units of study, especially in the launch units for each grade level, and in the small-group work, you'll find lots of attention given to moving children up levels of text complexity. Be suspicious of any reading program that teaches "the skills of the test" but doesn't acknowledge that all tests are mostly about the ability to read.

THE MISSION

The truth is that whether a district adopts the Common Core or not, the work we need to do is clear. Children deserve the richest, happiest, most powerful literacy education that we can give them, and for that to happen, teachers also need the richest, happiest, most powerful professional education that we can give them. Years ago, Seymour Sarason (1996), that great champion of school reform, wrote, "The notion that teachers can create conditions which are vital and alive for students when those same conditions do not exist for teachers has no warrant in the history of mankind." The most important thing we can do to help our children become the readers and writers that we want them to be is to turn schools into vibrant communities of professional learning.

Research is clear on the reason why commercial reading series and packaged reform programs haven't yielded results. Any reform effort that seeks to improve education by bypassing teachers, by trusting programs rather than professionals, will always fail. A U.S. Department of Education study showed that the single most important thing that can be done to lift the level of student achievement in our classrooms is to support the development and retention of good teachers. In fact, access to good teachers is more important to the likelihood that students will do well than anything else. It is more important than a student's background, than small class size, and more important than the fact that a school as a whole is a good one. A mountain of research confirms what all of us already know: the single most important resource a school can provide to its students is an effective teacher. And yet most of the money that has been spent over the past decade to improve the teaching of reading has been spent on large commercial reading programs that aim to teacher-proof reading instruction. What's needed is exactly the opposite.

In his book, *Time for Meaning*, Randy Bomer, a professor at the University of Texas, describes what it was like for him to enter teaching as a second career. On his first day of orientation, the district lined the new teachers up like children; Randy and the others marched single file onto a yellow school bus and were toured through the district. Randy and the other teachers didn't know each other. Each of them sat, as children are apt to do, one per seat, each in a separate box, with the seat ahead and behind walling each off in a fashion that Randy would later see as emblematic of his experience in that district. The new teachers were brought to the high school and led into the music room—an amphitheater of chairs on risers—where they sat as if in a chorus, although no one opened his mouth. The superintendent took his place on a swivel chair at the front of the room, sitting as if he was a conductor, and offered the new teachers some advice. "When anyone talks back to you, when a kid steps out of line, just write the person's name like so." To illustrate he called on Randy, elicited his name, and then wrote R-A-N-D-Y in large letters across the board. "Each time the kid talks back, just erase one letter," he said, and he proceeded to turn R-A-N-D-Y into R-A-N-D, R-A-N, R-A, R, and eventually, into nothing. "Kids identify with their names. They don't like to see themselves disappearing" (Bomer 1995).

Within a few years, it became clear to Randy that this was the district's way of working with teachers as well as with students. When he protested anything at all, he was dropped from committees and no longer referred to in decisions. "The longer I stayed in the classroom, the more my voice, my judgment, my creativity were erased" (Bomer 1995). What happened to Randy is what has happened to too many teachers. Too many teachers have felt that their creativity, their talent, their beliefs, and their dedication have all been erased—often by decisions that others have made to outsource reading, the heart of teaching, to corporations or to programs designed by state offices of education, dispersed through statewide websites. It hasn't worked.

The reading workshop offers an alternative, one where the emphasis is on providing students with the conditions that are supported by reading research (not by market research). The irony is that there are mountains of scientific studies that confirm what most of us knew just by thinking about the times in our own life when reading has worked and the times when reading has been the pits. The research confirms that kids get better as readers when they have time—lots of time—to read (to actually read, not to answer questions, fill in crossword puzzles, and circle the right answers). It is critical that kids read with engagement, and nothing supports engagement more than the opportunity to choose high-interest books within a reader's grasp. Learning to read isn't magic. It requires that teachers reflect on their own strategies as readers and reveal those strategies to kids. Good instruction involves demonstration and supported practice, and it is tailored to the learner based on the teacher's ongoing assessment.

Chapter 2

What Does the Series Contain?

E ACH UNIT OF STUDY includes minilessons; predictable conferences and small groups; mid-workshop teachings and shares; performance assessments, exemplar student work, rubrics, and anchor charts; extra teaching tools such as one-day charts or tools for conferring with readers; read-aloud texts; and lists of recommended titles for independent, partner, and club reading. There are four major units developed this way for each grade level: two fiction units of study and two nonfiction units. In addition, each grade has additional units of study in the *If . . . Then . . . Curriculum: Assessment-Based Instruction* book.

In each unit of study, you will learn a rich repertoire of ways to provide focused, explicit instruction for a handful of skills and strategies of proficient reading. Within one unit, for example, you'll learn that you can rally all your students to read expository texts, paying attention to the main ideas of those texts, creating little mental outlines as they read. The crucial work will be for you to teach in ways that support all children doing this work within their zones of proximal development. For children who are reading the most accessible texts, those main ideas will be apt to be spotlighted in headings and topic sentences. For children reading more complex texts, the main ideas may be embedded in paragraphs, and for those working with the most demanding expository texts, the main idea will be implicit, with the texts often containing a wealth of detail from which readers must learn to draw their own conclusions. Like any other essential reading skill, determining the main idea is not something readers learn to do once and for all. Instead, this skill, like every reading skill, develops along a pathway. This means that an entire community of readers can be invited to work toward a particular reading skill. No reader will ever stop working to determine the main idea, synthesize, read critically, and the rest. It's just that the texts in which readers do this work and the nature of the work itself will become increasingly complex, and the scaffolds you provide will vary.

To help you support diverse learners as each one works on her way toward shared goals, the series will show you how to collect data you value and to work together with colleagues to provide data-based instruction. You'll want to scaffold your learners so each works in his zone of proximal development. Once you have assessed children, you'll want to use the structures of the reading workshop to create individualized ways of supporting each of them in the particular skills they need.

One of the distinguishing features of this series is the way it welds theory and practice. Too often, practical, nuts-and-bolts instruction is divorced from theory on the one hand and from real-life classrooms on the other hand. The Units of Study for Teaching Reading and its two sister series in teaching writing instead weave theory and practice together in a new way. The books show state-of-the-art teaching, convey the logic and information upon which that teaching is based, and pull the curtain back from this teaching to reveal the principles that informed the teaching decisions. The books give you opportunities to learn teaching while receiving on-the-job support.

A SERIES BUILT ON DECADES OF TEACHING AND RESEARCH

This series builds on decades of teaching and research—in literally tens of thousands of schools. In states across the country, this curriculum has already given young people extraordinary power not only as readers but also as thinkers. When young people are explicitly taught the skills and strategies of proficient reading and are invited to live as richly literate people do, carrying books everywhere, bringing reading into every nook and corner of their lives, the results are dramatic.

The work has spread from one district to another, as school districts find that when teachers receive the necessary support to provide students with clear, sequenced, vibrant instruction in the skills and strategies of proficient reading, this makes a dramatic difference in their children's abilities and attitudes as readers. Powerful instruction produces visible and immediate results; when youngsters are taught well, the thinking, talking, and writing about reading they produce becomes far more substantial, complex, and significant. In fact, when I work with teachers, I often say to them, "If your students' reading skills are not visibly, dramatically improving after a few weeks in your reading workshop, you are doing something wrong." Good teaching pays off. When you provide students with constant opportunities to read and to write and when you actively and assertively teach into their best efforts, their literacy development will astonish you, their parents, the school administrators, and best of all, the students themselves.

It is not only *student's* work that is transformed when teachers are supported in the teaching of reading; *teachers'* work is also transformed. One of the beautiful things about teaching literacy is that no one needs to make a choice between responsive, student-centered teaching and results-oriented, data-based teaching. When young people talk and write about their reading, it's easy to track their progress in higher-level comprehension skills. Schools can be characterized by that cycle of continuous improvement that is the real source of good teaching.

The good news is that when a community of teachers embraces reform in the teaching of reading and writing, teachers often become reinvigorated and renewed in the process. And individual teachers find that workshop teaching taps new sources of energy within them. Over the years, teachers have repeatedly told me that this kind of teaching has given them new energy, clarity, and compassion, reminding them why they went into teaching in the first place. I understand what these teachers mean, for it has done all this—and more—for me as well.

As school systems come to realize that teachers are in fact the secret to higher standards and that schools need to participate in a cycle of continuous improvement, this creates an escalating demand for professional development. This series aims to meet that demand, providing what could be described as professional development in a box!

A SERIES PROVIDING BOTH CURRICULUM *AND* PROFESSIONAL DEVELOPMENT

Both the Units of Study for Teaching Reading and the sister publication, Units of Study in Opinion, Information, and Narrative Writing series, have been written to serve as both curricular support and professional development. Each day's instruction in both reading and writing is designed according to research-based principles. For example, you will see that all of the teaching follows the "gradual release of responsibility" model of teaching. Students first learn from a demonstration (accompanied by an explicit explanation), then from guided practice, and then finally they transfer what they have learned to another text, another day. When students attempt something new, they are given scaffolding, and this is lightened and then removed over time; they continue, however, to receive feedback on their independent work. Over time, strategies that are learned in concrete step-by-step ways become more layered and implicit, fluid, and responsive.

The progressions that undergird this curriculum are always carefully chosen and explicitly explained. Our goal is not just to provide you with a coherent, principled curriculum; it is to teach you methods of teaching reading and knowledge about reading development. Because my colleagues and I have spent thirty years helping hundreds of thousands of teachers learn to teach reading and writing, and because we have studied that work, reflecting on it as we engage in a continual process of revision, we know a lot about how to provide professional development in literacy—and that is the aim of this series. While the units scaffold your teaching, they also help you develop finesse and flexibility to invent other ELA units and to transfer this teaching to other disciplines.

The wonderful thing about learning to teach reading well is that there are just a few teaching methods that one needs to know and be able to use. Best yet, the methods are similar to those used for teaching writing, as well. This means that as teachers and students become adept at teaching within a writing workshop, those teaching methods become applicable also to a reading workshop. In this series, we provide crystal clear advice on how to lead efficient and effective minilessons, conferences, and small-group strategy sessions. We do so, knowing that as you travel through the series, encountering scores of minilessons, conferences, small-group sessions, book clubs, read-aloud conversations, and the like, you will learn not only from explicit instruction but also from immersion. *A Guide to the Reading Workshop, Intermediate Grades* details the architecture of all our minilessons, conferences, and small-group strategy sessions and articulates the management techniques that make reading and writing workshops possible. *Reading Pathways: Grades 3–5* provides you with an assessment system that can make teaching and learning robust, goal-directed, data-based, and responsive. The unit books put the methods, principles, and curriculum into your hands so that you can bring all this to life with your own students.

Ideally, you, and every other teacher in the world, should not only be able to implement exemplary teaching but you should also be able to do so with a coach nearby. Therefore, as you witness our teaching, I will from time to time act as a coach, underscoring aspects of the teaching that seem especially essential. The italic comments on minilessons are one of the many ways we help to extrapolate guiding principles from the specific details of teaching. This way, as you watch this teaching, you'll be positioned to invent more of your own teaching. The end goal is not the teaching that we've described here but the teaching that you, your colleagues, and your children invent together.

AN OVERVIEW OF THE SERIES' CONTENTS

The intent of this series is to provide systemic, schoolwide support enables the students across your school to become engaged, purposeful, strategic readers. To support this work, each grade level box for the K–5 series contains:

- *A Guide to the Reading Workshop, Intermediate Grades.*
- Four units of study: two units in reading fiction, two in informational reading.
- A book containing additional units: *If . . . Then . . . Curriculum: Assessment-Based Instruction, Grades 3–5* is written to help you adjust your curriculum to your standards, your interests, and your students' needs and interests. This book also helps you differentiate curriculum by supporting small-group work and one-to-one conferring.
- *Reading Pathways: Grades 3–5*, a book that puts a system for assessing reading into your hands and into the hands of your students.
- *Online Resources for Teaching Reading*, a treasure chest of additional resources, including bibliography, short texts, artistic renderings of charts, reproducible checklists, homework, mentor texts, videos, and Web links. A collection of these resources is available for each grade level.

An assumption behind this series is the idea that if you are truly going to bring all of your students to the ambitious levels of today's global standards, there needs to be vertical alignment in the instruction children receive, so that people who teach at any one grade level can count on students coming to them with some foundational skills that can then be built upon. Teachers and kids, too, need to speak a common language so they can reference and build upon the work each other has done.

The days of each teacher functioning as a lone ranger need to be at an end. Imagine how impractical it would be if each third-grade math teacher spoke of the numerator and the denominator by using different terms, and if each third-grade teacher also decided on her own whether or not to teach multiplication: fourth-grade teachers who received students from several different third-grade classrooms would find that half the class had no knowledge or vocabulary around multiplication, and the other half would be ready, with some review, to move toward multiplying fractions. Of course, almost every school *does* have a math curriculum that supports vertical alignment, allowing teachers to extend and build on previous instruction. This series provides a similar curriculum in support of skills such as close reading, inference, analytic reading, summary, cross-text synthesis, and interpretation.

In this series, instruction builds on itself. You might teach a skill first within fiction reading, then transfer that skill to a unit on high-interest nonfiction reading, and then help students also use that skill within a topic-based research project. You might say, "In your earlier unit of study in fiction, you learned that there can be tension between what a character says and what that character actually thinks or feels. Today, I want to teach you that this insight is also important when reading a nonfiction text, because there may be times when you read an article by an unreliable narrator and you doubt the trustworthiness of a quotation or a statistic." In this way, students are brought to higher levels of achievement, because teaching stands on the shoulders of prior instruction. One month's and one year's instruction recalls and builds upon the previous instruction. You might say, "I know that last year, you learned that when reading information texts, it is important to use cues from the text to signal the way the text has been structured. This year, I want to point out that many texts contain multiple text structures, and you need to be a flexible enough reader to note when those structures change midway." Because the units of study books fit tongue-and-groove alongside each other, they help students learn, then consolidate and apply what they have learned, doing so in ways that allow students to meet and exceed any iteration of global standards.

Later in this book, I will discuss a recent study by Bembry and others (1998) that shows that if a child has access to a strong teacher for three consecutive years, then that child's scores on standardized reading tests will be as much as 40% higher than the scores of students who meanwhile have not had that access to strong teachers. That data show not just the effect of a good teacher, but the effect of a good school.

This series aims to support good schools. We do so, believing that the children in Bembry's study who were taught for three years in a row by good teachers are not just the recipients of good luck; those "lucky breaks" happen in schools that are communities of practice, in schools that make teachers strong. These will be schools in which a spiral curriculum allows one grade level to stand on the shoulders of another. The teachers in such a school will meet across the grades to talk and think about how a unit of study in character will be different in first, second, third, and fourth grades. When will the emphasis on secondary characters move front and center, instead of being something for more proficient readers? At what grade levels will teachers tend to emphasize that characters sometimes play a symbolic role in a story? These will be schools that think carefully about special support services that children receive, making sure that a child's work with a reading specialist is aligned to and not disruptive of the classroom work. These will be schools with a systemic approach to assessment, where teachers at the end of one year make book baggies full of just-right books for each child, so that for the first two weeks of the new year, each child is reading books selected at the end of the preceding year.

I recall, during a visit to Portland, Oregon, when a principal spoke to me about the effects of our writing units of study—and what he said pertains, I trust, to reading units of study as well. He said, "What your series has done is that it has brought my whole staff into a shared conversation. Our school has become a community of practice. We started out working 'by the book' and now we're dancing on the edges, looping in some other work we also love, addressing some issues unique to our setting, but, because of the units, we're doing this together, in a cohesive community of practice." I can't imagine a more significant accolade.

It is critical that across a school, teachers take up shared methods of teaching, because this means that when one teacher has special finesse with that method, others can use a prep period to watch that teacher at work, learning from her. It means, too, that one teacher can head across the country to study from an expert, with everyone in the school waiting for the goods when that teacher returns, arms full of new information.

It is especially important for schools to become communities of practice because methods of teaching are also methods of learning. If every year, every teacher needs to induct kids into whole new ways of acting in a classroom, into whole new cultures and expectations, then kids spend half their time trying to adapt to the whims of each new classroom. How much better for a school to decide upon some shared methods and to think about how, over time, children's roles will become more proactive, more complex, and more responsible!

The Unit Books: The Heart of the Series

Each unit of study book represents about five or perhaps six weeks of teaching. Within that time, the unit supports students reading lots of books, with the assumption that those who are reading the shorter and more accessible texts will read them at a faster clip than those reading longer and more complex texts. So some students may read twenty books in a unit, and some five. That is, during every unit, students are matched to books that represent the high end of what they can handle, and they move through those books at different rates (see Figure 2–1).

The unit books capture the teaching that my colleagues and I, and our dedicated pilot teachers, have done. It is an understatement to say these units have been piloted many times. The teaching in these books has been planned, taught, revised, and retaught, through a cycle of improvement involving literally thousands of classrooms in schools dotting the globe. Earlier iterations of a few of these units were published in the Units of Study for Teaching Reading, Grades 3–5 series of books; summaries of some others were published in the "Curricular Plans" that the Teachers College Reading and Writing Project drafts each year. More to the point, each of these units

has had the advantage of input from scores of great educators who have lent their wisdom to the work.

The unit books are written to give you the opportunity to listen in on and observe a unit being taught at your grade level. Reading these, it will seem as if you were invited into a classroom to watch and listen as my coauthors and I teach and work with young people. You will draw close as we convene the class for a ten-minute minilesson, channeling the students to sit beside partners, calling for their attention, and you'll hear how we talk about and demonstrate the strategies and skills of powerful reading. Of course, you'll also overhear the stories we use to draw them in and the directions we give to send them off to their work time. Then, too, you'll hear the ways we confer and lead small groups—guided reading groups, strategy lessons, book clubs, and partnerships. You'll watch us teach readers to self-assess their abilities to synthesize, to compare and contrast, to interpret, and to read analytically for craft and structure. You'll see, too, how early in a unit of study we help students become familiar with goals for that unit, and you'll see the way that learning progressions and data weave through every unit of study.

Once you begin teaching a unit, you will find that each day's teaching—each *session*—within that unit is introduced with a prelude that helps you to understand why, out of all that could possibly be taught at that juncture, we decided on that particular session. The art of teaching comes from choice. The prelude, then, brings you in on the rationale behind the choices that inform the upcoming session. Why this minilesson? How will it fit with earlier and with later instruction? What are the real goals? What is the work students will be doing after the minilesson? The prelude highlights what matters most in the session and hopefully functions as a bit of a keynote speech, revving you up for the teaching that follows.

Then you can listen in to state-of-the-art minilessons, taught to students who are just the age of your own. Hear the language that the coauthors and I use, and hear some of the ways students respond. Each minilesson follows the same structure, which is described in more detail in Chapter 5.

After we send students off to their work, my colleagues and I fill you in on the conferring and small-group work we think you are apt to do during the work time that day. More often than not, this section will be like a miniature professional development workshop, showing you ways to anticipate the challenges your students are likely to encounter and giving you the opportunity to be ready to teach responsively. That teaching will be punctuated with

Level	Books I'll Need for the Week
J, K	📖 8–10 books
L, M	📄 4–6 books
N, O, P, Q	📖 2–4 books
R, S, T	📖 1–3 books
U, V, W	📖 1–3 books

FIG. 2–1 "Just-Right Book" chart

mid-workshop teaching that you will offer to the whole class, part way through reading time. Often this teaching builds on the minilesson, extending it by providing a next step or a follow-up point. Other times, the mid-workshop teaching counterbalances the minilesson or broadcasts lessons being taught in conferences or small groups. We also describe the whole-class share session that culminates the workshop. We know, of course, that you will very likely invent your own share sessions that respond to your own students.

By the time students are in the upper elementary grades, they can do substantial work at home, and they will be more eager to do this work if you are careful to craft homework that helps them outgrow themselves. The sessions also contain suggested *homework* assignments, written in pages that can be printed and sent home with students or displayed on your classroom homework site.

The Design and Rationale for the Curriculum

When you teach the units of study in this series, you will provide your students with instruction, opportunities for practice, and concrete doable goals so they can progress expeditiously to meet and exceed any set of high standards. The units will help you aim not only for grade level standards but also beyond them. Runners don't aim to stop at the finish line; they aim to run right through it, keeping up the pace until the finish line is well behind them. We, too, want to aim beyond the finish line—bringing every reader with us as we do so.

How were the four units a year decided upon?

The units of study books have been written with the assumption that a year-long curriculum will contain these and other units, taken either from the *If . . . Then . . . Curriculum* book or from other sources. The Teachers College Reading and Writing Project works with a number of schools. Those schools have been teaching seven or eight units at a grade level, and those units have changed somewhat over the years. As a result, when we decided to write units into books, we had many choices to draw upon. The units we selected seem to us most essential to students' progress as readers and to their mastery of the challenging goals that are required by the Common Core and by other global standards. We decided upon the units after PARCC and SBAC

assessments were in full swing, and we made choices with those and other assessments in mind.

You'll see that the units especially support the development of skills that students need to succeed in the twenty-first century. For example, starting in third grade and continuing through all the grades, much of the nonfiction reading work in these units involves reading across a variety of texts, comparing and contrasting what is learned, and synthesizing information. In fourth grade, readers become aware that the content they learn from the texts on a topic is sometimes conflicting. By fifth grade, students are well prepared to consider the perspectives of different authors, taking into consideration the assumptions, vested interests, and biases of those authors.

In a similar fashion, the units support students' emerging abilities to read fiction texts analytically, aware that the stories were written on purpose by an author who wants to achieve particular goals. By fifth grade, students are able to talk about the techniques—such as flashback, symbolism, use of figurative language—that fiction writers use and the goals they are aiming to achieve (supporting a theme, building suspense, establishing a tone, and so forth). The rigorous expectations in today's world cannot be met through a quick test prep–like curriculum. Instead, skills need to be developed incrementally, across years, and that is what this curriculum aims to accomplish.

At each grade level, there is equal support for fiction and for nonfiction reading. Some units (such as historical fiction) support reading across both fiction and nonfiction.

How are the units structured?

Each unit is structured into several "bends in the road." Think of a road winding up a mountainside, and a biker looking up the steep slope. Rather than thinking of the thousand-foot climb, it's easier to think of the first bend in the road, where you may stretch and regroup, readying yourself for the next bend. That's how these bends in the road go. For example, in the fourth-grade unit, *Reading the Weather, Reading the World* the first stretch of the unit supports students reading high-interest expository texts of their choice. Then the unit turns a corner, and students work for a time in small groups, studying one kind of extreme weather or another. Whether students are studying hurricanes or tornadoes, floods or drought, they research the causes, consequences, and scientific phenomena behind their weather event. In the final bend of the unit, students study a second topic, again under the larger umbrella of extreme weather, and they compare and contrast their topics—how are tornadoes and hurricanes similar? How are they different? Eventually, students study economic and political questions that undergird the subtopics the class has investigated.

The important thing to know about topic-based units is that when all or part of a nonfiction unit delves into a specific topic such as extreme weather, that topic is somewhat dispensable. You could substitute another topic and still maintain most of the teaching, because the focus of instruction is not on the topic itself, but on the skills. For example, while students are studying how to forecast hurricanes and floods, they are being taught how to synthesize as they read, drawing the graphs, charts, and illustrations into their understanding of an article. They're learning how to take notes across multiple sources, how to evaluate a source, and so on.

How do the units fit the needs of my students/school/district/assessments?

As you think over your students' interests and needs, your district and school's curriculum, and your high-stakes assessments, you'll need to make some decisions. You may decide, based on your particular situation, to teach a unit at a different grade level than it was originally intended. For example, you may choose to teach a unit that we have written for fourth grade to fourth-graders and then, with adaptations, again to fifth-graders. You may decide that some of the fifth-grade units are best taught, for the time being, in sixth grade, if your current sixth-grade students didn't get the fifth-grade teaching yet. Those sorts of decisions are all discussed in the *If . . . Then . . . Curriculum* book. In that book, we also point out that these units can be taught alongside other units, perhaps ones that lean on publications by literacy leaders such as Stephanie Harvey, Kylene Beers, Ellin Keene, Harvey Daniels, and others. Alternatively, some of the lessons and methods of those literacy leaders can be assimilated into these units. Certainly, the expectation is that your reading curriculum will always be an alive, changing, growing compilation of best practices.

Where can I find books for reading workshop that have engaging, relevant content and fit the needs of my readers?

Some units offer specialized book lists that will be helpful for you. For example, the book lists for the historical fiction unit include books at a variety of

levels, grouped by historical era. We have also created complete grade-level classroom library collections, and individual "shelves" on a variety of high-interest topics to support your reading instruction and the Units of Study.

The Relationship to Units of Study in Opinion, Information, and Narrative Writing

This Units of Study for Teaching Reading series aligns with the Units of Study in Opinion, Information, and Narrative Writing, although each can also be taught as a stand-alone unit. The most obvious alignment lies in the area of methods. Teachers who have learned to teach the writing units will find it is a small step to now also teach the reading series. Although people do not usually think about the fact that kids, as well as teachers, have jobs to do within a particular set of methods, they do—and kids as well as teachers will find it a small step to now work within reading units of study.

The sessions in the reading series are perhaps 20% briefer than those in the writing series, and texts play a more dominant role in the reading series, but other than those differences, the two series are very similar. The reading units all intersect with and reinforce the writing units and vice versa, connecting in how they develop content, skills, and/or habits.

There are instances in which the reading and the writing units are absolutely aligned to each other. For example, in the fourth-grade writing series, students do some research writing on the American Revolution. Meanwhile, the fourth-grade reading unit *Reading History: The American Revolution* provides the reading support that will make that writing unit far easier to pull off. Similarly, a fifth-grade book on argument writing contains a mini-unit in which kids research the pros and cons of chocolate milk. The fifth-grade reading unit, *Argument and Advocacy: Researching Debatable Issues*, provides the reading support to make that writing unit far more successful—and that will extend that unit, harvesting reading power from it.

In smaller ways, the reading units reference and rely on students' experiences as writers. For example, when teaching students to read analytically, realizing that an author has made the text they are reading and done things deliberately, students' own experiences as writers are called upon. When teaching students to structure their notes as they read expository texts, the term "boxes and bullets" is brought over from the writing workshop into their thoughts about reading. In these and other ways, there is reciprocity between the reading workshop and its sister, the writing workshop.

If . . . Then . . . Curriculum: Assessment-Based Instruction, Grades 3–5

In addition to the four units of study for each grade level, you will find *If . . . Then . . . Curriculum: Assessment-Based Instruction, Grades 3–5*, a book that helps you to go from assessing your students to planning your yearlong sequence of units. For example, the *If . . . Then . . .* book helps you to look at your data and to think about ways you might alter the suggested sequence in the units because of your data. If you are teaching fifth grade, for example, and your students have no experience with any of these units, what do we recommend? If your class is operating well below, or well higher than benchmark, should you vary the sequence of units that you teach? Our thoughts in response to questions such as these are in this text.

The *If . . . Then . . .* book also offers shortened versions of almost half a dozen additional units of study—units that you might decide to teach before, after, or in between the units we've provided in full. For example, if you worry that your students need to be prepared for poetry questions on your high-stakes test, you may decide to teach a unit on poetry. If you think your students need more experience reading narrative nonfiction, you might decide on a unit on biography. The curriculum we've described in the full-length books only supports a portion of your reading curriculum, so you will want to adapt and use some of these additional units of study.

Reading Pathways: Grades 3–5

The curriculum set out in these units is integrated into an assessment system that includes two grade 2–6 learning progressions, one in narrative reading and one in informational reading. These kid-friendly progressions support the development of essential reading skills, and accompanying rubrics allow students to self-assess their progress. An early version of this assessment system has been piloted in thousands of classrooms, and the entire system has been revised scores of times based on student, teacher, coach, and administrator feedback.

The most important thing about the learning progressions and the performance assessments that accompany them is that they enable you and your students alike to grasp where students are in their reading development, so that together you can figure out ways to help them move toward

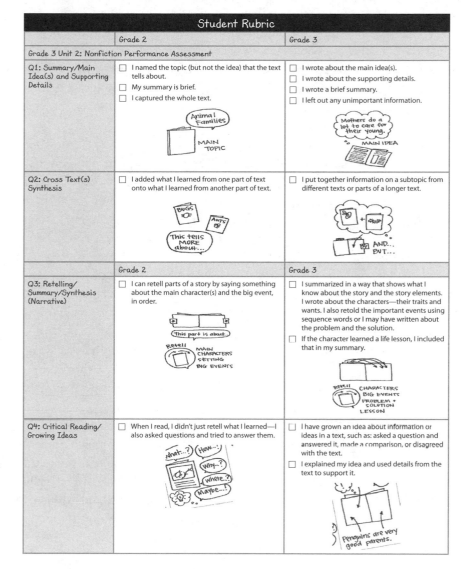

FIG. 2–2   Rubrics help students assess the work they do on their initial performance assessment.

next steps. The assessment system that undergirds this curriculum is meant as an instructional tool. It makes progress in reading transparent, concrete, and as obtainable as possible, and it puts ownership for this progress into the hands of learners. As part of this, this system of assessment demystifies the Common Core State Standards and other globally benchmarked standards, allowing students and teachers to work toward a very clear image of what good reading entails.

You will find that *Reading Pathways: Grades 3–5* contains information about leveling books, conducting running records, and instituting a system of running records and leveled books across the school as a way to track readers' progress. You'll find a chapter on using information gleaned from running records to help you guide instruction. The bulk of the book, however, is devoted to the two parallel learning progressions themselves and to accompanying rubrics and performance assessments. These progressions lay out pathways along which students develop skills. For example, you can see what a second-grade student should be able to do when comparing and contrasting two similar books, what a third-grader should be able to do, and so on as the progression takes you up the grade levels. These are written to be put into the hands of kids, and the message to a youngster is, "Reading well isn't magic. It is the result of hard work." You can use this learning progression to take your thinking about a text up levels in ways that make a big difference.

The learning progressions are accompanied by performance assessments that you can use before and after each unit of study. Each performance assessment contains an article or a story or two with questions embedded into the texts. The questions ask students to do some work on each of four skills that are highlighted in the unit. Students self-assess, and the performance assessments cue them into skills they especially need to develop across the unit. That is, an early question asking a fifth-grader to write about theme will almost paint a picture of later minilessons that help students develop the skills they need to do high-level work with theme. The assessments make students extra alert when those sessions are taught. This is deliberate because the skills that we assess in pre- and postassessments tend to be ones that are valued on high-stakes assessments and that are important in life.

Online Resources for Teaching Reading: A Grade-by-Grade Collection of Digital Resources

In the Online Resources for Teaching Reading, you will find a rich array of additional resources to support each unit of study and each grade level, including student samples, short video clips, Internet links, mentor texts, homework, and additional resources to go with particular sessions.

Also available in the online resources are videos that support Units of Study for Teaching Reading. These videos present views into reading workshops in a wide variety of school settings, featuring all kinds of teachers and children. The videos introduce the concepts of the reading workshop and help you create a vision for what is possible in the teaching of reading. They also convey how both master teachers and less experienced teachers bring the reading workshop's structures and rituals to life with children. For each unit of study you can observe how my colleagues and I initiate minilessons, teach reading strategies, conduct conferences, and guide small-group instruction. These videos can be used as a resource for introducing a reading workshop, but they can also be used later in a teachers' professional development as a resource for studying—and discussing, visualizing, and practicing—particular facets of reading workshop teaching.

In the online resources, you'll also find additional print resources, including reproducible learning progressions and rubrics, and links to websites that will help you and your students do research for your reading projects. These resources will support your teaching throughout the year.

AUTHORSHIP OF THE SERIES

Although the text reads as if one teacher created and taught the minilessons, mid-workshop teachings, small groups, and shares, the work that goes on behind a unit is actually much more collaborative. I am a coauthor of some of the books and the editor of others, but either way, the process has involved more people than I could ever name. Usually the genesis of a unit begins years before we actually begin writing it down. Either the entire unit or portions of it will have been taught in some form for years, often in hundreds of classrooms.

As the unit is being taught, my colleagues and I continue to learn new things, to adopt new standards; to take on new goals, and to make new tools—and all of that leads to revisions of the unit.

When the decision is made that out of all the many units my colleagues and I have created, a particular one is to be written down, then the unit is totally rethought from head to toe. The work begins with plans for the bends and the mentor texts. Implicit in the plans for a unit are literally hundreds of decisions, and our initial plans were always revised endlessly before becoming the backbone of the unit. Part of that revision process involved passing the plans among many of us because the units that we write will become essential to all the Teachers College Reading and Writing Project's work in schools, and we all needed to agree with the major decisions.

During the early planning portion of the process, we decide on mentor texts and on the bends of the unit. Then one of us drafts a minilesson or two, and that minilesson is placed on Google Docs so that we can all work with it. The lesson is revised, piloted, revised again, and principles from that revision are sent out from the work with that one minilesson to all the coauthors of all the K–5 books. Each book receives help from "elves," as we call writers who function like the shoemakers' elves, coming into the manuscript in the dead of night when coauthors have left it and keeping the forward progress going by lending their particular talents: one helps with "getting ready" sections and checks for consistency with other books at the grade level, another contributes to the small-group work and conferring write-ups, yet others triple-check the teaching against our best knowledge of reading development or of standards.

On the books for which I am a coauthor, I play a very major writing role, writing at least half and often much more of the final text. On the other books, for which I am an editor, I usually work intensely on the plans and also coach, revise, spot problems, and problem solve. I may write as much as half of those books, and I may write very little of them. One way or the other, the manuscript will go through four or five wholesale revisions and will be passed

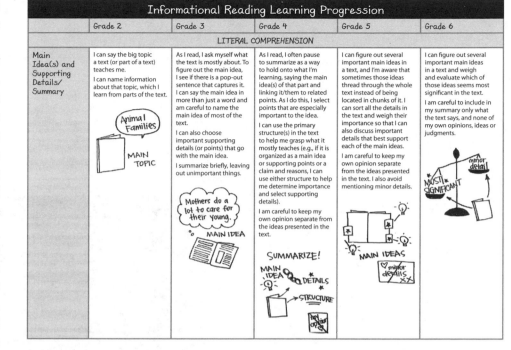

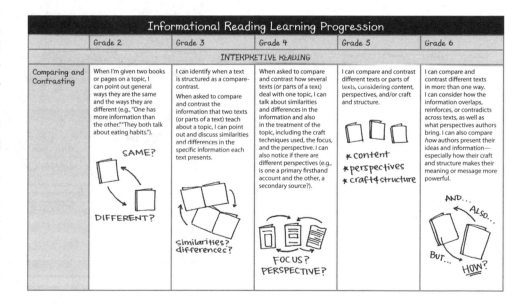

FIG. 2–3   Throughout the unit, students use kid-friendly learning progressions to set goals for themselves as readers.

among a number of hands before it is close to being finished. Many books were revised from head to toe even after we thought they were nearly finished. All of this work reflects the care and respect we have for teachers. We want your work to be easier, more efficient, and ever more effective, leaving you energy to give your students the attention they deserve.

In the same way, although the books read as if they draw on one classroom, depicting the true story of how that unit of study unfolded in that one classroom, in truth, the classroom depicted in these books is usually a composite classroom, and the kids' voices are captured or created from all of the kids we've taught.

Chapter 3

What Does Research Say that All Readers Need?

JUST AS DON MURRAY ARGUED that writers need three things—time, choice, and response—Richard Allington's research (*What Really Matters for Struggling Readers*, 2011) shows that readers need three things—access to books they find fascinating, time to read, and expert instruction. To make real progress, students need all three. No matter how expert your instruction, if kids don't get enough time to read, or they don't have enough *to* read, they won't progress. In the same way, if they have lots of books, but no one teaches them explicitly or confers with them about their reading, introducing them to new challenges and guiding the work they do, they also won't move up fast enough or with enough depth to their thinking. Neither "untouched" independent reading, nor expert teacher talk will shift readers adequately.

It helps to think of your readers a bit like a baseball team. You get better at baseball by playing baseball. In the same way, you get better at reading by reading. Still, a baseball team with a great coach is going to improve much more rapidly. You need to be that great coach, making sure your team has time to practice, planning the work you'll do with the whole team, and studying your players for the tips they each need.

WHAT ARE THE ESSENTIALS OF READING INSTRUCTION?

Twice, I've been part of a group of literacy leaders from across the nation who have met repeatedly for the purpose of constructing national literacy standards. Both times, the members of those think tanks were literacy leaders representing different thought-collaboratives and perspectives, yet each time I've participated in this work, I have been reminded that an important consensus has emerged around the bottom-line essentials that all children need to thrive as readers. Increasingly, people are coming together around the recognition that youngsters need a handful of key opportunities.

Above all, good teachers matter. It is important to develop teachers' abilities to teach by providing professional development and a culture of collaborative practice.

In the end, it's teachers that make the difference in kids' lives. Again and again, research shows what most of us already know to be true: good teaching makes a world of difference (Allington and Johnston 2002; Duffy 1997; Rebell and Wolff 2008, 90; Rivkin et al. 2005; Darling-Hammond and Sykes 2003; Pressley et al. 2003; Guthrie and Humenick 2004). Bembry has found that students who were, for three years, in classrooms that provide high-quality instruction achieved scores on standardized reading tests that were 40% higher than the scores earned by students receiving lower-quality instruction (Bembry et al. 1998). That is a staggering statistic, and it is an important one, because many people believe that reading comprehension boils down to intelligence and that some kids are predisposed to understand complex texts and others simply aren't. Clearly the research suggests differently. As Allington writes, "It has become clear that investing in effective teaching—whether in hiring decisions or professional development planning—is the most 'research-based' strategy available" (Allington 2002b).

Shirley Brice Heath, Margery Bailey Professor of English and Dramatic Literature at Stanford University, has gone so far as to suggest that the single most important condition for literacy learning is that a person needs mentors who are joyfully literate people, who demonstrate what it means to live joyfully literate lives. Some lucky children grow up in households where families demonstrate the richness of a life of books, but many of our children rely on school to provide them with that image of possibility. And so it is not just nice—it is essential—that teachers can bring their own love of reading into classrooms, talking about the books they love, sharing excitement over hearing an author speak, telling students that they can't wait to curl up with a book on a rainy Saturday while the rain pelts against the windows. As new global standards call for levels of intellectual work that many adults have never experienced, it is even more important that teachers are willing to become engaged in their own literacy, so they are able to say to students, "Let me show you a strategy that has worked for me." When teachers are public and transparent about their own efforts to outgrow themselves as readers, they can model that learning to read is a lifelong process.

Teachers grow stronger not only from their own experiences participating in adult reading groups and other sorts of literacy activities, but also from working within school-based learning communities. In his article "Improving Relationships inside the Schoolhouse," Roland Barth states, "One incontrovertible finding emerges from my career spent working in and around schools: The nature of relationships among the adults within a school has a greater influence on the character and quality of that school and on student accomplishment than anything else" (Barth 2006, 8).

It is critically important for schools to create communities of practice where teachers work together to learn from each other's best practices to position students to develop into skilled, proficient, expert readers and writers.

Learners need enormous amounts of time for actual reading.

When you teach reading, you are teaching a skill—like playing the oboe or swimming. And when anyone teaches a skill, the learner needs to be doing the thing. Students don't learn to play the oboe or to swim by filling out worksheets or answering questions or by listening to someone talk about playing the oboe and swimming. As Grant Wiggins said when he recently spoke at Teachers College, you don't learn to drive by taking a car apart and studying every tiny screw and cog that goes into making the car. You need to practice driving. The learner needs to be playing that oboe or doing the swimming. And in the same way, your students need to be reading.

A mountain of research supports the fact that teachers who successfully teach reading and writing provide their students with far more time for actual reading and writing. Allington reports that exemplary teachers of reading have their students actually reading and writing for as much as half the school day—whereas in typical classrooms, it is not unusual to find that kids read and write for as little as 10% of the day. In all too many schools, a ninety-minute "reading block" produces no more than ten or fifteen minutes of actual reading (Allington 2002b). Students in the classrooms of more effective teachers read ten times as much as students in classrooms of less effective teachers (Allington and Johnston 2002).

Success in reading is directly related to the amount of time a person spends reading. John Guthrie and Nicole Humenick's study, "Teaching for Literacy Engagement," (2004) illustrates that fourth-graders who read at the second-grade level spend just half an hour a day reading, while fourth-graders who read at the eighth-grade level spend four and a half hours a day reading. Krashen (2004) points out that 93% of the tests on reading comprehension that collect data on volume of reading show that kids who are given more time to read do better. Guthrie and Humenick (2004) found that reading volume predicted reading comprehension and that dramatic increases in reading volume are important for thoughtful literacy proficiencies. The NAEP Reading Report Card for the Nation (U.S. Department of Education 1999) shows that at every level, reading more pages at home and at school was associated with higher reading scores. Anderson, Wilson, and Fielding (1988) also researched the relationship between the amount of reading done and reading achievement. They found that the amount of time spent reading was the best predictor of reading achievement, including a child's growth as a reader from second to fifth grade.

It is important to note that even when the activity students are doing in lieu of reading has been shown to be useful, warning signs should go up when nonreading activities consume more than a few minutes of reading time. For example, although activating prior knowledge before reading has been shown to be useful (Pearson and Fielding 1991), spending most of a reading block doing so is not supported by research—and that is just one example. Allington suggests that three to five minutes spent activating prior knowledge is probably sufficient (Allington 2002b).

After reviewing the overwhelming amount of research on the need for students to spend a volume of time actually reading, Allington concludes, "So how much daily in-school reading might we plan for? I would suggest one and one half hours of daily in-school reading would seem to be a minimum goal given the data provided by these studies. . . . However my ninety-minute recommendation is for time actually spent reading" (2006, 47). Research by Guthrie shows what this call for more time spent reading will look like in practice. If *Stone Fox*, a level P book containing approximately 12,000 words, is an accessible text for a reader (if the reader can handle it with fluency), that child will finish *Stone Fox* (and other books like it) in two to four hours. This suggests that if reading fiction is even just half of what the child reads, she will still complete *Stone Fox* or another level P books in three or four days. Yet right now, many students spend several weeks reading a book like this! Similarly, a child reading a book in the Magic Tree House series will finish that book the day it is started and be able to read seven of those books in a week. Those books contain approximately 6,000 words, and for this to be a just-right book for the reader, the child would need to be reading the book at 100–200 words per minute—hence the calculation that these books should take no more than thirty to sixty minutes to read. Most level U–W books can be read in four hours, suggesting readers can certainly finish one of those books in a week. And the research is clear that if the volume of fiction reading done in school is something akin to those amounts, and students are doing an equal amount of nonfiction reading in their subjects across the curriculum, then that bodes well for a reader's progress.

The single most important thing we can do to make schools into places where youngsters thrive as readers is to clear out the time and space so that children can learn to read by reading. This means shoveling out the busy work: in some classrooms, a third of reading time is consumed with kids filling out dittos full of "text-based" questions and writing required summaries of every chapter! Speaking at Teachers College, Allington said, with a twinkle in his eye, "Crap is the technical term reserved for all the non-reading and non-writing activities that fill kids' days—the dittos, dioramas, papier-mâché maps . . . all that chases real reading and real writing out of the school day" (2008). Of course, sometimes kids spend their evenings doing more of the same. Remember, exemplary teachers' students read and write as much as ten times as much as kids in other classes. It is impossible to stress enough the importance of kids "just reading."

Learners need access to books that allow them to do a high volume of high-success reading.

One fairly obvious implication of the research that shows the need to provide students with enormous amounts of time for actual reading is this: students need access to books of appropriate complexity so they can engage in an enormous volume of high-success reading. That is, students need access to lots of books that they can read with high levels of accuracy, fluency, and comprehension. They need opportunities to consolidate skills so they can use them with automaticity within fluid, engaged reading. Readers need to work with texts in which they can orchestrate cueing systems so the magic happens and meaning is made. If a child holds a giant tome and stumbles through it, making swipes at some of the words, that's not reading. Novelist John Gardner (1991) describes reading this way:

> It creates for us a kind of dream, a rich and vivid play in the mind. We read a few words at the beginning of the book or the particular story and suddenly we find ourselves seeing not words on a page but a train moving through Russia, an old Italian crying, or a farmhouse battered by rain. We read on—dream on—not passively but actively, worrying about the choices the characters have to make, listening in panic for some sound behind the fictional door, exalting in characters' successes, bemoaning their failures. In great fiction, the dream engages us heart and soul; we not only respond to imaginary things—sights, sounds, smells—as though they were real, we respond to fictional problems as though they were real: we sympathize, think, and judge.

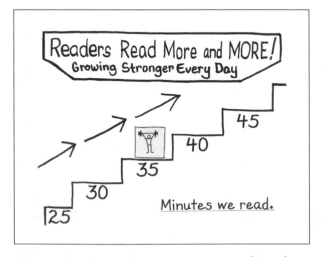

FIG. 3–1 Readers need enormous amounts of time for actual reading.

It's not surprising that children need opportunities to engage in high-success reading. Who among us brings giant pharmaceutical books on a long airplane flight or to the beach on a summer day? Adults rarely read a text that we can't read with 99.5% accuracy. We wouldn't read if we were constantly derailed by complexities that we couldn't assimilate, and kids aren't any different.

Over sixty years ago, Betts studied fourth-graders and found that low error rates led to improved learning (1946). In that research, independent reading levels were texts that readers could read with 98% accuracy or better, and instructional level texts were those readers could read with 95–97% accuracy. Swanson et al.'s (1999) meta-analysis of 180 intervention studies showed that for learning-disabled students, one of the three conditions that allow for achievement is that the difficulty level of the task must be controlled enough that the learner can be successful.

This is nowhere more important than for children who struggle. Too often, only the students who can read well are given lots of opportunities in school for high-success reading, and as a result they flourish. Kids who can't read well come to school ready for the promise of an education, and they're given impenetrable texts. They might as well be given sawdust. Many studies support this conclusion. For example, Ehri et al. studied a specific tutoring program to support struggling first-grade English language learners, and after tracking the daily oral reading accuracy of the students, found that "the reading achievement of students who received . . . tutoring appeared to be explained primarily by one aspect of their tutoring experience—reading texts at a high level of accuracy, between 98% and 100%" (2007, 441). O'Connor et al. found that greater fluency growth was achieved by sixth-grade readers whose reading was below grade level when they were provided with texts they could read accurately versus when they were provided tutoring in the texts used in the classroom. "Across groups," they found, "fluency was the strongest contributor to reading comprehension" (2002, 482). O'Connor et al. concluded, "Our results suggest that students with very low fluency will not improve their reading ability if they are taught with grade-level materials" (483).

The exemplary teachers in studies by Johnston, Allington, and Pressley rejected district plans that required one-size-fits-all mandates, wherein all students read the same texts and answer the same questions every day. These teachers instead recognized that such mandates contradict everything that is known about effective teaching. If need be, they spent their own money to provide multilevel texts, not only during language arts time, but in social studies and science as well. Allington writes, "A primary outcome of these exemplary teachers was the acceleration of literacy development in their lowest-achieving students (Allington and Johnston 2002, Pressley et al. 2001). While students at all achievement levels benefited from exemplary teaching, it was the lowest achievers who benefited most.

It is important to note that children need to read books they can read with fluency, not only during the reading workshop, but across the entire school day. This means rethinking the reading children are doing in social studies and science. Chall and Conrad (1991) found that only one of eighteen social studies and science textbooks they examined had a readability level that matched the intended grade in which the textbook would be used. Four of the textbooks were written for students who could read at a level three or four grades higher than the grade for which the book was written, and almost all were written for students two grades beyond the intended level. And this doesn't address the fact that even if the text was geared for that grade level—say, the fifth-grade level—*grade level* refers to what the average child at that grade can do. An average class will typically contain a spread of children, including many who are not able to read at the level that is determined to be average.

What does all this mean? It means that it is important to provision the actual children one has with books they can read. Publishers may advertise a set of books as appropriate for average fifth-grade readers, but some classrooms only have three or four kids who read like average fifth-grade readers! Some students will need easier books, and others, more challenging books.

It takes just a moment of reflection on our own reading lives to be reminded that it's important not only that young people have access to books they *can* read, but that they also have access to books they *want* to read. Choice matters, not a little but a lot. The goal, after all, is not only to teach kids to read, but to help youngsters grow up to be people who value reading. Luring kids to be invested in reading is not a small goal. After all, a 2007 National Endowment for the Arts study, "To Read or Not to Read,"

found that Americans are reading less, with people aged fifteen to twenty-four spending fewer than seven minutes a day reading. If we hope to bring up a nation of readers, it is crucial to allow them to choose among high-interest books that they can read. In fact, Guthrie and Humenick did a meta-analysis of twenty-two experimental or quasi-experimental studies of reading motivation and achievement, and they found several factors that were strongly related to student success. Ensuring that students had easy access to interesting texts was the single most influential factor, and providing children choice over what they read and whom they read with was the second most influential factor.

Learners need to read increasingly complex texts, and as part of this, they need to be stretched by being engaged with texts that are appropriately complex for their grade level.

College textbooks and scientific journals and magazines, as measured by Lexile levels, have increased in difficulty. American students who attend college are all too often encountering difficulty reading college-level texts with independence (Hayes and Ward 1992). A consensus has formed, therefore, around the resolve to accelerate students' progress so they can read increasingly complex texts and also to provide them with access to grade level complex texts even when students are not yet able to read those texts independently. Shanahan et al. (2012) liken developing reading muscle to lifting weights,

and write, "It is impossible to develop robust reading skills without reading challenging texts." Topping et al. (2007) found that the combination of high-quality books and a high quantity of books to read lead to high academic achievement gains among students in grades 1–12. Teachers are increasingly finding ways to provide students with access to complex texts, even if they cannot read those texts independently. Digital recordings and teacher read-alouds allow students to benefit from hearing, thinking, and talking about these texts (Elley 1989; Fountas and Pinnell 2012; Ray 2006).

It is especially important that students develop their vocabularies, not only by learning the domain-specific words that they are apt to encounter in content area classrooms (*erosion, adaptation, ecosystem*), but also through immersion in academic language such as *estimates, culminates, distinguishes,* and *classify*. Figurative language, too, is a hallmark of more complex texts, and students need to wrestle with the meaning of metaphors, similes, and personification. When students are given access to complex texts, they also are immersed in complex sentence structures, including longer sentences that contain subordinate clauses and embedded phrases. Complex texts are often organized in more complex ways: in narratives, time doesn't usually unfold sequentially but may be marked by flashbacks and flashforwards and by gaps in time and by a series of digressions. More complex expository texts are apt to contain multiple central ideas, hierarchies of categories.

Although nothing is gained from asking a student who cannot decode a complex text to sit in front of such a text, staring at the page, there are many students who *can* decode such a text and do not have the high-level strategies or the appetite for tackling this sort of difficulty. To help these students develop the muscles to handle complex texts, it is helpful to provide students with the instruction necessary to deal with complex text structures, shifting perspectives, figurative language, and the like. This instruction will involve opportunities to engage in repeated readings, to work in pairs, to pause often as they read to summarize and discuss meaning, and to explore word meanings (Shanahan et al. 2012).

In part, learning to tackle increasingly complex texts involves not just reading skills, but an effort-based stance on learning. Shanahan suggests that learning to read is similar to undergoing physical therapy. He writes:

> Initially, such therapy is often painful and exhausting, and it's tempting to cheat on the exercises a bit. Physical therapists have to focus not only on the muscle groups that need to be strengthened or stretched, but also on the patient's motivation. They need to keep the patient's head in the game, because working past the pain is beneficial. Similarly, it can be tough for students to hang in there and stick with a text that they have to labor through, looking up words, puzzling over sentences, straining to make connections. Teachers may be tempted to try to make it easier for students by avoiding difficult texts. The problem is, easier work is less likely to make readers stronger. Teachers need to motivate students to keep trying, especially when the level of work is increasing. The payoff comes from staying on track. (Shanahan 2012)

The challenge is to be sure that students are interested and invested enough in their reading that they are willing to work with some persistence when they encounter difficulty.

Learners need direct, explicit instruction in the strategies and skills of proficient reading.

Research shows that good readers are strategic (Pressley and Afflerbach 1995). Explicit instruction in comprehension strategies can make a dramatic difference in lifting the level of students' reading. Dole et al. (1996) study, "The Effects of Strategy Instruction on the Comprehension Performance of At-Risk Students," "demonstrates the value of strategy instruction in comparison to other effective instruction and the specific value of strategy instruction for far transfer." The results "demonstrated the value of strategy instruction when the goal was to understand particular texts and especially when the goal was to understand independently read texts" (82).

The National Reading Panel strongly supports instruction in comprehension strategies, suggesting that the teaching of even one comprehension strategy can lead to improved comprehension and that teaching a repertoire of strategies can make an even larger difference (National Reading Panel 2000). Allington's research yielded similar findings, noting that "exemplary teachers in our study routinely gave direct, explicit demonstrations of the cognitive strategies that good readers use when they read" (2002, 743). It is important that strategy instruction teach students *what* the strategy is, *when* it is used, *how* it is used, and *why* it is worth using.

This is important information because many teachers think of teaching as little more than assigning and assessing work. Assigning students a task—say one that resembles those on high-stakes assessments—and then assessing their abilities to do that work should not be confused with instruction. When imagining instruction, think instead of a progression of work that goes from "watch me, let me demonstrate" to "now you try and I'll support you." Many researchers have detailed this form of strategy instruction; among them are Duke and Pearson (2002), who point out that strategy instruction involves:

- Naming and describing the strategy: why, when, and how it could be used
- Modeling the strategy in action

- Using the strategy collaboratively
- Guiding practice of the strategy, gradually releasing responsibility to the student
- Providing opportunity for using the strategy independently

As Rosenshine (2012) found, "The more effective teachers do not overwhelm their students by presenting too much new material at once. Rather, these teachers only present small amounts of new material at any time, and then assist the students as they practice this material" (13–14).

Duke and Pearson (2002) make an important caveat in "Effective Practices for Developing Reading Comprehension," stating, "It is important that neither the teacher nor the students lose sight of the need to coordinate or orchestrate comprehension strategies. Strategies are not to be used singly—good readers do not read a book and only make predictions. Rather, good readers use multiple strategies constantly" (210). Allington (2002b) discusses this same point when he writes, "The instructional environment must foster independent strategy transfer and use. A real concern is that when instruction becomes too explicit too much of the time, children never acquire the independent strategy transfer and use. Use of a strategy in a highly structured, teacher-directed setting is not the same as knowing how and when to profitably and successfully use the strategy when reading independently."

Learners need opportunities to talk in response to texts.

Talking and writing both provide concrete, visible ways for learners to do the thinking work that later becomes internalized and invisible. Think about it. If you want to gain insights on your teaching, your family, your life—what do you do? You meet with someone to "talk things over." If you want become better at doing something, you bring in a coach, a tutor, or an advisor. Whomever the person is, what you will do is talk. In think tanks, study groups, inquiry projects, graduate courses, seminars—what do you do? You talk. Talk is the medium in which we all outgrow ourselves, over and over again.

It was Vygotsky (1978), more than anyone, who staked out the theory that accounts for the crucial role of social interactions in supporting learning. The key element in his theory of learning is that "all the higher functions originate as actual relationships between individuals" (957). The words that we say in conversation, the kinds of thinking we do in collaboration, become internalized. If you and I had a conversation about the ending of a book, mulling over why the author may have chosen to end it that way and weighing how the book might have been different had it ended differently, then another time, reading alone, I can reach the ending of a book and think to myself, "Hmm, . . . I wonder why the author decided to end this book this way?" The thinking that I'd be doing would be an internalized conversation.

Because teaching reading is teaching thinking, it is not surprising that social relationships are critical to a reading workshop. Conversations are especially crucial, because data suggests that few American students are growing up to be thoughtfully literate. The related finding is this. If one looks at what students spend their time doing in school, it is very easy to project the skills that they will master. If students spend their time answering low-level literal questions, filling in blanks, and recalling facts, then that will be the kind of thinking they can do well. And all too often, that is exactly what is being asked for and what is being learned in American classrooms. In study after study, researchers report that in the typical classroom the assigned tasks overwhelmingly emphasize copying, remembering, and reciting, with few tasks assigned that engage students in discussions about what they've read. Is it any wonder that many students do not seem adept at comparing and contrasting, analyzing, making connections, and thinking interpretively and critically? And yet this is exactly the sort of literacy that is required in the world of today—and of tomorrow. The New Commission on the Skills of the American Workforce (2007) describes the candidates that the best employers in the world will be looking for this way: "Candidates will have to be comfortable with ideas and abstractions, good at both analysis and synthesis, creative and innovative, self-disciplined and well-organized, able to learn quickly and work well as a member of a team and have the flexibility to adapt quickly to frequent changes."

One of the most powerful ways to teach children to think is to teach them to engage in thoughtful discussions, and especially discussions that incorporate thinking under, between, and around texts. In Allington and Pressley's research on exemplary teachers, they note that the nature of talk was fundamentally different in the classrooms led by exemplary teachers. These teachers fostered more student talk—teacher-student and student-student. The talk was not chatter, but problem-posing, problem-solving talk.

Talking well, like writing well, does not emerge *ex nihilo*, and it is helpful to explicitly teach students to make claims that are grounded in the text, to supply evidence for those claims, to talk between the example and the claim, to uncover assumptions, and to explore ramifications. It is also helpful to teach students to develop a line of thinking through sustained talk about one subtopic, and as part of this to elaborate using transitional phrases such as "The important thing about this is . . ." or "What is worth noticing about this example is . . ." Then, too, it is important to teach readers to be able to entertain ideas different than their own, to hold more than one idea in mind at a time, and to build upon the ideas of others, following an idea to its conclusion. Teaching youngsters to talk has a great deal to do with teaching them the skills of writing to think—and both are essential.

For this reason, reading workshops not only support talk, but also *teach* talk. Readers are generally matched to a long-term partner—someone who is able to read and is interested in reading similar books. Partners tend to read independently for most of the reading workshop, but in the last few minutes, they compare notes, raise and pursue questions, and learn to see the text through each other's perspectives. For something like half the year, readers work in small groups—inquiry groups or book clubs—so their talk can encompass not only a partner, but also other voices and other perspectives.

Partners Let Their Conversations Grow

Prompts can help... Try...

❀ "The important thing about this is..."

❀ "This connects to..."

❀ "An example of this is..."

❀ "I'm starting to notice..."

❀ "This doesn't seem to fit..."

FIG. 3–2   Learners need opportunities to talk.

The classroom community as a whole engages in extended conversations around texts that are read aloud.

Learners need support reading information books and building a knowledge base and academic vocabulary through information reading.

Adults read an enormous amount of nonfiction (Venezky 1982; Smith 2000). According to one study, 96% of the text on the World Wide Web is expository (Kamil and Lane 1998). This suggests that if we are going to prepare children for the world, we need to be sure they have strong skills for reading expository texts. Research suggests that until recently, students have not had enough access to information texts. One study of first-grade classrooms found that, on average, informational texts constituted less than 10% of classroom libraries and were supported by only 3% of materials displayed on walls and other surfaces in classrooms. This study also showed that first-grade classrooms studied informational texts for only an average of 3.6 minutes a day. Lower-income children logged just 1.9 minutes a day of exposure to informational texts (Duke 2000). A study by Goodwin and Miller supports these findings, suggesting that the average child in the United States spends just four minutes a day reading nonfiction.

One of the reasons that it is critical for students to increase the time spent reading nonfiction is that the strength of a student's general knowledge has a close relationship to the student's ability to comprehend complex nonfiction texts. Students who read a great deal of nonfiction gain knowledge about the world, as well as about vocabulary. Cunningham and Stanovich (1991) state that "the analyses of ability-exposure discrepancies (Tables 7 and 8) seem to indicate that even the child with limited reading skills will build vocabulary and knowledge structures through reading" (271). A similar study conducted by Krashen (2004) found that "conscious language learning does not appear to be as efficient as acquisition from input" and that "spelling and vocabulary are developed . . . by reading" (454).

Learners need assessment-based instruction, including feedback that is tailored specifically to their specific strengths and needs.

Learners are not all the same, and learners do not all need the same things to progress. Teaching, then, must always be responsive, and our ideas about what works and what doesn't work must always be under construction.

Certainly, when a teacher decides to angle her teaching in such a way as to support a cluster of reading skills (in expository reading, say, the ability to ascertain the main idea, to think between generalizations and particulars, and to synthesize within and across texts), then teaching begins with observing, listening, and making small informal assessments. Those assessments help us analyze what it is that our learners can do, can almost do, and can't yet do.

By taking the time to look at students' work and to theorize about their place along a pathway of development in a cluster of skills, we provide ourselves with the knowledge that enables us to provide explicit, concrete, doable guidance so that each learner is able to progress toward goals that are clear. This requires a stance on teaching that means teachers always behave in classrooms as researchers. We must invent ways to study kids' work, to research and reflect and discuss and imagine what good work entails. We must wrestle with what the pathways toward good work can look like, and we must help kids progress along those pathways. Assessment, then, like teaching, can't be outsourced. And assessment can't be something that occurs once or twice or three times a year. Instead, assessment is sewn into the fabric of our teaching. In this series, you'll see that units of study are book-ended with discussions of some of the formative assessments that inform these units.

Research suggests that the use of performance assessments embedded into curriculum can support building higher-order complex skills and can improve instruction (Goldschmidt et al.; Pellegrio et al. 2001; Wood et al. 2007).

In addition, a growing body of research supports the use of learning progressions to guide and raise the level of instruction. Research has demonstrated that learning progressions have important potential for educators, policy makers, and curriculum and assessment designers. Multiple policy documents and research reports published recently (see, for example, Daro et al. 2011; Corcoran et al. 2009; Mosher 2011) and related to learning progressions argue that the development of the Common Core State Standards has created a strong need for learning progressions. For students to have a hope of meeting these standards, teachers will need to monitor student progress and know when and how to intervene to support students in reaching the standards. They will need to be aware of when students are encountering difficulty in working to reach these standards and of how to support students in getting back on track. In short, teachers will need to know "when to teach what to whom" (Daro et al. 2011, 12). Learning progressions, as research-based maps or pathways, can help offer that sense of where to go next.

Of course, assessment is never more critical than when it allows us to take our cues from students who struggle with reading. If a child enters our classroom already encumbered with labels, then we need to be clear from the start: it is our job to turn that child around so that he begins immediately to see that, in fact, learning and progress are within reach. Readers who struggle cannot wait even a week before we begin to show them that reading can make sense for them, and they can get better as readers in a palpable, observable fashion, achieving multiple years of growth in just a single year. The first step is for the most knowledgeable person around to assess these readers to find what the reading work is that this child can do with success. If this is a fifth-grade child and he needs to be reading books at the level of Frog and Toad, then absolutely nothing is gained by taking him instead to Captain Underpants. Halfway measures are good for naught, because with texts he can't read well, the child still won't feel everything clicking together into reading and still won't have the chance to read in ways that allow him to learn from reading. If the various stakeholders who are invested in this child—the people who care about him—disagree, then these adults need to come together and talk longer and think harder so that a single, coherent plan is made that will allow this child to be a successful reader (with the texts that are within reach) and then to move forward in giant steps.

Children who struggle with reading cannot be taken from the language arts classroom—from reading, writing, word study, or reading aloud—for extra help in language arts.

It is especially worrisome if children who are below benchmark in reading are taken out of the general classroom for reading once or twice a week and left within the room the other days. The result of this is that when the child is in the classroom, she won't understand the read-aloud book or know the shared reading texts or grasp references in the minilessons to prior instruction because she will have missed a third of reading class, leaving her with big gaps. How much better if the child can receive supplementary support before school, after school, or during a time other than reading class. For these particular children to achieve success, they would benefit from a cohesive intervention program, where all the adults work together and collaborate regularly to ensure positive outcomes for the child's reading progress. This is what makes programs like Reading Recovery so successful in achieving accelerated progress with their struggling readers. Interventions that utilize methodologies that are congruent with classroom practice support effective teaching and learning.

Children who read below grade level need to spend 100% of their time reading books they can read with ease.

This means that guided reading can't be about propping a child up to struggle valiantly through a text that is too hard. Anyone who uses guided reading in such a fashion should reread Gay Su Pinnell and Irene Fountas's important books on the topic! It is critical that children who read below grade level are reading books within their zone of proximal development, not just during reading time, but across the day. For these readers, 90% of their reading time should be spent on books that are easy for them, books they can read with 99% accuracy, and, perhaps as much as 10% of the time, they can be reading books that they read with 96% accuracy, fluency, and comprehension.

During extra-help time, children who struggle with reading need help that is assessment-based, tailored to that particular child, and in sync with what is happening in the classroom.

It cannot be that all children who struggle with reading receive the same one-size-fits-all help during this intervention, because what we know about each one is that they are more different, one from another, than most readers are. Kids who struggle with reading need something, but not necessarily the same thing! For starters, some children in grades 3–5 who struggle need help in comprehension and fluency; others need help in phonics and word work. The instruction these readers need will be utterly different.

For any learner to grow stronger, that learner must be provided with informative, responsive targeted feedback. Hattie's research perhaps best supports this claim (2008). He reviewed 180,000 studies involving 20 to 30 million students and found that of 100 factors that contribute to student achievement, providing learners with feedback rates in the very top 5–10% of influences. The feedback is especially valuable if the teacher helps the learner know where he is going, what progress he has made so far, and what specific activities he can do next to progress toward the goal. Ideally, learners also receive help in refining and seeking more challenging goals. This is what conferring—working one-on-one with an individual child—is: listening and looking to understand a child's work and intentions and then helping that child take all of the instruction that is in the air and use it in ways that connect precisely to him, making sure he is working with direction and feedback.

Above all, children who struggle with reading need access to good teachers, and that means that teachers need high-quality professional development. This subject is such an important one that I devote an entire chapter to it.

Eight essentials of reading instruction are woven into the reading workshop structure.

In summary, these tenets, then, have led to the reading workshop structure for teaching reading:

- Learners need teachers who demonstrate what it means to live richly literate lives, wearing a love of reading on our sleeves.
- Learners need long stretches of time to read.
- Learners need opportunities to read high-interest, accessible books of their own choosing.
- Learners need explicit instruction in the skills of proficient reading.
- Learners need opportunities to talk and sometimes to write in response to texts.
- Learners need assessment-based instruction, including feedback that is tailored specifically to them. Strugglers especially need instruction that is tailored to their specific strengths and needs, as well as extra time and extra help.
- Learners need teachers to read aloud.
- Learners need a balanced approach to language arts, one that includes a responsible approach to the teaching of writing as well as of reading.

Chapter 4

The Big Picture of a Reading Workshop

I N MANY WAYS, reading workshop can be compared to the process of knitting a cardigan. The structure of a cardigan is simple and basic: a cardigan has a left front, a right front, a back, and two sleeves. But that simple structure allows the designer to incorporate a seemingly infinite variety of elements: different necklines, sleeve lengths, textures, and colors. This flexibility allows the designer to tailor the cardigan to the person who will wear it.

Likewise, the reading workshop has a simple and basic structure. This predictable structure accommodates the ever-changing and complex work that students will do, and it allows you, the designer, to tailor each day's teaching to the learning needs of your students.

For the bulk of time during each reading workshop, students carry on with their reading. As they do so, they draw upon a growing repertoire of skills, tools, strategies, and habits. The whole-class instruction adds to that repertoire of skills and strategies, and the units of study organize the larger projects that give direction to students' reading. Perhaps for one unit, students are reading across a stack of books to develop expertise on the habitats, eating habits, and methods of protection for first one animal and then another. For another unit, students are reading shared books with a club comprised of four readers, and together the children are synthesizing nonfiction and historical fiction texts related to a time period and learning to see symbols supporting themes. Whatever the unit of study may be, the bulk of students' time during the reading workshop is spent reading, in the fullest sense of the word: reading, imagining, thinking, recalling, questioning, talking, writing, reviewing, comparing, researching, and reading some more. If you have taught within a writing workshop structure, the reading workshop structure will be very familiar to you. It will include minilessons, independent work time, conferring and small-group work, mid-workshop teaching, and shares during which partnerships or clubs work together.

As I describe it, you'll see how the structure upholds the tenets we all know are necessary to teach children to read. You'll find separate chapters in this book on each of the major components of a reading workshop.

FIG. 4–1 The structure of a reading workshop

A CURRICULUM INVOLVING A SEQUENCE OF GRADE-SPECIFIC UNITS OF STUDY

The structure of the reading workshop remains largely the same throughout the year and across years, but in reading, as in writing, the actual work that kids do and the instruction teachers teach varies as the year unfolds. The top level of structure is your units of study. The grade level cohort of teachers will have planned a yearlong sequence of units of study, each lasting four to six weeks. For instance, the third grade might be as follows: *Building a Reading Life, Reading to Learn, Character Studies, Research Clubs*, mystery clubs,

biography clubs, social issue text sets. Embedded within these units will be strands of skills. Teachers will think of the units more specifically in terms of skills. For example, teachers will approach the third-grade character unit knowing that the unit focuses not only on using story elements to summarize, but also on inference and interpretation. Other units will extend some of those skills and highlight others. You want to ensure that your units and your reading skill progressions and assessments match clearly.

We suggest planning for a roughly equal division of fiction and nonfiction units, although a number of units straddle those categories. Usually the units taught in the fall support students working in swap-book partnerships (so perhaps for a week, the two members of one partnership read Gary Paulsen books, with titles being passed between the two readers). When a unit supports partnerships, this usually means that the reading workshop ends with five minutes for partner conversations. Often there are also partner conversations during the minilesson or midway through the workshop, during a mid-workshop teaching point. Units in the spring usually support students working in research teams to investigate a topic (such as the battles in the American Revolution) or in clubs to read multiple copies of a sequence of books. The research teams and clubs are apt to meet for longer chunks of time less often—perhaps meeting for ten minutes at the end of three workshops in a week.

MINILESSONS AND INDEPENDENT WORK TIME

Reading workshops open with the teacher teaching everyone a minilesson that usually includes a quick demonstration of a powerful reading strategy. The minilesson is meant to equip learners with a strategy they can use not only that day but whenever they need it. Each unit of study book contains seventeen to twenty-two minilessons, written in the words I used—or a coauthor used—to actually teach that lesson. In most reading units of study, there is a read-aloud text or two that thread through the sequence of the unit. There is a pacing guide for the way the read-aloud interfaces with the unit. It may be, for instance, that to teach the first minilesson, you need to have finished reading aloud the first two chapters of the read-aloud book (and no more), and then the next time the read-aloud book threads into a minilesson, a few days later, you need to have read aloud five chapters. You could decide to substitute another book for the suggested read-aloud, but we tend to suggest that the first time you teach a unit, it will be easier for you if you stay with the book we recommend.

Some nonfiction units are built not around a book but around a topic: extreme weather, the American Revolution, the debate over whether schools should serve chocolate milk. Again, you are welcome to alter the topic—doing so (like altering the read-aloud book) won't be hard to do—but I again suggest that when possible, you stay with the topics and texts we recommend the first time you teach a unit.

After the ten-minute minilesson, you say those all important words: "Off you go!" And now students turn to their ongoing independent reading work, which might be a club book, a partner book, or an independent book. In the reading workshop, that means readers get their self-chosen, within-reach books out of their backpacks, and they settle down to read.

Teachers who are new to workshop sometimes wonder what kids are doing during reading time—after all, they are supposed to be working, not reading! The truth is they are working at their reading. Reading is a skill, like any other, and it takes work to get better at it. That does not mean that these readers are left on their own during this time. You will be actively conferring and teaching small groups, making sure that children have chosen not only their books, but their reading work wisely. Every reader has work to do, and that work grows in part out of assessments and in part out of the cumulative impact of minilessons. Imagine this is a unit of study on tackling nonfiction complexity. Some readers are working together to compare the main ideas in the texts they are reading. You'll see them reading quietly, jotting notes, underlining, and getting ready to defend their thinking. Others may be working on reading slightly more difficult texts, and you'll see them previewing the texts, using what they've learned about getting ready to read to orient themselves not only to the topic, but also to the text structures. Still others may be working on teaching about what they've learned, and you'll see them giving mini-lectures about the topic, referring to what they've read, and using the charts and illustrations to highlight their teaching.

CHILDREN ENGAGE IN ONGOING READING WORK (AND WRITING ABOUT READING)

When children disperse from the minilesson, they bring with them bins or baggies or some kind of carrier containing the books they are reading and the ones they'll start reading soon—or some children may be reading digitally on Kindles or Nooks or other smart devices. Regardless of the container, the books in this collection may be ones selected from the classroom library or may have been brought from home or from the local or school library. Not all of those books will have been leveled, of course, but you'll be teaching your readers how to choose books wisely and monitor their comprehension, so they should become adept and confident choosers of books from any source. (More about that in *Reading Pathways: Grades 3–5*, Chapters 4 and 5.) When a child who has been reading level P books in your classroom turns to a book that has not been leveled—say, one from home or a digital version—you expect the child will select a book that is comparable to those that she's been reading in the classroom. Children will generally select a few books at a time, filling their collection with these books, which means that when they finish one book and are ready to start another, they need not head to the library for fifteen minutes of roaming about. They can simply turn to the next book without missing a beat. Some teachers refer to the books in children's baggies as "books by the bed." Most teachers send books home every night; sometimes children have take-home baggies or other carriers.

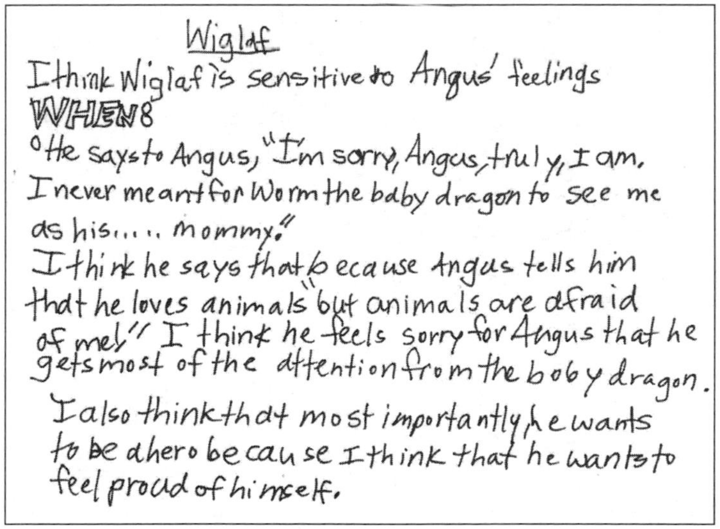

> Wiglaf
>
> I think Wiglaf is sensitive to Angus' feelings WHEN:
>
> ° He says to Angus, "I'm sorry, Angus, truly, I am. I never meant for Worm the baby dragon to see me as his...... mommy."
> I think he says that because Angus tells him that he loves animals "but animals are afraid of me." I think he feels sorry for Angus that he gets most of the attention from the baby dragon.
>
> I also think that most importantly he wants to be a hero because I think that he wants to feel proud of himself.

FIG. 4–2 A student's notebook entry explaining a character's motivations

Later in the year, children will often read books with members of a book club, drawing from text sets that contain multiple copies of a title. These might fall under categories such as historical fiction or fantasy, and these sets of multiple copies are apt to rotate among classrooms so that perhaps the fifth grades have the historical fiction books in January and early February, and then these sets of books are brought into the fourth-grade classrooms. Don't worry about children reading the same book as they move up grades. They'll have changed level by then, so even though they may be reading the same genre, they won't be reading the same titles.

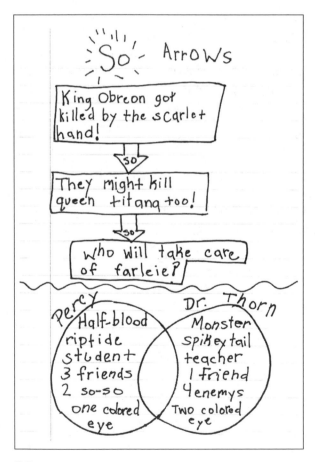

FIG. 4–3

Provisioning a Classroom Library

Walk into any Williams-Sonoma and pause to look around. Whether or not you consider yourself a chef, when you are surrounded by the newest gadgets, copper-bottomed pans, and monogrammed aprons, it's easy to find yourself wanting to cook, and, since the tools are easily accessible, grabbing what you need to bring any project you imagine to life. Now, walk into your classroom and study your classroom library. Like Barnes and Noble, Goodreads, and Amazon, we are in the business of marketing books to kids. Your classroom library must make students want to read, selling all your readers—both the avid consumers of books and those who have never before picked up a book by choice—on the texts it holds.

One of the things reading researchers have clearly shown is that kids need access to a volume of books. Nowhere is this more true than in a reading workshop. Supporting students with reading requires a volume of books. Richard Allington suggests that schools have at minimum 1,000 books per classroom, with at least 500 unique titles included in the collection (Donnalynn Miller's keynote, August 2014 Reading Institute).

Provisioning a classroom library is an ongoing process, and teachers work tirelessly to ensure students have access to a volume of high-interest, within-reach texts that represent the genres, topics, and series their students love. Take an inventory of the titles you currently have, consider the levels of students in your classroom and the types of topics and texts they love, and then grow your library. You will want to draw on the titles available in the guided reading library of your school and the school library, if you have these resources available. Know that books will need to be an ongoing budget item for your school and classroom, as book loss is certain to occur. Look for the silver lining in this situation. As books leave your classroom, they become permanent features in kids' personal collections.

We have created complete grade-level classroom library collections (and a separate library for each grade for classrooms where students are reading dramatically below benchmark), carefully designed to serve as the bedrock of powerful reading instruction. But we also know that many schools and districts will need to build up your collections over time—or you may already have good classroom libraries that you will want to shore up with specific "shelves" on a variety of high-interest topics, or shelves developed to support specific Units of Study.

Teachers may also work creatively in other ways to acquire books for their classrooms. Teachers scour tag sales and thrift shops to find titles their students will love. Some submit short grant proposals requesting libraries or books alongside a brief description of how these texts will be used in their classroom. Other schools hold a variety of fundraising activities, involving students and parents.

Consider how to best arrange your classroom library. It is important to level a big portion of your classroom library and to level both fiction and nonfiction books. Many teachers use the Fountas & Pinnell Leveled Books website to support this work, which houses a regularly updated database of book titles by reading level. Others draw on Scholastic's Book Wizard, which includes a book-leveling app that can easily scan and level books in your library. Of course, not all titles are featured in this database, so teachers draw on their knowledge of the leveled books in their libraries to help them estimate levels for other texts.

All readers should see themselves represented in your classroom library. This means it is necessary that your classroom library include texts that represent the range of readers in your classroom. The classroom library should feel inviting and allow students to easily access within-reach texts. To achieve this goal, teachers establish fiction and nonfiction sections in their libraries. Many teachers arrange a chunk of their fiction library into bins by level and label the bins so children can access their within-reach texts. It is important that students see themselves not just as a level M reader, so teachers divide the remaining books into bins by series, author, and genre, and label these the "39 Clues" bin or the "Gary Paulsen" bin. Some teachers even create special bins featuring books: "Hot Off the Presses!", "Award Winners," or "Books in the Theaters." What we do to organize our fiction library, we should also do to organize our nonfiction library. Teachers divide their nonfiction library into leveled bins, as well as bins that represent the topics, series, and authors your students love. Think about the most enticing displays in the public libraries and bookstores you frequent, and look for ways to mirror those arrangements in your classroom.

As part of his theory of five laws of library science, S. R. Ranganathan states that "a library is a growing organism." It grows and evolves as your readers change interests and move levels, as you transition into new units of study, and as new texts are published. That is, the classroom library is not a static organism. When designing your classroom library, look ahead to the units you will teach across the year. Many teachers decide to leave titles related to genres or topics studied later in the year out of the classroom library. If, for instance, you will be teaching a unit on *Reading the Weather, Reading the World*, you might choose to tuck bins of books on weather away in the library, unveiling them at the start of the unit. This can breathe new energy into your classroom library and expose students to books they might otherwise not have read. Of course, if this decision will dramatically limit the number of texts students have access to, you would be wise to leave the classroom library as is.

Your classroom library is one of the most visible features in your room, and it sends a strong message to your students about your views on literacy and learning. Regular investments in your classroom library and attention to physical layout will ensure your library sends the message that reading is important and that books are meant to be treasured.

Writing about Reading

When writing about reading during any one day's reading workshop, readers typically jot half a dozen Post-its® or a few brief entries in a reader's notebook or make digital annotations. In many cases, teachers allow the reader to decide which format to write in. In book clubs in which students read texts in synchrony with each other, many teachers ask readers to write a page-and-a-half response to their reading once a week or so.

Either way, the writing that readers do as they read is meant to capture thinking, and that thinking (that jot) is typically then put at the center of a partnership or book club conversation that follows independent reading time, during what is often referred to as teaching share time. If you are also teaching writing workshop and your students are learning to draft and revise literary essays, you may want to provide your students with time to do the reading and thinking that supports the writing during their reading time. However, the writing generally occurs during the writing workshop.

CONFERENCES AND SMALL GROUPS

Reading workshop is structured so that you can give students feedback while they are in the midst of their work. The simplicity and predictability of the workshop is designed to free you from constant choreographing so that you have time to observe, to listen, to assess, and to teach into each student's zone of proximal development. Like an artist in a pottery studio, a soccer coach in the midst of a practice scrimmage, or a physicist in a physics lab, you will circulate among your students. You'll pull close to observe, mull over what is and is not working, and intervene to coach, demonstrate, encourage, and celebrate with individuals and small groups. This teaching may reinforce the minilesson, or it might address the unique needs and goals of a child or a group of children. The teaching in a conference or a small group, like the teaching that occurs within minilessons, aims to support not just today's work, but also children's reading from that point on.

We've found that it can help you enormously to prepare ahead for conferences and small-group work. That is, while you'll want to respond to the individual needs of your learners, those needs are often predictable. Also, sometimes you'll want some tools with you—a learning progression or a certain text or a some exemplar jots—and you don't want to be searching for those while deciding what to teach. One of the great gifts of these resources, we hope, is that you'll feel prepared not only for the first ten minutes of class, but also for the next forty minutes. You'll have on hand a series of predictable small groups and conferences you may want to teach that week, as well as the tools with which to teach them. Then you can focus on how your children respond to your teaching, rather than trying to invent it all in the moment, which can feel variously beautiful and desperate on different days!

Conferences and small groups are essential in a workshop. The small groups often feel like one-to-one conferences but involve a cluster of children instead of just one child. These forums allow you to tailor your instruction to match the needs and goals of individual learners. Reading conferences are very similar to writing conferences, and both are essential not only for the student but also for us as teachers. It is by conferring that we develop the knowledge, the insight, and the methods to be able to reach learners. A teacher-student reading conference often provides the material for the small-group strategy lessons and the minilessons we teach later. During reading time, you will tend to lead several small groups. Some of these will be guided reading groups; others will be small groups of other sorts. The ideal situation is to be able to select the method for small-group work that best suits your particular learners and the moment. Both conferences and small-group instruction are important enough that I devote an entire chapter to each later in this guide.

On any given day, you will move among many readers, helping many to settle and channeling many toward work they feel as if they chose independently but that was really through negotiation with you. Then, you will be apt to lead a four- or five-minute conference with two or three individual readers

or partnerships of readers and to coach a small group or two. By this time, you generally will pause to briefly address the whole class, usually through a mid-workshop teaching point that sometimes channels kids to work with a partner for a few minutes before they resume reading—and then you resume teaching. Don't worry, we'll help you with all of this, so that you can focus on what really matters—your readers.

Mid–Workshop Teaching

The mid-workshop teaching can be a way to peel kids' attention from their books for just a minute while you make a point that has wide implications. You'll see in the units that often we suggest a small point that may move readers' work forward. Sometimes it extends the minilesson, and other times it may be a reminder of ongoing habits. For instance, you might have taught a minilesson on how characters in a story can be more than one way, teaching children to notice how and why characters seem nuanced or complex. Then in your mid-workshop teaching, you might mention that it's not just people, but also places that can be more than one way, and that readers notice the way places are complicated as well. What you don't want to do is offer a mid-workshop teaching point that is really a whole minilesson, because this is meant to be a quick "eyes on me, here's one way to deepen or sharpen your work" moment. Implicit in this interruption is our long experience that some children simply need a moment's respite to refocus again with new zeal. Just as a soccer coach might notice his forwards are tiring and call a huddle for a moment, you too can ask kids to raise their heads, consider some new options, and then return to reading.

We've helped you plan these, because they can make a difference in deepening kids energy and thinking. Often when your small groups aim to support students who need extra support, your mid-workshops aim to give ideas to readers who are ready for new thinking. If you and your students are deep in engaging work, though, you may forego a mid-workshop teaching point. Or on other days you may offer more than one, especially at the start of the year or a unit. This, of course, is exactly the same situation in a writing workshop.

SHARE

The workshop ends with a small amount of time for readers to work collaboratively with partners or with a bit longer time for readers to work with clubs. This time is framed by a teeny bit of teacher talk, and this sometimes takes the form of celebrating what a few readers have done in ways that apply to other readers in other instances, providing you with a chance to balance instruction. You can often angle the sharing that children do during this time. You may do this in ways that provide follow-up to the topic addressed in the day's minilesson. For example, if the minilesson demonstrated a few ways to evaluate evidence of an author's main idea, during the share you might suggest that readers compare their evidence, determining which is most compelling and convincing. Or you might introduce a simple rubric built off of the Informational Reading Learning Progression and invite students to self-assess their own work, asking them to write their best thinking about an author's ideas and then evaluating that work against the rubric.

We help you to plan these shares, because how a workshop ends can be as important as how it begins. Those minutes set your children up for the work they'll continue outside of class. It's often a perfect time to reinforce transfer, agency, and independence.

PARTNERSHIPS (AND CLUBS)

Partnerships are a cornerstone of workshop—and you can't be the partner for each reader in your class! These partnerships will be strategic. As soon as you know a little bit about your readers, you'll help them settle into a stable partnership, which will endure probably for the length of the unit of study, and perhaps longer. Partners help each other with reading work and act as cheerleaders and teammates. Whenever it's feasible, it's helpful if partners are reading the same book, series, genre, or books about the same topic. It's just easier to talk about books when you are reading about the same thing, and the conversations will be higher level because readers don't need to retell basic facts.

When you don't have enough pairs of titles for readers to read the exact same book, often readers can be in swap-book partnerships (that is, they are both reading Gary Paulsen books, one reading *Hatchet*, the other *The River*, and then they swap). The advantage of swap-book partnerships is that half the time, children are able to talk about books that their partner has recently read and knows well. Meanwhile, swap-book partnerships do not require that classroom libraries be in duplicate. Clearly, there will be some issue with kids not finishing books at exactly the same time, and children will need to manage that, having an extra book on hand, rather than not reading at all as they wait. There is no question, however, that reading shared books in synchrony with another person is preferable, whenever you can swing this, and most of us make a point to channel our students who struggle with reading into same-book partnerships.

Children do a variety of sorts of sharing within partnerships. On the Teachers College Reading and Writing Project's Vimeo web page (vimeo.com/tcrwp), you can watch two fourth-graders in a same-book partnership who have just read *Old Yeller* (vimeo.com/album/2777084/video/55954403). You'll see that the readers decide to go to a startling passage in the book, to read it aloud taking parts (roles), and then talk about the emotions in the passage before rereading it with more feeling. Finally, the readers close the book and ad lib the passage. In other partnerships, readers might regularly share words that they found challenging and work together to pronounce and understand the words. The mainstay of partnerships, though, is that a partner rereads her jottings, chooses either a single jot that seems especially important or two jots that go together, puts that Post-it (or entry) on the table between the partners, and then the two children try to talk for as long as they can about the ideas sparked by that one reader's thought. To do this, readers often use "thought prompts" such as "I agree because . . . ," "I disagree because . . . ," "That connects with another part of the book because . . . ," "I think that is important because . . . ," "I used to think . . . , but now I realize . . . ," and so forth. Of course, once these scaffolds are no longer necessary, they fall away, and children simply talk with depth, referencing the text and traveling along a journey of thought.

The partnership conversations that are a mainstay in the fall give way to reading clubs—also called book clubs or literature circles—usually in the spring (Chapter 11 discusses book clubs in some detail). Now the reading workshop still involves a minilesson, time to read, and time to talk. Usually the clubs across a classroom will all be engaged in a genre-based study, as when all the clubs are reading historical fiction books, or a topic-based study when readers are in research clubs. When children are reading a genre like historical fiction in clubs, clubs don't all have to be reading about the same historical era. It will be more interesting, and you'll be able to find a wider range of titles, when children are comparing and contrasting across eras. You will absolutely want to watch the club meetings that are captured in the fourth-grade historical fiction segment (see vimeo.com/album/2777084/video/55950554). You will find this video useful no matter which grade level you teach, because your partnerships and read-aloud book conversations at the start of the year all need to work together in ways that enable children to participate in this sort of conversation by the end of the year.

When clubs are in research groups, children will be working together on a shared topic, building understandings across texts. When they do this work, your readers will often make strategic decisions about when they want to read the same text together and when they want to read different texts. Often, even though children are reading in the same topic, they will find themselves interested in different aspects of that topic. Nonfiction clubs need to meet as often, or more often, than literature clubs, because children are processing a lot of information, and they need to clear up misinformation, share what they've learned, and point each other to great sources. That said, whenever children are in clubs, you'll have to carefully balance the amount of talk, so that they get enough reading done. Ideally, your students will internalize this judgment, so they will learn to say to each other, "It feels like we should get back to reading!"

FIG. 4–4

to offer a writing workshop that lasts a similar length of time. Literacy instruction can continue through those shorter periods of time (twenty minutes) for read-aloud/accountable talk (or for shared reading) and for word study. And, of course, reading and writing thread through the content areas of social studies, science, and to a lesser extent, math.

BEYOND THE READING WORKSHOP

Literacy instruction continues, of course, outside the reading workshop. In addition to the fifty- to sixty-minute reading workshop, many teachers choose

Chapter 5

The Architecture (and the Principles) that Inform Minilessons

WHEN I WAS A BRAND-NEW TEACHER, my colleagues and I had a time in our day that we referred to as DEAR time—Drop Everything and Read. For fifteen minutes, we and the kids would all get out our books and settle down to read, read, read. There was a big emphasis on us, as teachers, reading during this time, so I'd settle down alongside the kids and sink into my novel. It was a peaceful time, a lovely interlude in the midst of a busy day. The room had a camp-y "Kum-Ba-Yah" feeling to it.

Sometimes, today, when I try to explain the reading workshop to a teacher from my generation, her eyes will light up and she'll say, "Oh! I got it! So it's sort of like DEAR time, is that it?"

That's a sign to me that I have a lot more explaining to do because there are important differences between the DEAR times of yesteryear and today's reading workshop. And the biggest difference is that although it is crucially important that we, as teachers, live in our classroom as richly literate adults, carrying our books and our love of reading with us, we've come to realize that youngsters need not only large stretches of time to read books of their own choice, but also explicit direct instruction in the skills, strategies, and habits of proficient readers. That instruction happens during every minute of the reading workshop, from the first to the last minute, but it starts with the minilesson.

Just as the art instructor pulls students together to learn a new glaze or a new way to mix paints, just as the football coach and his team huddle over a new play, just as a writing workshop teacher convenes kids to show them techniques for exploring different leads in a fiction story, so, too, the teacher of reading pulls children together for a minilesson that opens the day's reading workshop and powers the curriculum.

Because children are gathering in and dispersing from the meeting area at the start of every day's reading workshop (and then again at the start of every day's writing workshop), most teachers that I know well have found it worthwhile to take a bit of time at the start of the year to make sure that children can move to and from the meeting area efficiently and calmly. Teachers literally teach children to walk directly from their work spots to the meeting area, sitting themselves down in their assigned spot, sitting on their bottoms

I generally suggest that struggling readers work in same-book partnerships whenever possible, because this allows a friend to provide extra scaffolding for a child's reading, and it means that your time working with one of these readers will do double-duty, helping the other reader as well.

Although the teachers with whom I teach often worry over the content for their minilessons, your first priority should probably be to master the *methods* of teaching minilessons. I'll discuss the content of minilessons—reading skills and strategies—later in this volume, but in general, the biggest challenge is learning not the *content* but, rather, the *methods*. And while the content of minilessons changes from day to day, the architecture of minilessons remains largely the same, and it remains consistent whether you are teaching writing or reading. The architecture of a minilesson is easy to learn and provides enduring support across any minilesson you might ever write. You'll note in the units of study that occasionally we'll offer an inquiry minilesson, which has a very slightly different structure, and every now and then, we may offer a guided practice lesson. We'll look at those shortly as well. To achieve maximum efficiency combined with clarity, most minilessons will be direct instruction, and for those, we suggest this particular architecture.

SAMPLE MINILESSON

The minilesson that follows illustrates the major components of most minilessons. Let's read a sample minilesson, then discuss its component parts. It's a minilesson teaching strategies for determining main ideas when they are implicit in nonfiction texts.

instead of kneeling in ways that block other children's view. In some classrooms, teachers always ask children to bring the same materials to each day's workshop so that children are sure to have whatever they need on hand. In other classrooms, when teachers say, "Let's gather for our reading minilesson," the teacher gestures toward the white board that lists that day's materials. No one way of managing a reading workshop is more correct than another, but it is important for you to take seriously the challenge of managing workshop instruction, bearing in mind that this method of teaching calls for learners to do more self-management than some children have been asked to do before. I write in some detail about the management of a writing workshop in *A Guide to the Writing Workshop*, and the management systems you develop to support a productive writing workshop will transfer perfectly into the reading workshop as well.

Usually children sit in the meeting area alongside a long-term partner, clustered as closely to the teacher as possible. This is not usually a time for children to sit in a circle, because conversations among the students are minimal. This is time instead for the teacher to teach as efficiently and explicitly as possible. So children sit alongside a partner, at the teacher's feet, facing the teacher. Those partners need to be able to read the same books, either in same-book partnerships or swap-book partnerships. So partnerships tend to be homogeneous groupings of children who can read books at the same level.

CONNECTION

Tell a very, very short story about how you researched how to get past the tricky parts of a game.

"Readers, when I was a kid my favorite video game was *Mario Kart*. Have you ever played it?" I began an animated description, acting things out as I described them. "We raced these tiny cars around tracks, dodging enemy racers, trying not to take turns too tightly, and, of course, avoiding the dreaded bananas that would make a car lose total control.

"My brother and I would study the racetracks for hours to figure out the hard parts—especially Rainbow Road. The name sounds friendly, but it wasn't. It was this flashy track in the middle of outer space, and what made it so tough was that there were a ton of places where you could fall off the edge.

"My brother and I thought that if we could just figure out where the tough parts were to Rainbow Road, we'd be able to beat that track. But, it turned out, just knowing what made it tough wasn't enough. We had to develop strategies— like eventually we learned to stay a foot away from the edge and to go slower on the third turn.

"I know that you have games or sports or activities that you've studied this way as well, where you figured out what you needed to do to overcome difficulties. Well, when you're reading, you need to do the same thing with nonfiction texts. You need not just to know the hard parts, but also to come up with strategies to help you with them. In fact, right now, tell a partner *one* thing you know how to do when you're trying to figure out a hard nonfiction text—like you want to get what it's really teaching you."

I waited just a moment for partners to share their ideas.

❖ **Name your teaching point.**

"Readers, today I want to teach you that once readers know how a nonfiction text is complex when it comes to main ideas, they can develop and draw on a toolkit of strategies to support them in determining the main ideas."

TEACHING

Suggest that many students reported that they invented a strategy for discerning the main idea when none is stated explicitly. Detail that strategy.

"As you were talking, I heard some of you say that when the main ideas in your texts aren't stated straight out, when they are instead implicit, it helps to chunk the text into parts and then to pause after each part to say, 'What does this chunk seem to be about?' After that, you read on through another chunk and do that same pausing. After a bit you think about how the chunks fit together."

Recruit students to study a video clip. Set them up to note the multiple main ideas forwarded in the video and then to determine which main ideas are most supported by the text.

"You game to practice this? I'm going to show you a video clip of a public service warning that New York City shows its citizens. As you watch this, think, 'What is one main idea that is being put forward in this text?' Just like you discovered last night, you'll have to chunk the text to do this, noticing what different chunks seem to be about and then seeing how those chunks fit together.

"But here is the challenge. Think also, 'And what else? What is another main idea that is being put forward?' You will probably find yourself jotting four or five possible ideas, but in the end, for these to be *main ideas*, you will want to choose just a few—say, just two. You ready to watch? This lasts less than two minutes, so get ready to watch with some intensity." I showed the clip, which explains how cities are vulnerable to emergencies because of their geography and densely populated area. The video asks New York residents to consider if they are prepared to respond to natural or manmade disasters.

After the clip was over, I said, "So what are the two main ideas you felt were most advanced in this video? Try to decide on two *main ideas*." Students began talking with their partners to hone in on the main ideas they'd found. I noticed there was overwhelming consensus about one main idea and some disagreement about the second. I decided to name two that had the least overlap with each other.

Record two main ideas the video forwards. Ask students to record the main ideas they found and to find the strongest details that support those main ideas. Show the video clip again.

"Let's come back. When we come to a text expecting it to be about more than one thing, a lot jumps out, right? For the first main idea, you were pretty much all saying the same thing—you need to be prepared for disaster to strike at any time. For the second main idea, many of you said it was that cities are dangerous places (or that New York City is a dangerous place)." I quickly jotted those main ideas down on chart paper.

> You need to be prepared for disaster to strike at any time.

-
-

> Cities are dangerous places to live.

-
-

Then I said, "Record your two boxes. They might be the same as mine, or you might have your own—maybe that New York's aging infrastructure makes it especially vulnerable or that weather extremes can have devastating effects on a city. We're going to watch the video again, and this time, will you find supportive details for your two main ideas? These details might come in any order, so sort them as they come! Again, you will probably notice a bunch of them, and in the end, I'm going to ask you to choose the most important supportive details—just two for each main point." Again I showed the clip, modeling how I jotted notes furiously in my reading notebook as I watched.

"Yikes! I've got a ton of details!" I said, holding up a filled page in my notebook. "I've got to prioritize, make sure these details actually fit with this idea. Will you do the same?" I hunched over my notebook, crossed out some details, and starred others.

ACTIVE ENGAGEMENT

Name the transferable reading work students just engaged in, and set students up to try similar work with the texts they've been reading.

"Readers, I'm thinking it will pay off for you to try this work in the texts you're reading now. With longer texts like yours, we can't just say back every little thing the text is teaching in every chunk and all the teeny, tiny supportive details. Instead, we've got to notice individual chunks and then put them together, thinking, 'What are the *main ideas*? And what are the strongest supportive details?'

"Right now, will you find a familiar part in your nonfiction text where you could try this work? Make it a part you've read before so you can quickly skim it again, thinking about what the *main ideas* are that the author's trying to teach. As

soon as you find that part, get started reading and jotting those main ideas and supportive details down."

Coach in to support individual readers as they work to find the main ideas taught in their texts. Voice over with feedback to support the entire class based on your students' needs.

As students skimmed, I leaned into one cluster, then another, offering tips to individual readers. Giovanni had found a main idea that was explicitly stated in the text. "You've got the explicit main idea, the one that was popped out in a sentence," I said. "Look again and ask, 'What other less obvious main ideas are advanced in this text? What else is this text teaching?'"

I saw several students writing all the details the text taught in order, so I offered a tip to all the students. "Jot critically. Really study the supportive details and think about which are strongest before you start writing."

Highlight the work one reader did as a model for other students, restating it if needed to elevate it.

"Readers, listen to what Iris just did! She was rereading the start of *The Most Beautiful Roof in the World*. At the very start she noticed this chunk that seemed kind of small and insignificant, about how this scientist had wanted to study the rainforest canopies since she was a little girl. It was so tiny, just two sentences, that she didn't even jot it down. But then she noticed, as she read on, that the author really supported that idea on the next page. In fact, the author spent almost a whole page talking about it. Iris said to me that sometimes the main ideas are all woven together. Like, the text taught about one thing, and then a second thing, and it went back to the first thing. Instead of chunks of main ideas it was more like threads, so she followed those threads."

LINK

Remind students to pull flexibly from their repertoire of main idea strategies and to begin taking notes that mirror the main ideas and supportive details in the text.

"Readers, as you head off to read today, draw on (and invent) strategies that will help you determine the main ideas your text is teaching. Keep in mind that often the main ideas won't be stated clearly. They'll be implicit, or less obvious, and often there will be multiple main ideas across a text. Prioritize as you read on, pushing yourself to identify the main ideas and supportive details that are most dominant in the text.

"I still don't want to see you reading with pencil in hand and pausing to take notes every fourth line. Instead, pause only when you reach the end of a big, meaningful chunk. Think a moment, and *then* jot the main idea—or ideas—in that chunk of text and the most important supportive details. You'll probably work in a boxes-and-bullets structure, but remember that if your text is structured in a compare-and-contrast way or in some other structure, you may want to mirror that. Do anything that helps you find and capture the main ideas and most important supportive details."

COMPONENTS OF A MINILESSON

Each minilesson has the same predictable structure and is designed to be completed in ten minutes. The minilesson consists of the following components:

- **Connection:** Contextualizes the day's teaching by connecting it to work students have already been doing

- **Teaching point:** Crystallizes what you plan to teach in that day's minilesson

- **Teaching:** Teaches a particular strategy, using one of several teaching methods

- **Active engagement:** Provides students with guided practice as they try out what they learned in the teaching

- **Link:** Restates what children have learned, doing so in a way that is transferable to another day and another text

I invite you to continue reading as I provide more details about each of these components in the sections below.

CONNECTION: Contextualize the Learning of the Day

During the first two or three minutes of a minilesson, I try to connect the content of today's teaching with the work the class has already been doing, so that this new bit of instruction does not come out of thin air but is instead contextualized, nestled into the prior work the class has been doing or to work

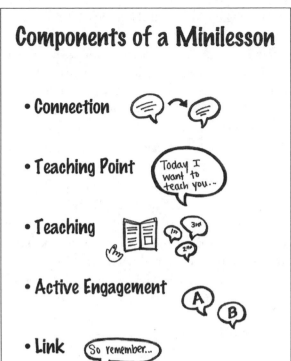

FIG. 5–1

that they do in the real world. Recalling what children have already been learning and doing also reminds them of the whole repertoire of strategies that they've learned, so that at the end of this upcoming minilesson, children leave not with one single strategy in hand, but rather, with an expanded repertoire at the ready.

Although minilessons are a form of whole-class instruction, when taught well, they have an intimacy and immediacy, and that tone is established in the connection. "Come close," we say. "I've been thinking and thinking about what the one most important tip I can give you might be, and it is this." Alternatively, I might say, "Readers, can I tell you a secret? I want to let you in on something that I do, something I haven't really told too many people about." Then again, I might say, "Last night, I couldn't sleep. I kept thinking about your work and thinking, thinking, thinking about what I could say today that might help. Suddenly, in the middle of the night, an idea came to me. I got out of bed and wrote it on a Post-it. You ready to hear my idea? This is it." Or

I might say, "Last night, I was telling my family all about the cool stuff you've been doing. I told them . . ." Then as we talked about you, my sister said, 'Hey, Lucy, why don't you show them . . .'" In these and other ways, I try to help children know that my teaching is personalized, tailored to them.

Over the years, I've developed a handful of ways to help children connect with our message. Perhaps the most common thing I do is that I use the connection as a time to recruit students to recall what they have already learned—strategies they may draw upon that day—so that I can then add to this repertoire. I sometimes recruit them to do this recalling by saying, "You all have learned so many things about . . . Right now, will you list three things you've learned about . . ." Then I say, "Turn and tell the person near you what you have learned!" and the room erupts into conversation. I listen for a minute or two—not long enough for the two children to each exchange ideas—and then say, "Holy moly. You have learned a lot!" Then I name the things I either heard or wish I had heard. In my teaching point, I am then apt to say, "Today I want to teach you one more way readers . . ." and I add to the children's repertoire.

I can easily vary my methods for accomplishing the job of surfacing what children already know related to today's teaching point. For example, I might again suggest that kids have learned a lot and then say, "Let's reread our anchor chart. As I read a bullet from it, will you signal with a thumbs up if this is something you do a lot, a thumbs down if you have never tried the item, and a thumbs in between if you have used the strategy once in a while?" If I want to be creative. I might create a scenario. "Imagine that a reporter heard about the brilliant work you have been doing and the reporter came to interview you to learn all that you do as a reader of fantasy books. Will Partner 1 be the reporter, and will you interview Partner 2? Partner 1, hold an imaginary microphone," I made one with my fist, "and pass it to the subject of your interview."

In all of these examples, I am recruiting kids to do a little bit of talking during the connection. It's critical that that invitation to talk doesn't swamp the minilesson. You are setting kids up to talk to a partner and to talk for just a minute or two. Be sure to keep the talk contained, and remember, there are other possible ways to start a minilesson.

For example, I sometimes start a minilessons by sharing tiny excerpts of student work. I'm always playing Johnny Appleseed as I teach, finding one youngster who does something that can nourish other readers' imaginations of what's possible. But I also keep a file of work from previous years and, frankly, from other people's classes. Kids are interested in other kids, even if I need to preface my story by saying, "Can I tell you about something that one of last year's readers did?" I save work that is funny, especially, and that represents problems many people encounter. Once the author of the problematic work is no longer in the school, I find it effective to show children some of the work another child did that might be problematic, rallying the class to provide ideas that could help that reader.

When I talk about children, I know that what I say will be interesting to other kids if I'm detailed, so I zoom in on a very few tiny specifics. In one minilesson, I told children that the day before, Joel had given me a lecture on penguins. "Did you know that all the boys are called king penguins?" he said. "All you gotta do is be a boy, and you're called king penguin!" I knew that detail would connect with listeners in a minilesson, because it is a fascinating bit of penguin trivia and also because I told the story using direct address. Chances are good that I did not actually remember the exact words that Joel said to me, but I know from my work in the writing workshop that when characters talk, the text tends to be livelier. This may seem unimportant, but actually, minilessons are much better if we tell stories fairly well—and including the actual words that a person said and thought usually ramps up the liveliness of a minilesson.

It is not at all unusual for me to launch into a minilesson by telling a story that will seem to the kids to have nothing to do with reading, but which, in the end, will become a metaphor for whatever I want to say. For example, one of the minilessons in historic fiction begins with the story of how that day, when I'd come as a visitor to the children's school, I first met a five-year-old from my neighborhood. She gave me a tour of the school, showing me the swing that she'd fallen from and the child-sized drinking fountain. At that point, the principal appeared on the scene, and she proceeded to give me her tour of the school, taking me to an entirely new set of paces: the mailboxes in the front office and the book room. The children, listening, will probably be entertained because they generally like to hear little true-life vignettes, but they'll think the story is unrelated to reading until suddenly, in the teaching point, I make explicit the fact that we can see a place through one set of eyes and see one thing, but when we look through another set of eyes we see something entirely different. This, of course, leads right into the fact that when reading stories, it is helpful to notice the perspective from which a story is told and to consider how the story would be different had it been told from another perspective.

When I tell stories, whether it is a true story from my life or a story about something a student said or did, I rely on what I know about writing compelling personal narratives to make my stories engaging. I know that it generally works to tell a story bit by bit, letting it unfold chronologically. Listen, for example, to the start of this story, and you will see that I'm telling my story very much as I would write it if I was in a writing workshop, working to write personal narrative well: "Yesterday I watched a tiny ant as he made his way across my paper. To see what he'd do, I lay my pencil across his path. I thought he'd climb over it, like one of those monster tractor toys that climb up and go over a hurdle. Instead, the ant turned left, walking patiently along the length of the pencil. My pencil felt so high to the ant that he didn't even consider climbing over it." Of course, before that story is over, I'll show students that actually this story has a lot to do with reading. For now, I'll let you guess that connection!

When watching teachers work with the Units of Study in Opinion/Argument, Information, and Narrative Writing, Grades K–8 series, I find myself wishing I could gather those teachers in a huddle and offer a few tips about minilessons. What I'd want to say is that we really mean it when we say that minilessons should be ten minutes in length. (Okay, sometimes twelve minutes.) It will help if you approach a minilesson knowing that the lesson written in the books can actually be delivered in just about ten minutes. For that to happen, you must move briskly. If the minilesson suggests that you say during the connection, "Will you tell each other three things you have learned so far about . . ." and then, as students talk, that you listen in and then call for students' attention, saying, "I heard you say . . . ," know that you actually don't give students time enough to tell each other three things they've learned. They think of those things, they begin talking about them, but by then, you are saying, "I heard you say . . ." And know that actually, you won't have time to continue listening until you have heard a whole collection of wise comments. Listen to a student or two, and then ask for the class's attention. Then, too, you needn't wait for all eyes to be on you before you start saying, "I heard you say that . . ." There are countless little ways to shave minutes off your minilesson, and you absolutely need to do that.

There are several other predictable problems that you will encounter if you attempt to author your own minilessons. Some teachers have been taught that it is better to elicit information from kids than to say anything to them in a straightforward way. The result is that sometimes the connection to a minilesson is filled with a barrage of questions. "Class, during the last session we talked about . . . what, class?" the teacher will ask. "And you were having trouble with . . . what, class?" she'll ask. You will notice in the connections we described that some of them do recruit bits of input from students, but on the whole, for minilessons to be only ten minutes long, those bits of involvement need to be very brief. The most valuable place for student participation is later in the minilesson, once you have shown kids how to do something and now want to give them a chance to try that new work out, with support. I suggest, therefore, that you avoid launching minilessons with questions and, above all, avoid asking known-answer questions to which you're looking for a particular answer. It's just not an effective use of time, and you'll get frustrated because kids can't read your mind, so their answers will tend to take you off in different directions, turning a minilesson into a conversational swamp. You have the floor. Try to speak in interesting and clear ways.

TEACHING POINT: Crystallize the Day's Teaching

The teaching point is actually a subordinate part of the connection. In the teaching point, we crystallize what it is we hope to teach in that day's minilesson. I work hard to make teaching points crystal clear and, when possible, memorable and worth remembering. Here are a few examples of teaching points:

> "Today I want to teach you that every nonfiction reader reads with energy, with power. One way that nonfiction readers do that is we rev our minds up for reading. Even before we shift into 'go' and read a sentence, a paragraph, we read the title, subtitles, look over chunks of the text, and we think, 'I think this book is mostly about . . . and then it will also tell . . .'"

> "Today I want to teach you that a good argument has reasons to support it and evidence to back those reasons. When you analyze an argument, it helps to ask, 'What is the claim being made? What reasons support that claim? What's the evidence to support those reasons?'"

> "Today I want to teach you that as readers tackle more complicated books, the stories will begin to have multiple plotlines. Often readers find it helpful to use charts, timelines, and other graphic organizers to track the problems that arise in a story and to follow the multiple plotlines."

"Today I want to teach you that readers mark up a text in purposeful and deliberate ways to help them remember the big ideas of the text, as well as the things they were thinking when they read it. The annotations that readers make should help them use that text in conversation."

An effective teaching point conveys what readers often try to do, and also how we often go about doing it. Very often, the teaching point starts with a sentence or two about a goal that a reader might take on, and then the teaching point conveys the step-by-step procedure the reader might go through to accomplish those goals. Notice, for example, the first teaching point above: "Every nonfiction reader reads with energy." That's the goal. And the way to do this: "Even before we read a sentence, we read the titles, the subtitles, we look over the chunks of text, and we think, 'I think this book is mostly about . . .'" That's the strategy.

I wouldn't feel that my teaching point had earned its keep if it went like this: "Today I am going to teach you that readers make theories about characters." Such a teaching point wouldn't be worth posting as a bullet on a chart or reiterating several times within the minilesson. That is, a teaching point doesn't simply name the terrain that the minilesson will cover; it actually crystallizes the most important lesson from the day.

I want to point out that there is a huge difference between teaching a strategy and giving an assignment. Sometimes teachers will angle their teaching points in ways that sound more like assignments than replicable teaching points. For example, if a teacher prefaces what she thinks is a teaching point by saying, "Today I want you to . . ." or "Today you will . . ." or "Today I want to talk about . . . ," I'm immediately wary that instead of giving a minilesson, the teacher is probably laying out an assignment. A teaching point is a tip that learners can draw on often, whenever they read or write. So again—be wary of any teaching point that sounds like this: "Today I want you to collect Post-its about the theme of the story" or "Today I want you to take notes on how your character changes." Those are assignments, not teaching points.

How different the message is if you instead say, "Today I want to teach you that whenever you are reading informational texts, it helps if you figure out the main ideas that are advanced in the text and then think about whether the diagrams, charts, or other visuals either support those ideas or offer another perspective on them." The difference is not just a matter of words. It's a difference of intent. In a teaching point, you crystallize a technique that you

expect your students will draw on repeatedly, perhaps today, and certainly for the rest of their lives.

Seymour Sarason, a scholar who has written on school change, points out that very often in schools today, people take revolutionary new ideas and stretch, chop, splice, and twist those ideas so they fit into the ongoing assumptions and norms of their teaching. He suggests that it is for this reason that American schools are characterized by a constant frenzy of change and by an underlying sense that the more things change, the more they remain the same. "New math," Sarason (1996) writes, "ended up as very much like old math." Your reading workshops can end up as very much like traditional whole-class instruction if you don't guard against your teaching points becoming one-day assignments.

TEACHING: Provide Concrete Instruction Using One of Many Methods

Usually when teaching reading, one or two read-aloud texts will thread through just over half of the teaching sections of your minilessons. In the units in this series, for example, *Stone Fox* threads through the first unit of third grade, *The Tiger Rising*, the first unit of fourth grade, and *Home of the Brave*, of fifth grade. Each of those units has another text or two that weaves through a few minilessons—usually this is a picture book or a poem—and minilessons sometimes revisit familiar texts: a fairy tale, a familiar song, a novel from the previous year. Also, of course, some things are taught using texts that the students are reading as the basis for the minilesson.

If I'm using a text like *The Tiger Rising* as the touchstone for the unit, I'll read the text, noticing the reading work I do that pertains to the focus of the unit—inference and interpretation, especially around characters—and then I'll think, "Is the work I am doing with this text pretty universal? Do I hope that all kids will be doing variations of the same work with their various texts?" So, for example, I found that when I first met Sistine, I created a mental portrait of her as a feminine girl dressed in a pink dress. She was named after Michelangelo's painting, featuring angels and white puffy clouds. Only when I got a bit farther into *The Tiger Rising* did I realize that Sistine was entirely different than I'd expected; this required me to rethink the way I'd read an earlier scene involving her. After spying on myself reading this book, I then thought, "Are my students, when reading whatever they are reading, apt to do what I've done—to create impressions of their characters and then, as they read on, find that something is awry—either their image of the person is off or the person suddenly acts out of character?" My answer to that was yes, many students would probably be required to do similar work as they read, and so I wrote a teaching point addressing this, and found a chunk of *The Tiger Rising* that I could use within either the teaching or the active engagement component of the minilesson.

Once I have decided generally what I will teach and the text or other material into which I'll embed my teaching, I need to decide on the method I'll use to teach. As far as I can figure out, there are only four main methods available to any of us, so I'm going to teach using one of those four methods. Those methods are demonstration, guided practice, explicitly telling and showing an example, and inquiry. To help teachers grasp what it means to teach using those four methods, I often ask them to get into pairs, and I then ask one teacher to teach the other how to put on her shoes, and to do this bit of instruction using a specific teaching method. (I don't discuss what those methods might be just yet—I simply suggest teachers use a specific teaching method, not naming it to their student.) After two minutes, I stop the group and suggest that the student and teacher reverse roles, and now the new teacher plan a way to teach her student how to put on shoes, only this time, I ask the teacher to use a different teaching method. I continue this until people have had four opportunities to teach that one putting on-your-shoes lesson, and then I ask teachers to list the methods they used.

As mentioned earlier, I have come to believe we have only four options. One person may name one of those options differently than another person does, but if we discount the various names people ascribe to a method, I think it is fair to say that when asked to teach someone how to put on his shoes, the teacher will probably rely first on the method of demonstration. This method involves the teacher starting off by removing her shoe and then proceeding to narrate the step-by-step process of putting that shoe on and tucking in little pointers. That is, at one point the teacher adds the tip, "Sometimes you need to wiggle your foot from right to left a bit to get it actually into the shoe. Don't step down too hard on the heel of your shoes or it might fold in on you." Later, the teacher may add another tip.

Then again, a teacher can decide to walk her students through the process. If the teacher subscribes to the method of guided practice, the teacher's shoes can stay securely on her feet, and attention shifts to the learner. "Okay," the teacher says. "Start by pointing your toe." Then the teacher waits for the sock-footed learner to do that action. "That's it. Now stick that pointed toe right into the shoe, all the way to the far end of it." That's guided practice.

Another method involves giving a little lecture, complete with illustrations, on the topic of foot insertion into shoe. The teacher following such a method could even use PowerPoint to illustrate the four stages of foot insertion. That's the method I call "explicitly telling and showing an example."

Then again, a teacher may ask, "If we laid out a lot of shoes, like these, what would be involved in getting those shoes on? What steps would each shoe involve? You figure it out." And that's inquiry.

Each of those methods can be used to teach readers within a minilesson. Let's go back to my example of the time when I created an image of Sistine that needed to be revised in light of further reading. Before I can show you how I might develop the teaching point for such a minilesson, let's pin down a way to word the teaching point. Perhaps it is this:

> "Readers, today I want to teach you that after you've developed a theory of a character, you read on, and as you learn more stuff about the character you say, 'Yep, I was right,' or 'Huh? That doesn't fit with my thinking.' When you have a theory of your character, but he or she doesn't act according to your theory, you rethink, asking, 'Might I need to revise my theory?'"

Okay, now I want to shift to the teaching component of this minilesson. So I want to think about how I can teach just this one specific point. Ninety percent of our reading and writing minilessons rely upon demonstration as the method of choice, so let's devise a minilesson that uses demonstration to teach this. I do *not* recommend that you simply summarize what you want to tell people, like this:

> "Readers I want to tell you about how yesterday, when I was reading this book, I realized I'd created an image of Sistine that actually wasn't borne out as I continued reading . . ."

That's not teaching by demonstration—that's teaching by leaving one's shoe on and simply looking back to explain (and perhaps showing an example). No, if I want to demonstrate, the first thing I need to do is to take off my shoe, to un-do the reading work I have already done so that I can "put my shoe on" (that is, read the passage and encounter the character acting out of character) in front of the learners. Now, I also do not want to demonstrate the entire process of reading. I do not want to show readers how I grow a theory about Sistine, read with the theory in hand, and revise the theory all in one minilesson. So to demonstrate, I already need to have this theory about Sistine that I know will prove erroneous. So we are getting closer to writing an effective minilesson. The teaching portion of the minilesson might start like this:

> "Readers, you'll remember that yesterday we talked a bit about Sistine and how we could really picture her. I know I picture her with that frilly pink dress, and her name—Sistine—reminding me of the angels in the painting for which she is named. Remember that once readers have a theory of a character, we read on, and as we do, we learn more about the character. We either say, 'Yep that fits,' or we find that sometimes new parts of the story challenge our theory. Watch as I read on now and see if, in the upcoming story, Sistine does prove to be a girly girl, with a pink dress."

Then, of course, as I read on, we could come to a place in the book that defies that image of Sistine. "Whoa! This is definitely not what I expected! Is it the same for you?" we say, and then show students how we think, "Might I need to revise my theory?" "Might the character be changing?"

This is beginning to be an effective bit of teaching, but there are a few more fine details that make a big difference. Most of all, when I'm demonstrating, there are things I can do to make sure kids learn as much as possible.

First, kids will learn more if they see themselves doing what I'm trying to do. Brian Cambourne, the great Australian educator, once told me that people fly hang gliders on the field outside his office. On many days, he can look out his office window and see the people strapping themselves into harnesses and running pell-mell toward a cliff, whereupon they throw themselves over the cliff, into the air. Brian pointed out that although he has watched this perhaps several hundred times, those hang gliders aren't functioning as mentors to him, because he does not watch them as one would watch a mentor. He has absolutely no intention of ever strapping those machines onto his back and racing toward the cliff, so he does not vicariously experience what those hang gliding people are doing, nor does he learn from their actions.

This story hit home for me, and I am very careful to try to make it as likely as possible that when I do something in front of kids—performing, if you will—I've tried to get the kids to join me in the work so that they're trying to

do the same thing and watching me make moves that either match theirs or that show them what they could do. So in this instance, I'd say to the kids,

> "Readers, let's remember for a second what we know about Sistine." I leave a space for them to think. "Hmm, . . . I'm thinking about that pink dress, her name—Sistine—like the painting with the angels on it. I'm trying to crystallize my sense of what she's like. Umm, . . . What are you thinking? To me, she seems like a girly-girl type, sort of feminine. Remember that once readers have a theory in mind of a character, then we read on, either finding more examples that support our theory or finding evidence that makes us go, 'Whoa!' Let's read on with our theory of Sistine in mind, and let's all of us listen for whether the upcoming part of the story fits with that theory or goes against it. You ready to do that thinking?"

I'm hoping that you see that I've gotten the kids to join me in imagining Sistine in one way, and of course, as I read aloud, I'll want them to join me in saying, "Huh?" Then, once students are doing this work alongside me, I'll step ahead of them and show them how I handle moments of discordance.

There is one more point I want to make as we take this little bit of reading and turn it into a demonstration. If you look back over this example, you will see that I've been explicit with children about what I hope they notice and do. There are instances in which I have not yet been explicit, however, such as when the children and I crystallized our image of Sistine. It would be best to revise how I did that (see the transcript above) so that my teaching highlighted the moves I want kids to make when I am not with them:

> *"Readers, I want to remind you that it helps to pause as we're reading to think, 'What do we know about the character?'* We already read a bit about Sistine. Let's remember for a second what we know about Sistine. Hmm, . . . I'm thinking about that pink dress, her name—Sistine—like the painting with the angels on it. I'm trying to crystallize my sense of what she's like. *Usually I find the author tells me details, but I need to come up with words for what the person's like.* To me, she seems like a girly-girl type, sort of feminine. *Remember that once a reader has a theory in mind of a character, then we read on . . ."*

Of course, later in this bit of teaching, I'll show children that when the character acts in ways that are totally surprising, I need to either change my image of the character or to realize that she's changing.

Although I've shown how you devise the teaching component of a minilesson using the teaching method of demonstration, I could have used different teaching methods. As you read and use the series, you'll find minilessons that use those other methods.

ACTIVE ENGAGEMENT: Give Students a Chance to Try Out Their New Learning

This is the time when you say to your kids, "Now you try it," and you provide them with just a little bit of guided practice. In this minilesson, I searched the book to see if there was a second example of a character who could easily be pegged as one way and who then acted out of character. Fortunately, the protagonist of the story, Rob, introduces himself to readers as a fairly timid character, one who cannot stand up for himself, but we no sooner crystallize this impression than Rob acts in ways that belie our expectations. This makes it very easy to create an active engagement section that is very similar to the teaching section, only now the kids will do 95% of the work. You'd set them up to do this work by saying something like "Let's think a bit about Rob. Yesterday we talked about how Rob is sort of a timid kid, right? Remember how he let the bullies pick on him and he didn't protest? So let's do what readers do, and carry our theory of Rob with us like it's a football, tucked under our arm, and let's read on. Remember, we're going to see if we find more stuff that helps us add onto our theory of Rob or if we end up saying, 'Huh?' and changing our minds, as we did with Sistine."

Then you could read aloud, and at the perfect moment, when Rob has just acted in ways that belie your theory, you could show an astonished look on your face and say to the children, "Turn and talk. What are you thinking? Does this fit with your idea of Rob as a scaredy-cat?" After children talk with partners for a minute or two, with you coaching into their efforts, you could repeat what one or two of them said.

The important thing to realize is that in this example, you would have provided kids with lots of assistance,

and that is your intention during this section of the minilesson. You would have first crystallized a theory about Rob that you knew was going to be relevant to today's passage. You would also have read aloud, so that simply "getting" the text wouldn't be a problem for anyone. You would have selected the passage that *does* upset the apple cart and created a talk interval at the exactly key moment. You would have channeled children to work in the supportive safe harbor of a partnership. And, of course, after children have done the work, you'll use this to convey an example or two that is clearly within reach of most of your readers.

In this example, the actual activity that children participated in was that of talking with a partner (which you refer to as "turn and talk"). You could instead have set children up to "stop and jot" or to "list across your fingers" or to be active in other small ways. And this example involved children with a continuation of the text used in the previous section of the minilesson. You could, instead, have asked children to think about a character in their own independent reading book (or, if they are in book clubs, their book club book) and to read that book, looking to see if the character acted out of character. Alternatively, you could have turned to a second text during the read-aloud— to a familiar poem, picture book, or different novel. You could even have turned to real life, setting children up to practice a reading skill by doing a bit of shared reading about life itself. For example, had you taught children to use clues to predict, you could say to them, "Will you practice this reading skill, only instead of doing so with this book we've been reading, will you practice the skill away from a text? Right now, work with your partner and see if you can collect enough clues to solve the mystery of my missing glasses. I had them at the start of school today but can't find them now."

There are a few principles to remember when constructing the active engagement section of a mini-lesson. First, you will be aiming to give children a two- or three-minute interval to practice what you've just taught in your teaching point and in your teaching component of the minilesson. This will only be possible if you take some time to set them up to have success quickly. For example, although theoretically I could have asked children to use their independent reading books as a place to practice the strategy of reading onward to see if a theory about a character continues to fit the evidence or not, that would have been time consuming. It would have taken each reader a few minutes just to crystallize his theory of a character, and chances are that had each reader had time to read on in his independent book, there would be nothing in the passage the reader was poised to read next that would have challenged the readers' theories. So in this instance, the only way to provide readers with a really *brief* chance to experience the content of the minilesson was to do so in a shared text, with me articulating the theory of the character and then channeling readers to read a passage that was preselected so that it would set them up to do the work.

There are other ways to scaffold readers, and as you read through this series, you might collect a list of possible ways to do so. You'll find that you use the same scaffolds in the active engagement section of a minilesson and in conferences and small groups. For example, one scaffold you can use in all these instances is that once you've set children up to do the work, you can also set a few kids up to simultaneously do the work aloud, publicly, on chart paper. That way, if anyone is stumped, that child can shift from doing the work to watching another child do it. While readers are working, another scaffold you can use is to call out brief prompts to remind them of what you want them to do or of the next steps. Sometimes your prompts provide the actual words you think they might think or write to get themselves started. In this instance, for example, you might call out, "I used to think Rob was . . . but now I'm realizing that maybe he's . . . ." If you wanted to do so, you could leave a bit of time and then call out, in a voiceover as children work, "I think this because A, because B."

It's also helpful to remember that kids are ravenous learners, and you can usually tuck some helpful tips into either your teaching or your active engagement. For example, if you are helping readers revise their theories of a character, you might tuck in the tip "Remember, when you are trying to find the precisely right word to capture your theory about a character, it helps to try saying this one way, another, another, 'til you get it right." In addition or alternatively, you could say, "If you are looking for the one word that will sum up your whole character, try using more than one word. Usually people are too complicated to be shoehorned into one word. Sometimes it helps to compare the character to someone you know or to something else. So-and-so is like an apple, hard on the outside, soft on the inside."

Finally, you want all of your readers to be actively involved during this section of the minilesson. Had you asked the whole class to work together, joining you in thinking about ways your theory of Rob did and did not hold true as you continued to read, you could have asked everyone to do this in their mind, and then elicited a few people's answers while the class watched on. Don't do this! It may feel to you as if the whole class is actively participating, but the fact is that when you call on two or three members of the class to do the work while others look on, this is a way to involve two or three kids, not every member of the class.

The active engagement section of a minilesson generally ends just like the teaching section ends, with you extrapolating what you hope the students have learned in ways that are transferable to another text, another day. If you scan minilessons throughout the series, you will see bold headings that say, "Debrief in ways that are transferable to another day, another text," or some variation on that. If you read half a dozen examples of the text that follows those headings, you'll quickly learn how to do this important work.

When restating what you hope children have learned that applies to another day and another text, you'll often restate the teaching point. I find it helpful to actually look back at the exact wording of the original teaching point and use those same words again. The goal is to make the minilesson and the teaching point stick, and one way to do this is through making the keywords of the teaching point into almost a mantra.

LINK: Remind Kids that Today's Learning Is Transferable

The minilesson ends with you restating what you hope children have learned, doing so in a way that is transferable to another day and another text. "Readers, from this day on, whenever you are reading a novel and you've developed a theory about a character, remember that your theory is tentative. It's your best guess. As you read on, you will learn more stuff about the character, and you'll say, 'Yep, I was right,' or "Huh? That makes no sense.' When you have a theory of your character, but he or she doesn't act according to your theory, remember, you can rethink, asking, 'Might I need to revise my theory?'"

Often at this point, the teaching point gets added to a class chart that compiles what you have been teaching.

Usually before sending children off to do their reading, you'll also want to recall other things you have been teaching that you hope they are doing today, perhaps gesturing to the same chart. You might say something like, "So readers, you've been learning so many things about what it means not only to read stories, but to read characters. You've learned to do A, you've learned to do B, and today I hope you have learned to do C. Today as you read, I'll be dying to see you do all of these things."

Sometimes you'll also add on instructions: "If you do this work, would you bring it to your partner talks later? I'm going to ask all of you to start today off by doing this for just a minute. Then you can continue . . ." or "You'll see I've put some purple Post-its on your table. If you do this sort of thinking, would you leave a purple Post-it there so we can find that place easily when I come around and when you go to share with your partner?"

Overall, your link aims to increase students' sense of agency. You remind them of what you just taught, fit it into what they've been learning, and invite them to make smart choices about the work they will pursue. Even when most students will, in fact, do the work you've just taught them, they'll feel as if they've been part of that choice, and they are more likely to make a similar choice when they need to make their own decisions without your guidance.

Letter to Teachers

Occasionally in these units, you will see a session that begins "Dear Teachers." This is a letter to teachers that will guide you to try developing your own unit of study. This may occur two or three times in each unit.

We've written the units in ways that reveal the tools, methods, and assumptions that underlie a unit or a session. Our work is purposeful: we want you to be able to author portions of your own curriculum. The letter to teachers provides some support and suggestions as to how your session might go, but you will make many of your own decisions. Often, the letter provides a place to pause during the unit and gives you and your students a chance to practice a just-learned strategy, or perhaps to approach it from a slightly different angle.

Chapter 6

Management Systems

O TEACH WITHIN A READING WORKSHOP, you need to establish the structures and expectations that ensure that all students will work with engagement and tenacity at their own important reading projects. Otherwise, your entire attention would be focused on keeping kids working—and you therefore wouldn't be able to devote yourself to the all-important work of assessing, coaching, scaffolding, and teaching. Yet teaching young people to work with independence is no small feat!

You make an important start by recognizing that teaching your students to work with independence is a sizable challenge. You'll need to give careful thought to the systems and expectations that will make it likely that your students sustain rigorous reading work without you microcontrolling their every move. That is, as you approach a new school year with your students, you should be mindful that the minilessons—the words that you say for ten minutes at the start of reading time—are nowhere near as important as the structures you put into place to shape the work your students do.

The good news is that the reading workshop, like the writing workshop, is deliberately kept simple and predictable, because the work itself is ever-changing and complex. Students can approach any day's reading workshop as artists approach a studio, planning to continue with their important ongoing work. Each day's teaching in a workshop does not set up a new hoop for the students all to jump through, in sync, on that day. Instead, for the bulk of time during each day, students carry on with their work. As they do so, they draw upon a growing repertoire of skills, tools, strategies, and habits. But the bulk of students' time during the reading workshop is spent reading.

Workshops, by definition, are places in which you are engaged in continual assessment. The simplicity and predictability of the workshop will free you from constant choreographing, allowing you time to observe, listen, and teach into each student's zone of proximal development. Like an artist teaching in a pottery studio or a physicist running a physics lab, you circulate around the room. You pull close to observe, mull over what is and is not working, and intervene to coach, demonstrate, encourage, and celebrate. In short, you teach.

But this sort of teaching is only possible if your workshop hums along without you micromanaging everything. Thankfully, thousands of teachers have worked for years to devise the management structures and systems that make it possible for children to carry on as readers and as writers working productively with independence and rigor. When you institute simple and predictable structures and systems, you will be freed from choreography—and free to teach.

You can start by recognizing that you need to give careful thought to how you will institute the systems that make it likely that your students will sustain rigorous work. When you plan your instruction, plan not only the words out of your mouth—the minilessons and the small groups—but also the management structures and systems that make it possible for children to work productively.

THE IMPORTANCE OF STRUCTURES AND SYSTEMS

Why do so many people assume that classroom management is a concern for novice and struggling teachers but not for master teachers? Is there really a good teacher anywhere who doesn't think hard about methods for maximizing students' productivity, for inspiring the highest possible work ethic, and for holding every learner accountable to doing her best? I get frustrated when I hear some people say with disdain, "She has trouble with classroom management."

Who doesn't have trouble with classroom management? How could it *not* be tricky to build an environment in which twenty or thirty youngsters each pursues his own important project as a reader, working within the confines of a small room, each needing his own mix of silence and collaboration, time and deadlines, resources and one another?

Corporate management is considered an executive skill, and high-level executives are often coached in methods for maximizing productivity. Directors, managers, and executives attend seminars on developing systems of accountability, on providing feedback, on organizing time, space, and personnel to maximize productivity. If the people working under your direction were grown-ups instead of children, the job of managing the workers would be regarded as highly demanding leadership work. But all too often in schools, classroom management is treated as a task akin to doing the laundry. That's wrong.

As a classroom teacher, you absolutely need to give careful attention to methods of managing young people so they sustain high levels of purposeful work. You and your colleagues would be wise to assume from the start that classroom management will be a challenge and to give careful thought to instituting systems that channel your students to do their best work.

And the good news is that you needn't invent systems from the ground up. Thousands of teachers have worked for decades to develop simple and predictable structures and systems that can free you from constant choreography and allow you to teach.

LEARNING CLASSROOM MANAGEMENT SYSTEMS AND STRATEGIES

I recently visited the classroom of a first-year teacher. This teacher was teaching a writing workshop, but he could just as well have been leading a reading workshop—his methods were largely transferable. "Students," Manuel said, "in a moment, I'd like you to bring your notebook and your pen to the meeting area. Put everything else away and show me you are ready." As he counted ("Five, four, three, two, one."), children hurried to clear off their workspaces of everything but the materials they would need during the upcoming hour. "Table 2," Manuel signaled, "let's gather." Soon Manuel had signaled four other tables as well, and each time he gestured, his children stood, pushed in their chairs, walked swiftly and directly to the meeting area, and sat cross-legged, shoulder to shoulder with their reading partner. Manuel had soon taken his place in a chair at the front of the meeting area.

"Can I have your focus?" he said, touching his eyes to signal that he wanted children's eyes on him. Almost every child turned in his direction. Manuel then began a ten-minute minilesson in which he named a strategy, demonstrated that strategy, gave the children a few minutes of guided practice with the strategy, and invited them to add that strategy to their repertoire. Soon the children had dispersed to their work spots, each hard at work on her ongoing work. None of them required Manuel to come to their side and provide a personalized jump start.

As I watched all this, I marveled that Manuel, a novice teacher, was teaching in such efficient and effective ways. I remembered with a pang my first years as a teacher. "How did he get to be so good?" I wondered, but then I knew. Although Manuel is a new teacher, his methods are not new. His methods have gone through hundreds of drafts and have benefited from the legacy of experienced teachers. He learned from the countless others who went before him. This is how it should be!

The best way I know to learn classroom management strategies is to visit well-established reading and writing workshops to study the infrastructure that underlies this kind of teaching. Both reading and writing workshops are structured in such predictable, consistent ways that the infrastructure of most workshops remains almost the same throughout the year and throughout a student's elementary school experience. This means that when you visit one hour of a workshop, you peek in on not only today's but also tomorrow's teaching. In this chapter, you and I will visit a few upper-elementary-school reading workshops when they're in full swing, and we'll pay special attention to the nitty-gritty of classroom management. I'll be at your side on this tour, commenting on what we see together. We'll pay special attention to the management of each component of the writing workshop.

- Managing the minilesson: the beginning of each day's reading instruction

- Managing reading time: the heart and soul of the reading workshop

- Managing conferring and small-group instruction

- Managing the mid-workshop and share session: workshop closure

- A word about other components of balanced literacy

MANAGING THE MINILESSON: THE BEGINNING OF EACH DAY'S READING INSTRUCTION
Convening the Class for the Minilesson

Most teachers find that it is helpful to circulate around the room five minutes before a workshop begins, saying, "Five more minutes until we gather on the carpet," or something similar. This gives students time to finish up whatever they are doing. The workshop itself begins when you use an attention-getting signal to secure students' attention and then ask them to convene. It is remarkably important for you to develop such a signal and to teach children that it is a meaningful one. The signal can be obvious. Most teachers simply stand in the midst of the hubbub and say, in a voice one notch louder than usual, "Readers." Once students have given you their full attention—and don't hesitate to wait until they literally stop what they were doing and look at you—then you'll convene them. Experienced workshop teachers know that attention to procedures early in the year pays off, so they are apt to start

the year by demonstrating—acting out—their hopes for how students will gather for minilessons. To do this, show children that you expect them to push in their chairs, to make a beeline for their spot on the meeting area rug, to sit (rather than hover), to handle materials however you expect them to be handled, and to begin rereading the anchor charts containing teaching points from previous days.

Some people use a countdown as a scaffold to move students expeditiously along. "Let's take the count of four to gather for a minilesson. Four: I love that you are getting your books and your notebook out of your knapsacks and finding your My Reading Life folders." If there are some materials that you want brought to the meeting area, you may want to hold those materials up, and then your countdown can continue. "Three: I love that you are grabbing the materials you need and pushing your chairs in and coming quickly. Two:

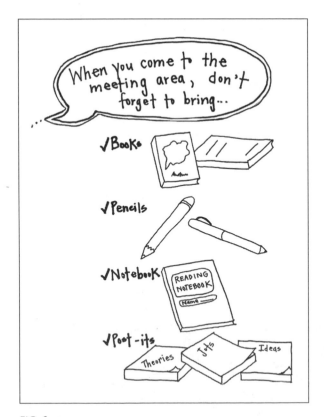

FIG. 6–1

I love that you are sitting on your bottoms, in your spots. One: Nice to see you opening your notebooks so you are ready to jot, if need be, and to see you rereading our anchor charts."

Of course, before long this behavior becomes automatic, and you need only say, "Blue and green tables, please come to the carpet," and then while you gesture to the next two tables, the first group of children push in their chairs, come quickly and quietly, sit in their assigned spots, open their notebooks to the first available page, and begin rereading charts from previous minilessons. This is very efficient!

You may question this detailed attention to transitions, and some teachers may prefer a more organic, easygoing approach. But for many teachers, transitions can be a source of delay and tension, and neither is advisable. A fiction writer once said, "The hardest part of writing fiction is getting characters from here to there," and this can be true for teaching as well.

If you want students' attention but don't need them to gather—which will be the case for your mid-workshop teaching points and for most of your share sessions—you can use the attention-getting device again. Most teachers simply stand in a certain part of the room and say, "Readers," with a commanding voice. After saying that (or whatever you choose as your signal) give the classroom a 360° survey, waiting for absolute silence and for all eyes to be on you before proceeding.

The important thing is that you use the signal you settle on consistently and teach children to honor it. This requires that after you say, "Readers," you wait as long as necessary until every child has put his pencil or pen down, stopped talking, and looked at you. You may need to wait as long as three minutes before further addressing the group, although if this is a schoolwide procedure and if other teachers maintain high standards around this, then it will be easy to institute.

Some teachers are uncomfortable insisting on utter silence, and therefore they speak over still-murmuring children. I'm convinced you do your students no favors when you collude with their tendencies to ignore your words. If your goal is to teach children that words matter, then your words, for a start, must mean something. When you ask for attention, you should expect that children will comprehend and honor your request. The same children who are Teflon listeners, regularly letting instructions roll off without getting through, tend also to be Teflon readers, regularly moving their eyes but not their minds over the words on a page, then looking up to say, "I read it, honest; I just don't remember what I read." If you regularly repeat yourself several times to be sure children take in what you've said, you are enabling your students to live as if they have comprehension problems. The first step to remedying this is to develop a way to signal for children's attention, and the second step is to resist repeating yourself.

It helps, then, for you to keep in mind that there will be times when you speak to your whole class and you do not need everyone's full attention. Your children could be deeply immersed in their reading and you don't actually want to stop them; you just want to float a reminder across the landscape of the classroom, rather like those blimps that fly over crowded beaches with advertisements trailing behind them. Use an entirely different voice, then, if you simply want to say something like, "We'll gather in five minutes. By then, make sure you have recorded a couple of Post-its or entries about the theme of your story."

I find it striking that in classrooms in which the transitions are long and mired in tension, teachers often assume this is par for the course. They shrug and say, "What are you going to do?" as if they assume this is how workshops proceed in most classrooms. But many aspects of classroom management are shaped more by our expectations than by anything else. When teachers make a point of teaching classroom management, thirty children can come and go quite seamlessly between the meeting area and their workspaces.

Establishing Long-Term Partnerships, Research Teams, and Clubs

When children gather on the carpet, they usually sit in assigned spots beside an assigned, long-term partner. Because your children will read the same books as their partners—usually in swap-book partnerships but sometimes in same-book partnerships—these relationships need to be ability matched. Partnerships generally last at least the length of a unit of study and often longer. If one reader is ready to proceed to more challenging texts before the other partner is, you may need to finesse this by creating temporary triads. There is another reason for triads—if children are English language learners, the partnerships or maybe triads often contain a more and a less proficient speaker of English. For new arrivals, the partnerships may be language-based—two speakers of Urdu working together, for example.

Usually teachers assign students to sit beside their partner during the minilesson and workshop time. Partners often talk during the active engagement section of a minilesson, during the mid-workshop, and during the share session. These are brief interludes for talking, and often the teacher will give directions, such as asking for either Partner 1 or 2 to do the talking that particular time. "Partner 1, will you teach Partner 2 what you learned from your nonfiction reading today? As you do this, remember to organize your teaching into categories and to elaborate about a point before moving on to the next point. Reference illustrations, charts, and diagrams from your book as you teach. Go!"

Some teachers organize students so they work within mixed-ability partnerships during the interactive read-aloud and matched partnerships during the reading workshop. That's a terrific idea if the logistics aren't too complicated, because research is clear that students benefit from heterogeneous pairings, when possible.

Some units support not just partnerships but clubs. Usually a club consists of two ability-based partnerships, and usually the four readers are roughly similar in their reading abilities. This is important, because a club usually reads the same book in sync with each other, meeting perhaps two or three times a week to talk about the portion of the text that the club members just read. Usually those conversations are during the share time at the end of a workshop, and they usually last a bit longer than the standard five minutes for partner sharing. Typically, a club conversation ends with club members deciding how much they will read before they meet again and what lens they will bring to that reading. A club might say, "So let's continue to read this book, looking for themes, and let's each make at least five Post-its a day. They can be about the theme or anything else that we notice, but we should be sure to come to the next club, ready to talk about two themes we see in the book and the evidence that best supports that." The clubs are a source of agency, giving themselves tasks to do and deciding how to continue one day's conversation with reading and writing about reading that extends that conversation.

Management during the Minilesson

The biggest challenge you will encounter when teaching a minilesson is achieving that magical balance wherein your children are wide-awake, active participants—and yet their involvement does not turn a tight, economical bit of explicit instruction into a free-for-all, with chitchat and commentary, questions, and free associations overwhelming lines of thought. Over the years, my colleagues and I have recommended different ways for you to walk this delicate balance, and frankly, you'll need to do some self-assessment to decide on a plan that works for you and your students.

For years, we suggested that the best way to keep minilessons streamlined was for you to essentially convey to kids, "For ten minutes at the start of most reading workshops, I'll pull you together here on the carpet and I'll teach you a strategy that you can use to become a better reader. For most of the minilesson, this is my time to talk and your time to listen. I'll tell you what I want to teach and show you how to do it. Then you will have time to talk to a partner as you try what I've taught."

I still believe that many teachers would be wise to convey that message and to teach minilessons in which children are essentially seen and not heard until midway into the minilesson. I say this not because I think it is the perfect solution, but because I think the perfect solution is hard for mere mortals to achieve. It is a real trick to allow for more active involvement while still modulating—limiting—that involvement.

But in this series, we go for the gold. We send a more nuanced message to youngsters. We say to youngsters, "I'll often channel you to talk, and then, before you finish talking, I'll ask you to hold that thought and to listen up while I make a quick point. This means you need to watch my signals. There will be times to talk to the group, times to talk with a partner, times to talk to yourself silently, and times to be quiet."

Thus, the minilessons in this series offer many more ways for students to be actively involved in the frontal teaching than there were in the earlier units of study books. In the chapter on minilessons, I described ways some teachers involve kids in the connection of the minilesson, and also ways you can recruit kids to actively participate in your demonstrations. The challenge is to demonstrate something that the youngsters are also imagining themselves doing, or are doing in their own minds, so that as they watch you, they notice how you do things differently—better—in ways that inform their practices. To recruit students to be engaged in your demonstration, you are apt to get them started trying to do the same thing that you will soon demonstrate. You start the demonstration with some guided practice. "How would you do this?" you ask, and you get children started doing the work in their minds. Then—just when they are beginning to do something—you will say, "Watch me for a sec'," and you'll pull ahead of their actions to show them how you would do this particular thing.

For your performance to function as a demonstration, the learner needs to be about to do the same thing, so he is primed to notice how you do things differently. This requires a keen level of engagement by the learner, which you can get if you recruit kids to be on the edge of doing something, and then, instead, you take the lead, pointing out what you hope they notice in your demonstration. You'll need to be accustomed to signaling to students, saying, "Watch and see if the way I do this matches what you were doing as well."

There are some management issues you will want work out with your whole class. Children need to know what to do if a partner is absent (join a nearby partnership, without asking you to problem solve). When you want them to talk to their partners in a minilesson, you will want to show them how to make a fast transition from facing forward and listening, to facing their partner and talking. They can't spend five minutes getting themselves off the starting block for a turn-and-talk (or a stop-and-jot), because the entire interval of that interlude usually lasts no more than three minutes!

FIG. 6–2

All of these things are worth explicitly teaching. I've watched teachers practice the transition from listening to talking to a partner by saying, "What did you eat for breakfast this morning? Turn and talk," and then, after a minute, saying, "Back to me." If you take just a minute or two to coach into the behaviors you want and then remember to hold to those expectations later, you'll find this all pays off in giant ways.

MANAGING READING TIME: THE HEART AND SOUL OF THE READING WORKSHOP

While the minilesson sets the tone for the workshop and provides students with another teaching point to add to their repertoire, the main work of the day happens during reading time, when students are bent intently over their work, pages turning, or are alternating between reading, jotting, and rereading. It is during reading time that you are free to support, scaffold, and foster students' growth as readers in whatever ways seem most important for each individual. In this section, I'll provide an overview of the structures to consider so that your students are not distracted during reading time, including how to effectively send them off to work, the nature of their work, and how to teach and organize for a collaborative work environment.

Sending Students Off to Work: The Transition from Minilesson to Work Time

Just as you explicitly teach children how to gather for a minilesson, you will also teach them how to disperse after the minilesson and get started on their work. Students need to learn how to go from the minilesson to their workspaces and then to fill out their reading logs, open up their books, decide what they are going to do, and get started doing it. If you don't teach them otherwise, some children will sit idly by until you make your way to that table and give that child a personalized jump start. It's worthwhile to come right out and teach children how to get *themselves* started reading. Sometimes you will disperse one cluster of students at a time. While one cluster goes off to work, you may say to those still sitting on the carpet, "Let's watch and see if they zoom to their reading spots and get started right away!" Sometimes you will speak in a stage whisper. "Oh, look, Toni has her reading log out and is filling in the time and her page number. That's so smart! I wonder if the others will do that? Oh, look. Jose is getting his log out too!" This reminds both the dispersing and the observing youngsters what you hope they will do.

Your students are apt to "just read," and your hope is that they are deliberately working on goals as they read. The way you send readers off to work can make it more likely that they will deliberately try new strategies, working toward goals they take on as important. Sometimes you will find it helpful to ask children first to tell each other the new reading work they plan to be doing that day. You might even ask them to envision how they will go about doing that work. "Picture yourself leaving the meeting area. Where will you go, exactly? What will you do first? Thumbs up if you can picture yourself leaving and getting started," you might say, signaling to the children who seem ready, that they can go back to their seats and get started. Sometimes you disperse children by saying, "If you are going to be doing (one kind of work), get going. If you are going to be doing (another kind of work), get going. If you are not certain what goals you can work toward today and what strategies you can try using and need some help, stay here and I'll work with you." Soon you are leading a small group of children who've identified themselves as needing more direction.

Other times you will say, "Get started doing that right here on the rug," and then you'll watch to see when a student is engaged in the work, tapping that student on the shoulder and gesturing to say, "Go to your work spot and keep reading." Again, this allows you to end with a group on the carpet who need some help.

Transitions are smoother if children always know where they'll sit during reading time. You will probably give your students assigned spots. You'll want to avoid, however, making it a habit not only to tell children where to sit but to also to tell them what to do. This may surprise you. You may think, "Doesn't the teacher tell students what to do during the minilesson? Isn't that really the role of the minilesson?"

Those are very important questions, and it is true that in traditional instruction, you would use the whole-class instruction at the start of the lesson as the time to show everyone what they are expected to do that day. In traditional instruction, during the whole-class instruction at the start of work time, you would assign the day's work, perhaps demonstrate it, and then youngsters could practice that work in the minilesson, with support, before being sent off to do that same thing with more independence during work time. But during a workshop, your whole-class instruction aims to add to students' repertoire, teaching them how to do strategies that they will then draw on over and over as they read. So you generally end your minilesson by saying, "So when you are ready to work on . . ." (or "when you reach that part of your text . . ."), "remember this tip . . ." Or "So remember that today, one of your options is to do (whatever you've just taught). But you can also draw on all you've learned to do prior to now." That is, fairly often students will leave the minilesson and still need to reflect on their progress, consider their goals, look over their book, and choose a way of proceeding. In some classrooms, youngsters are expected to give themselves an assignment (also referred to as a planning box) each day. "Decide what you are going to do, record your plans in a self-assignment box, and get started!"

The Nature of Children's Work During the Reading Workshop

The rule during a reading workshop is that during reading time, everyone reads. So there is no such thing as being "done." If a reader completes one text, then he begins the next text. You should expect that as your young readers progress along through their sequence of work, some of them will come to places where they feel stymied. "I'm stuck," they will say.

When a youngster feels stuck, her first instinct is usually to find the teacher and ask, "What should I do next?" You will want to approach those interactions being clear that your job can't be to dole out all the little things that every reader is to do. A big part of being a skilled reader is noticing the work that a text wants you to be doing, reviewing possible strategies for doing that work, monitoring and assessing how that effort works, and so on. You will not want to remove that responsibility from your students' shoulders by allowing them to make you decider-in-chief. Almost always, you'll respond to requests for assistance by either turning students back onto their own resources or by teaching them to assess and to identify goals and teaching them several possible strategies they might draw on to reach those goals.

If youngsters seem overly reliant on you for direction, you will probably want to teach them to help each other. "Readers, can I stop all of you? Would you look at all the people following me! I feel like a pied piper. Readers, today I want to teach you that there is not just one reading teacher in this classroom. Each one of you can be a reading teacher. And you need to become reading teachers for each other because this is how we learn to become reading teachers for ourselves. In the end, every reader needs to be his or her own reading teacher. So, right now, let me teach you what reading teachers do for each other. Then those of you in this line behind me can help each other."

MANAGING CONFERRING AND SMALL GROUPS: MAKING ONE-TO-ONE CONFERENCES AND SMALL-GROUP INSTRUCTION POSSIBLE

When you confer, you will probably find it works best to move among children, talking with them at their workplaces, dotting the room with your presence. Although you won't come close to reaching every child every day, you can hold individual conferences with three children a day (four or five minutes per conference) and also lead several small groups, and this will allow you to be a presence in every section of the room. You make your presence matter more because, when talking with one child, you can encourage nearby children to listen in. For most of a conference, you'll probably want to deliberately ignore those listeners, looking intently into the face of the one child, which often spurs the listeners to eavesdrop all the more intently. Often, as your conference ends, you will want to generalize it to the others who've listened in. "Do any of the rest of you want to try that too?" you might ask. "Great! Do it! I can't wait to see."

If it seems that your children are not able to sustain work long enough for you to do much conferring, you first of all need to congratulate yourself for identifying and naming this as a problem. You are far closer to a solution once you have looked this in the eye and said, "This is important."

The next step is that you need to think about ways you can scaffold children's independent work. You can angle your conferences so that you are teaching children how to carry on with independence not just this time, but every time. For example, you can be sure that some conferences will begin with a reader coming to you and saying, "I'm stuck." In those instances, your first job will be to learn what the reader has already done and to turn the reader back on her own resources. Then you will need to help the reader extend her work in ways that make that youngster more self-reliant in the future. I might say, "When I'm not sure of a good book to read next, what I do is I think about people I know who like the same books as I do, and I go to them and ask them what they've enjoyed reading lately. You could try that instead of coming to me for help."

One of the decisions you will need to make in relationship to conferring is this: with whom will you meet? Teachers develop their own idiosyncratic systems here. Some teachers enter a reading workshop with a little list in hand of readers they plan to see. The list may come from studying assessments or conferring/small-group records and noticing the children they haven't worked with for a while and from thinking about previous conferences and small-group work that need follow-up. Alternatively, the list may come from thinking about children's data and deciding on children who especially need help.

Personally, although I do enter a workshop with a list of the children with whom I hope to confer, I find it is important to be able to improvise based on the signals children give me. So, if youngsters at one table seem unsettled, I'm apt to confer with a child at that table, knowing that my presence can channel the entire group to work rather than socialize. Then, too, if one child is especially persistent about needing help, I generally assume he needs to be a priority—unless he is always at my elbow, in which case I'll respond differently.

I tell children that if they need my help, they should get out of their seats and follow me as I confer. I find this keeps the child who feels stymied from derailing his companions as well; in addition, the children learn from eavesdropping on conferences. The line that forms behind me also provides me with a very tangible reminder of how many children feel confused or stuck at any moment, and this keeps me on my toes. If I have six children in tow, I'm not likely to overlook them for long.

You will definitely want to record your conferences and small-group work, and it is important to develop a system for doing so that fits intimately into the rhythms of your teaching. The important thing is that this record of your teaching must help you teach better and help your students learn better. This record keeping needs to be attuned to your teaching, reflecting, and planning. You will probably go through a sequence of systems before settling, temporarily, on one. Five or six systems are especially common among the teachers with whom I work.

Many teachers use digital systems for keeping notes on their work with students. Notability and Evernote let you keep digital files, with quick inserted photographs of students' Post-its and notebook pages. You can even tuck in audio files of kids reading. Some teachers like the Confer App, created by David Lowe in Seattle, which is designed to help teachers record their conferences, tag and sort children for small groups, and keep track of which children you've been meeting with on your calendar.

Other teachers keep a page on a clipboard that looks like a month at-a-glance calendar but is, instead, the class-at-a-glance. For the period of time this page represents (which tends to be two weeks), they record the compliment and teaching point of any conference they hold. They use a grid that has light lines dividing each child's square into several parallel slots, with alternate slots labeled either C (for conference) or TP (for teaching point).

Alternatively, some teachers create a record-keeping sheet that culls some main goals from the learning progression and use it to remind themselves of their goals for children's learning as well as to record their observations of children's work and their teaching. Some teachers use learning progressions and unit plans to create a prewritten list of possible compliments or teaching points and carry these prewritten teaching points with them, checking off what a child is doing that merits a compliment, what they will teach, and what they recognize they could but won't be teaching.

Some teachers have notebooks divided into sections, one for each child, and record their conferences and small-group instruction with each child that way. Others do a variation of this, recording the conferences and small-group sessions on large sticky notes and later moving the note to the appropriate section of their notebook. Some teachers use an enlarged version: they post their conference notes on a wall-sized grid, which reminds every child what she has agreed to do and serves as a very visible record of which children have and have not received this form of intense instruction.

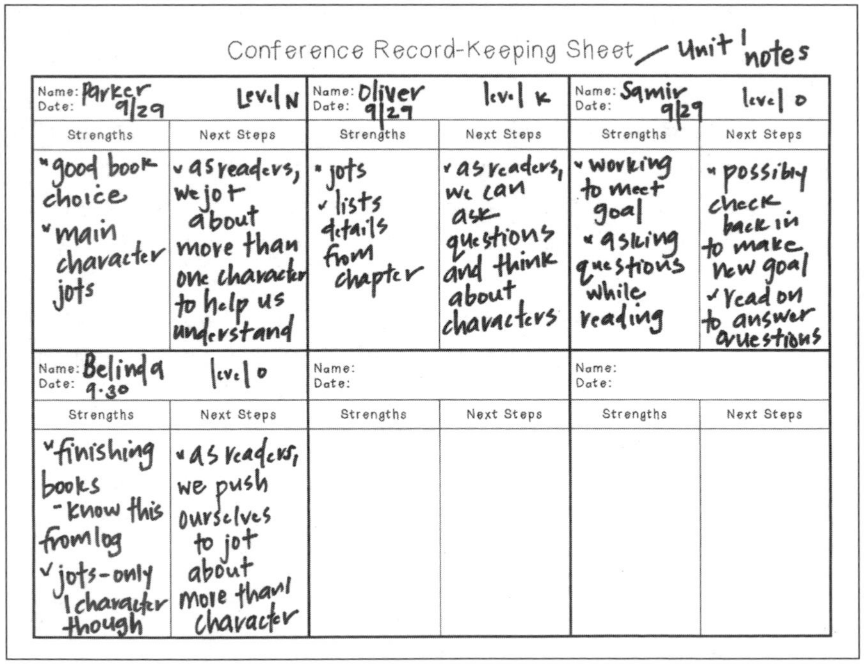

I like to record conferences and small-group work in a final section of students' reader's notebooks, the logic being that this way when I return for another conference or small group, I can look at both the conference notes and any available work. At the same time, the child has this very tangible record of the agreed-on work and the pointers I have made, and this is alongside the child's own goals for himself.

MANAGING THE SHARE SESSION: WORKSHOP CLOSURE

You will want to draw on a handful of alternate ways that share time generally goes in your classroom and to induct children into those traditions right from the start. When it is almost time for the class to stop work for the share session, one child might circle the room, letting the other children know it is time to finish up. Alternatively, you could intervene to announce, "Three more minutes." In any case, readers will need a bit of time to finish what they are reading or writing. Then you'll decide whether for this share, you want to bring children to the meeting area, or if you'll work with them while they are in their reading spots. Nine times out of ten, teachers in grades 3–5 leave kids in their work spots for the share.

Either way, you'll probably begin the share by talking with children for a minute or two. You may plan to share an entry a child has written in her reading notebook, or a set of Post-its she's made. You'd mention that the work is exemplary and demonstrate the strategy the reader used. Then, typically, there is time for children to talk with their partners or their clubs.

Don't underestimate the power of the share. Research shows that it matters what you read or think about right before you go to sleep, for it is this final thing that your brain remembers and processes. That research has always made sense to me, for I know, from decades of studying professional development, that the ending of keynotes and workshops matter as much as the beginning. No matter how busy and rewarding a workshop has been, if it ends with a rushed sense of "Oh my gosh, it's time to go," that ending diminishes the force of the prior hour. Tom Corcoran, a leader with CPRE (Consortium for Policy and Research in Education at Teachers College), studies science

FIG. 6–2   Conference record-keeping sheet

A GUIDE TO THE READING WORKSHOP, INTERMEDIATE GRADES

classrooms around the globe, and he has often spoken to me about how important the last few moments of a science class are. He laments that instead of engaging in reflection, classes are often engaged in "clean up and pack up."

You want your share to give students an opportunity to reflect on what they've learned, and/or take that learning a step farther. You'll see that in a share, for instance, you might suggest readers compare and rank the themes they've entertained in their book, deciding which is more compelling across the entire story. Then again, you might ask students to name the skill they have worked on especially that day—choosing from a small list—and then to look at the learning progression for that skill, noting the nature of the work they have done and setting goals for next steps. The point is, the share is the true ending of workshop, and you'll want to be prepared for those final few minutes so they give coherence and increased power to the work.

Chapter 7

Conferring with Readers
Intense, Intimate, Responsive Teaching

WHEN PEOPLE want to learn to do something, we consider ourselves very lucky if we can get ourselves a coach. A young person hoping to qualify as an Olympic swimmer gets herself a coach, and that coach begins to watch her swimming, noticing her needs and channeling her to work on them. The coach also notices her strengths and does everything possible to maximize them. Someday, when that swimmer makes the team, when she walks to the pool and climbs into the water at the Olympics, the camera will scan to show her mother's face, and it will scan to show her coach's face as well.

When I wanted to get better as an organizational leader at the Teachers College Reading and Writing Project, I got myself a leadership coach. For an hour once a week, my coach talked to me on the phone about the work I'd been doing to become a better leader. One of her first questions was "Where do you want your organization to be five years from now? One year from now?" She then asked, "What's standing in the way of that?" and "What positive steps forward could you take?" Having established a trajectory of work, she was able to start our weekly conversation by asking questions like "How's it going?" and, "What new work did you try?" and "How'd that go for you?"

Young readers, too, benefit from coaches who are invested in their progress over time and who help them take all the instruction that is in the air of a rich reading workshop and use that instruction in ways that connect precisely to the individual learners, making sure the learners are working with direction and feedback in ways that make a palpable difference.

Conferring is every bit as important for readers who are working to become stronger as it is for swimmers, dieters, leaders, writers, runners, and teachers, too. As mentioned earlier, the research is clear that one of the factors that contributes most to any educational achievement is feedback. Hattie reviewed 180,000 studies involving 20 to 30 million students and found that of 100 factors that contribute to student achievement, providing learners with feedback rates in the very top 5–10% of influences. That feedback is especially powerful if the teacher helps the learner know where he is going, what progress he has made so far, and what specific activities he can do next to progress toward the goal.

Ideally, learners also receive help refining and seeking more challenging goals and adopting self-assessment strategies (Hattie 2008).

There are some principles and some methods that can guide your conferring whether you are working with readers or with writers. In this chapter, I'll discuss those guiding principles and essential methods for a reading conference, and then I'll discuss the challenges you face when conferring when you don't know the text that the child is reading.

THE ARCHITECTURE OF A CONFERENCE

Conferences, like minilessons, tend to follow a predictable architecture. That may sound odd—the idea that these intimate, responsive conversations have a structure or, you could say, a formula to them—but actually, in life, there are predictable structures undergirding many of our common interactions. For example, traditional teaching often follows a question-response-evaluate structure, with the teacher asking a known-answer question, "What is the capital of New York?", to which the child responds, "Albany," and the teacher assesses that response, saying, "Very good." Teachers who follow this question-response-evaluate pattern of interaction may not realize they are doing so because the content of their teaching presumably changes, minute to minute, day to day. But the architecture or pattern of this teaching interaction is all-important because as long as that pattern of interaction remains the same, the instruction itself will convey many of the same messages.

There are two kinds of conferences: research-decide-compliment-teach conferences and coaching conferences. Each kind of conference has a structure, or an architecture, that undergirds all these interactions. So although conferences are in some ways informal, they are also highly principled teaching interactions, carefully designed to move readers and writers along skill development pathways. Of course, the teacher who is experienced at conferring will adapt the architecture as needed, but for someone learning to teach within a reading (or a writing) workshop, it is important to understand the principles that underlie the design of conferences.

The Research-Decide-Compliment-Teach Conference

This kind of conference is the mainstay of the writing workshop and is critical to upper-grade reading workshops as well.

The Parts of a Research-Decide-Compliment-Teach Conference

- **Research:** This may involve questioning the reader, looking at his work, or thinking back over all you know of the reader, his process, goals, text level, and all the other data you have collected about him and his reading.

- **Decide and Compliment:** This involves making a decision about the most helpful lesson to teach this reader, and it includes offering the reader a compliment that is meant to support and instruct.

- **Teach:** This phase may take various forms, depending on the method of teaching you choose. It includes a teaching point and the reader's active involvement. This phase will also be where you help the reader

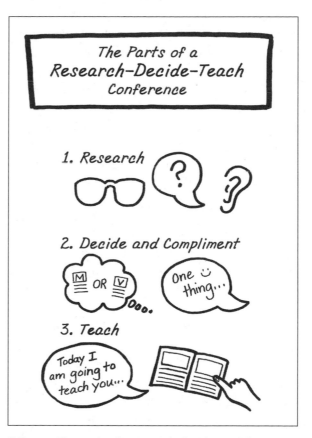

FIG. 7–1 The parts of a research-decide-compliment-teach conference

link your teaching in this moment to her ongoing independent reading work.

The Research Phase

Think for a moment about a time you have gone to an expert for guidance, for coaching. Perhaps you have gone to your minister, your rabbi, your doctor, your hairdresser, your fitness coach, your principal, or your staff developer for assistance. When you go to that person—the person in authority—how do you want the interaction to begin? My hunch is what you want in those instances is no different from what you want your principal to do when he or she does an observation of your teaching. You expect a question such as "What have you been working on lately?" or "What sort of help could I give you?"

Your conferring will be light-years more powerful if you draw on your memories of all the many times someone has conferred with you, using all that you wanted from those interactions to guide you as you frame your interactions with your kids. Because the truth is that kids are not all that different from you and me. If a child has been reading and working on becoming a better reader, then it makes sense that you need to do some research before you can teach in a way that will really make a difference. So chances are good that you'll begin your reading conference by asking something basic, such as "How's it going?" or "What have you been working on as a reader? or "What new work have you been doing as you read this?"

Listen wholeheartedly.

If you've had the good fortune of having a person you respect—perhaps someone coaching your teaching, your writing, or your marriage—say to you, "What new things have you been working on lately?" or "Can you walk me through what you have been trying to do?" you will have found what I have found. The question alone has led me to reflect, to dig deep, and even sometimes to create dawning insights about myself. Has that been true for you as well?

Of course, there are also times when someone asks, "What new things have you been working on?" and you respond with a perfunctory answer. You probably did that because you sensed the person wasn't really interested and sympathetic. We all know there are ways a person can listen, leaning in to hear more, nodding in ways that convey, "Say more," signaling for us to amplify what we've said, responding with gasps or little interjections that make us feel heard and understood—and all those signals make us want to talk. A good reading conference begins with deep listening.

Draw on all the information you have.

Journalists have a rule of thumb that guides their research. "The more you know, the more you can learn." Conferences benefit from information. So, for example, if you know a reader has been abandoning books shortly after starting them, you wouldn't ignore that information and begin the conference by asking, "How's reading been going for you lately?" Instead, you'd probably want to say, "I've noticed you started and stopped three books in the last few days. That's unusual for you. You aren't usually a picky reader. What's been going on for you, do you think?" Then, too, if you began a line of work during a previous conference, you're apt to bring readers to that vicinity and to say, "I know last time we met we talked about . . . How's that been going for you?"

Of course, you'll use whatever reading records you use to help you recall what you have taught and observed during previous interactions. You'll rely on those records more in reading conferences than in most other forms of one-to-one instruction. After all, when you draw alongside a *writer*, as opposed to a reader, and ask, "How's it going?" you have the evidence right before you, so it matters less if the child can articulate how it's been going. But when you ask a reader, "What new work have you been trying to do as a reader?" there won't be any reading sitting there on the table for you to look at. There will be some bits of evidence—reading logs, Post-its or other sorts of notes, perhaps entries in a reader's notebook—and you'll want to pore over these, deducing whatever you can from them. But ultimately, you will rely on your record keeping and the cumulative history of your work with this child more in reading than in writing. And you will need to mine whatever children do say or show you for all it's worth.

Follow up on information readers offer.

When I studied research methods early on in my professional training, I was taught that it is always important to "unpack" what an informant means with follow-up questions. If a reader says, "I've been finding evidence to support my theory about sharks," you might ask, "What do you really mean by 'finding evidence?' What sort of evidence are you looking for, and how do you look for it?" Alternatively, you might unpack a different portion of what the child said to you, saying, "You said you are finding evidence to support your *theory* about sharks. What is your theory—and can you explain to me what you mean by *theory*? Is a theory the same thing as an idea, or is it different?"

You might feel foolish at first asking such questions, because, of course, you know what the term *theory* means to you. The child is only using the term because he's parroting back something you've taught! But you truly do *not* know what the youngster means, and when a child has the opportunity to explain a literary term or a strategy to you, that illuminates a child's understanding—or lack thereof.

An even more powerful way to unpack what a child really means is to channel the child to shift from telling to showing. So if the child says that she is collecting evidence to back her theory, you could say, "Could you walk me through that work?" Alternatively, if the child doesn't have evidence of the work or is just about to embark on it, you could say, "So, will you get started doing that right now while I watch?" Then as the child sets to work, you can inquire, "So I see you are skimming this page. What are you thinking?"

Pursue a second line of questioning, and take into account as much information as possible.

For a minute, imagine a reading conference with a reader who is part way through one of Beverly Cleary's Ramona books. You asked him what he was working on, and he said he is trying to read faster and more. He is pushing himself to stop less often, to read with stamina. You asked what he means by *stamina*, and he told you about how runners have stamina, and he is trying for the same thing. You smiled to hear your own analogy coming back to you, but mostly you have been thinking furiously about what you can teach and what you can compliment. Here is an important tip—and it holds true in instances like this, when the reader is less experienced and less metacognitive, but also in instances when the reader's discussion of his goal leaves you dazzled. Always remember that after following a line of questioning, you need to go back and start a second line of questioning. Doing so will allow you to take in

additional information that gives you more options about where to go next. Starting a second line of questioning can be as simple as saying to the reader, "So one thing you have been working on is increasing your stamina. What else are you trying to do as a reader?" Then again, you can launch your second line of questioning differently. "Will you think about yourself as a reader? Would you say that the last few days have been a really good streak for you as a reader, or so-so, or not too good?" Then again, you can say, "There are some things that we've been studying as a class. Can you talk to me about the work you have been doing around . . . ?"

Not only do you need to launch a second line of inquiry, but you also need to gather information from many sources. So as that child explains that he is reading Ramona and working on his stamina, your eyes will go to his log. You'll note whether he's been reading within this series for a while and what he read before this. You'll check on how many books he is reading in a day and whether he is reading at home. If you have taken running records recently, you glance at them and recall the sources of difficulty he finds in books. You notice the writing about reading he has or has not been doing. All that information comes into your brain at the same time that you pursue your second line of questioning, and often what you see sparks that second line of questioning.

Help the child understand her role in the conference.

Of course, you can follow all my advice, do all these things, and the child can look at you like you are crazy. "What do you mean? What new work am I doing as a reader?" The child might say or think, "I'm reading, can't you see (or I would be if you'd leave me alone!) I'm on page 92. What am I working on next? Page 93."

Alternatively, when you ask those sorts of questions, the child could easily launch into a prolonged retell of whatever she is reading. Taking a giant breath, she starts, "Well, see, in my book, there's this guy, and he . . ." If you know the book, you may be able to extract from the retell some information about the sort of thinking the child has been doing as she reads, but if you do not know the book, you're apt to feel a bit at a loss. The child can go on and on, and try as you might to make yourself listen with rapt attention, you can feel your eyes roaming the room, checking on who is and who is not working.

So, if you ask a question like "What are you working on as a reader?" and the child launches into a retell of the book, you need to stop her. It is okay to hold up your hand like a crossing guard does to stop oncoming traffic. "Wait, wait," you'll want to say. Then you steer the child in a different direction, but also explicitly say why you are doing this. "When I ask, 'What have you been working on as a reader?' I'm not really wanting to hear the whole story of your book from beginning to end. When I ask, 'What are you working on as a reader?' I'm wanting to know what new stuff you are trying to do to become an even stronger reader. I'm wondering if you have been trying any of those things on our chart. Like, for example, have you been . . . ," and then I might fill in some of the answers I anticipate the child producing.

Much of what we do as readers is done with automaticity, inaccessible to conscious metacognitive thinking, so it will not be utterly surprising if your children are not particularly articulate about their reading goals and strategies. As Marie Clay points out, "Most things we do as readers need to operate below the conscious level most of the time, so that fast and effective processing of the print is achieved and attention is paid to the messages rather than to the work done to get to the message" (2001, 127).

If your teaching brims with ways you teach children how to take on deliberate goals, it will be important to work in purposeful and strategic ways to lift the level of thinking they are doing as readers. If you have been teaching youngsters how to read fiction interpretively, and you have taught them to be alert for ways that authors advance a theme across a novel, and if that child also knows she needs to keep track of minor as well as major characters, thinking about the role that minor characters play, and she also knows that in fiction, a problem is introduced and then the trouble often intensifies, all of this teaching should disrupt the child from a "just reading" relationship to a text. So if many of your children truly have no answer when you ask, "What are you working on as a reader?" then you'll want to look at the sticking power of your minilessons, mid-workshops, and shares.

Still, there will be times when a child can't name what he's doing as a reader, so you'll say, "Will you do that work right now, as I watch?" Then after the child does whatever it is—say, orienting himself to get ready to read an expository article—you can name what you have seen the child doing, "So to

FIG. 7–2

me it looks like you are the kind of reader who doesn't just pick up an article and sort of drift into reading it," I say, feigning a sleepy, passive approach to the text. "No way! You turn your mind on to high even as you just get the article into your hands. And it looks to me like when you look over the article, you are already thinking about what the big ideas might be that it will teach readers. Am I right?" And the narrative could continue, either with you continuing to talk through what you have seen the reader do or with you passing the baton to the reader, who could resume the narrative, taking up the story where you leave off.

Readers benefit from teaching you about their reading work.

Inviting children to reflect on and articulate what they have been doing as readers allows them to verbalize their strategies, which is helpful to them for a number of reasons. This puts them in a position to teach you. This is important in a learning community because this means that they can also teach other students. Your classroom will be transformed if young people, as well as you, are the source of knowledge. As Peter Johnston writes, in *Choice Words*,

> The side benefit of the "How did you . . . ?" question is that as children articulate their strategic action, they teach their strategies to other students without the teacher being the authoritative-source-from-which-all-knowledge comes. It arranges for instruction without hierarchical positioning. Naturalizing this sort of conversation opens the possibility that students will continue such conversations among themselves, thus increasing the level of "explicit" instruction without increasing the extent to which children are being told what to do. (Johnston 2004, 32)

There are other reasons as well that asking a child to teach you what she has been doing as a reader can, in and of itself, help that child. To really understand this, imagine that I came to your school. You know I'm an authority figure, and you expected me to come and teach you some things about using these units of study really well. I arrive early in the day, before the kids have come, and we're alone in the staff room. We each get coffee and then sit for a minute. "So," I say, "Can you fill me in on your teaching of reading—how's it been going for you over the last year or two?" You talk and I lean in closer, blown away by what you are saying. "Whoa," I murmur. "Geez." Then I ask a question or two. "So how has that really affected your interactions with kids, do you think?" "Has anything helped?" and then, a follow-up, "So what do you think helped so much?" After some more talk, "So how do you think these units of study are going to fit into that whole story of you and your teaching reading?" And finally, "While I'm here, are there things I could do that might help, do you think?"

A conversation like that reverberates. Later, afterward, we ask ourselves the same questions that the teacher asked us, beginning to internalize this line of thinking as we work independently. How has my teaching changed over these years? What do I want for myself? What might be the first steps I could I take?

In the same way, your questions to your young readers are gifts, in and of themselves. There is abundant research that shows that just doing a thing—just reading—is not the best way to accelerate one's development. Instead, it is through deliberate goal-driven work that people improve at almost anything. Your questions can promote that conscious, deliberate, goal-driven approach to reading.

The Decide and Compliment Phase

If you return to the memories of times when people in authority have come into your life, assessed your work (or your hair or your physical fitness) and then intervened in ways that aim to help you improve, my hunch is that some of those times ended up being incredibly destructive, and other times were incredibly helpful. It's important to think, "What was the difference? Why did the one interaction hurt me for life, and why did the other help in ways that still matter to me?"

I think that mostly, the way you feel about a conferring interaction will depend on whether the coach gives you the sense that you have the capacity to do the work, to rise to the occasion. If someone watches you teach or reads your rough draft writing or studies the records of your reading or hears about your marriage or looks over your hair and then, having seen you, says, "Geez. This is a bigger problem than I realized. I don't know . . . ," then this one interaction can seal the deal, making you totally convinced that you are not cut out to be a teacher, a writer, a reader, a spouse, or a beautiful person. Marie Clay has written extensively about the fact that sometimes, without meaning to do so, we can actually teach children that they *can't* solve problems, *can't* help themselves, *can't* get better. Clay's classic paper, "Learning to Be Learning Disabled," shows that just as a teacher can help a child learn to be an active agent of his own learning, a teacher can also teach children to be passive victims, filled with self-doubts (Clay 1987).

After researching what a child has already done and has been trying to do, I try to do two interrelated, intertwined things. I decide and I compliment. Sometimes I compliment first, then decide, and sometimes the sequence is the reverse. But either way, I take a few moments to name what the child has already done that I hope she continues forever more, work that I hope becomes part of the child's identity. And I think, "Out of all that I could possibly say and teach, what will help the most?" That decision influences the compliment, often, as well as the teaching that follows. In this section, I'll discuss the decision first and then the compliment.

Decide

To an outside observer, my conference may seem fairly relaxed. But meanwhile, I am listening with every cell in my brain activated, and I am thinking, thinking, thinking. Malcolm Gladwell, the author of the bestselling book *Blink: The Power of Thinking without Thinking*, talks about how an expert can thin-slice and, in the blink of an eye, make critical judgments. As the authors of *Breakthrough* point out,

> Instruction is powerful only when it is sufficiently precise and focused to build directly on what students already know and to take them to the new level. While a teacher does and must do many things, the most critical is designing and organizing instruction so that it is focused. Without focus, instruction is inefficient, and students spend too much time completing activities that are too easy and do not involve new learning or on tasks that are too difficult. (Fullan et al. 2006, 34)

As I listen to the reader and take in all the evidence I can see and all that is available in my reading records, I'm theorizing, predicting, and connecting this reader to other readers I've known, determining priorities, imagining alternative ways to respond, and lesson planning! Meanwhile I am smiling genially and nodding warmly enough that I keep more data coming my way.

Some words of caution: there are a few temptations to avoid when deciding what to teach the reader.

First, remember that before you can select the most powerful way to teach, you need to be able to imagine a variety of possible options, and to do that, you need to have taken into account lots of sources of information. Have you glanced at the reader's log as he talked to you? Doing so is pretty crucial, even if you don't bring the log up in discussion at all. Have you thought about what you know about the level of books the child is reading (What are the challenges that tend to dominate in those books?). Have you glanced over the child's writing about reading?

It is tempting to listen just long enough to know the kind of work that reader is engaged with and then to leap to an instant conclusion about what you will teach.

Try to take some time to think so that you are actually *selecting* the most powerful thing to compliment and to teach, not just grabbing at straws. And remember that doing this involves not just identifying the goal you'll take up, the skill you'll support, but also understanding where the reader is along that learning progression. So you may be teaching kids to determine the main idea in an expository article, but you need to know what it is the learner can already do and can't yet do. (Perhaps she can identify the main idea when it is supported in headings and topic sentences but can't do so when it is more implicit.) The real decision involves not what terrain one is teaching in, but rather what precisely it is that the learner doesn't yet know how to do and seems ready to learn—and how you'll teach that next step.

It is tempting first to study and name what a reader is doing and then send the reader off to new territory, in a new direction.

Be wary of this. All too often, a teacher will read over a reader's Post-its and notice that she does a lot of something—say, raising questions about the main character—and then the teacher's instinct will be to point out something the reader is not choosing to do—say, predicting what will happen next.

Consequently, the teacher then says, "I love the way you are asking questions as you read. Now, though, can I teach you that in addition to asking questions, you can predict?" (or do whatever else strikes the teacher's fancy). When a learner seems to be "on about" one line of work, you'll want to be hesitant to redirect that learner. There are endless sorts of work that a reader can be doing, and if there is no particular reason why a reader needs to drop the kind of thinking she is doing so as to do whatever you have in mind, then resist the temptation to pull her off course. Honor her intention, as much as possible, or if you have a reason to want the reader to do a different kind of thinking, be sure to explain your logic and to lure the reader to take on the new goal you suggest.

Remember that it is important that learners have a sense of agency, authoring learning lives for themselves. So, for example, if this reader tended to ask lots of questions about the main character, I might look over those questions and show her that there's one kind of question she's not asking too much, and that's "Why?" When characters do something or want something, an astute reader can usually discern why the character has said or done this, and to do so, we generally need to locate earlier parts of the text that link to the part we're reading now. So this is important work. Alternatively, I could notice that the reader asks questions that are important ones and well worth trying to answer. I could talk to the reader about ways to go from asking questions to entertaining them, using phrases such as, "Could it be that . . . ?" Or I could show the reader that the questions she is already asking could encompass minor as well as major characters. One way or another, I try to stay with and extend and build off from a reader's own intentions rather than redirecting her.

Use the learning progression to help you decide—and develop your own additional learning progressions.

Throughout human history, people have become smarter through the use of tools. Tools of the hand become tools of the mind. There is one tool that will help your conferring and small-group work more than any other, and that is the learning progression. If you listen to a child and determine that what she is trying to do is to retell a biography, a bit of narrative nonfiction, then glance at the learning progressions for summary. Listen to the reader, and check out where she is on the learning progression.

Compliment

As I listen to readers, another key decision revolves around the question, "What is it that the reader has already done (or almost done) that I could compliment?" I know that I can teach as much through finding, recognizing, and celebrating good work as by issuing challenges, so that is one reason that the compliment portion of a conference is an extremely important one. The compliment also allows readers to sense that you have confidence in them. If you can't convey this message, it is unlikely that a reader is going to be willing to listen to what you have to say.

Make the compliment transferable.

The trick is that a good compliment applies not just to today's work, but to tomorrow's as well. I'm wanting the reader to go through life remembering, "I'm good at . . . I need to remember to do that." So if a reader's book tells about how a character journeys from one town to another and the reader has recorded the names of the towns on Post-its that dot the book, I'm not going to say, "I love the way you recorded the towns your character visited. You are really great at recording those towns," because I don't really want to say, "Whenever you read a book, remember to record the towns where the character visits." But I could recast what the reader

has done, by saying, "It's really helpful that you think about the main things that are happening in your book and record them so that later you can look back over your jottings and recall in your mind the time line of big events in the book." That compliment is transferable. That is, I could say, "Whenever you read a book, remember to do this."

Make the compliment centered on new learning.

There are a few ways to make a compliment especially significant. One is that I try to compliment work that feels as if it represents the cusp of a learner's trajectory. If the learner has just begun to do something and is still a bit shaky at this new work and I can celebrate that brave new work, that's especially powerful. Peter Johnston has written,

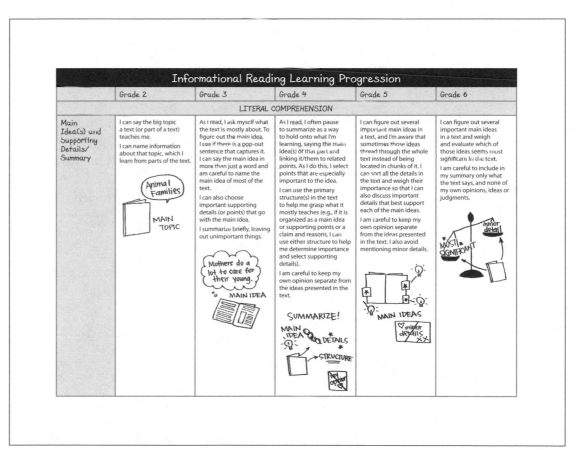

Focusing on the positive is hardly a new idea. It is just hard to remember to do it sometimes, particularly when the child's response is nowhere near what you expected . . . Much more important is noticing and helping the students notice—what they are doing well, particularly the leading edge of what is going well. This leading edge is where the student has reached beyond herself, stretching what she knows just beyond its limit, producing something that is partly correct. This is the launching for new learning. (Johnston 2004, 13)

Sometimes, when I try to notice and name what the student has done that represents the leading edge of the student's learning, I end up complimenting what the student has almost done or is just about to do. In this instance, for example, I might say to the reader, "I am blown away by your decision to mark the important steps that your character made on her journey—the big things that happened, the places she visited. I know you did that so you can look back over the whole journey, sort of retelling it in your mind and to others, and that is just so smart—not just to read forward but to stop from time to time to recall the path the book has taken so far." I might say that, knowing full well that the reader had no intention of pausing to look back, or of using the Post-its in that way.

Make the compliment personal.

Then, too, I can make my compliment more significant if I personalize it. I tell teachers that in general, when I am complimenting a child on doing something, I do not want to reuse the words of my own teaching point. If I have taught readers that when predicting, it helps to think, "What do I know about how stories like this tend to go? How can remember that? Help me think what might happen next in this story?" Then, in a compliment, I do not want to say, "I love the way you thought, 'What do I know about how stories tend to go?'" Such a compliment is really no more than saying, "I love the way you did as I told you to do," and no child is going to phone home and share that compliment with a parent! Instead, the challenge is to find new words to use to capture what, precisely and uniquely, this learner has done.

An example of a reading compliment.

When I spent a bit of time with Kobe during a unit on character, I definitely wanted to support the hard work he'd done to lift the level of his predictions and his envisioning. So I said to him, "Kobe, you are so determined! I remember that first day when you and your table looked over your envisioning Post-its and you told me the group had decided that yours just repeated the stuff that was in the book. Other kids might have gotten all discouraged and said to themselves, 'I'm not going to do this kind of thinking. It is not my style.' Others might have folded their arms in a huff and said, 'I'm not the type to envision.' But you—you have been so determined, and bit by bit, you have worked harder and harder. Look at the difference in your envisioning. At the beginning, you just wrote, 'He is a good basketball player.' Now look at your envisioning!" We looked together at the progression in his work.

Then, continuing, I said to Kobe, "To me, you are a lot like Sassy, in *Dancing in the Wings*. Remember how when Mona and Molly told her she had no talent, that there was no way she'd get picked to go to the dance festival, she didn't let them discourage her? No way. Remember how that very night she dreamed that she was dancing on the Milky Way and she went right on to those tryouts and didn't let Mona and Molly's snickering get to her? You are just the same as Sassy because the two of you never give up."

The Teaching Phase

After complimenting the reader, I name my teaching point and teach. This aspect of the conference feels a bit like a minilesson. The difference comes in that in a conference, just as in small-group work, the time spent teaching is less and the time spent guiding children's active engagement is more.

My suggestion is that you guard against the tendency to slip between a conference and the teaching part of the conference because I find that often, the reader doesn't even grasp that the conference has taken a turn. For example, if I complimented Kobe on his envisioning becoming much more detailed and on working with resolve to accomplish that goal, and now I wanted to teach him to be more attentive to tone and mood in that envisioning, the best way to make my point wouldn't be to go from the compliments to ask, "Do you know what *mood* means? When you envision what's going on, do you think about the mood?" Instead, I'd ask permission to teach him a tip. "Do you mind if I give you one small but important tip?"

When our teaching is especially subtle, kids often miss it. If we are not explicit, the chances that they'll learn something they can use again another day is unlikely. So in the example above, I'd be much more apt to conduct my interview, perhaps give a compliment, and then crystallize whatever I wanted to teach about questioning into a single, straightforward teaching point.

After that, you are apt to do a tiny demonstration. You will probably carry with you the class read-aloud, a short stack of other books that your children are familiar with, the relevant reading checklists, and the learning progression. If you are super-prepared for conferences, you might even have gone through those books, mining them for possible illustrations of teaching points, and jotting these on Post-its so that you're able to quickly say, "For example, let's read this page of this book that we were reading last week. This is the part where . . . I'm thinking . . . Now let's read on together and see if we can . . ." Then I demonstrate and name what I have done in the demonstration that I hope is transferable to the kids.

The conference then turns as I say, "So try it." As the reader tries what I have just demonstrated, working either in the text I've pulled out for the occasion or in the reader's own text, I coach into his work, giving lean pointers that help him do the work successfully.

The conference ends with my suggesting the reader try this not only today, with this text, but often. I might give the reader some sort of a cue card or reminder—a bookmark, perhaps, containing a summary of what we've just gone over together or a special color of Post-its to mark times when the reader does this over the next few days, making it easy for us to see the traces of that work. By then, it is time to record what I've taught and learned and to scurry on to another reader, another lesson—for the child and for me.

The Coaching Conference

When you coach readers, you act rather like a running coach acts, running alongside the athlete, interjecting brief bits of advice: "Today, remember to breathe from your stomach," the coach says just before the jog begins. Then the runner begins to run, and the coach jogs alongside, watching. As the runner reaches a hill and begins to strain, the coach interjects, "Stomach." When the runner begins to breathe faster, the coach says, "Breathe deep."

Similarly, when you coach a reader, you read along with the reader, watching the reader move across the terrain of the text.

Similarly, when you coach a reader, you read along with her, watching her move across the terrain of the text. Your first interjection might be a bit longer than the ones that follow. Instead of "Breathe from your stomach," you might say, "You're skipping past words. Work on them a bit. Word solve." Then as the reader continues to read, you watch. "Check it." you might say when the reader skips past a difficult word. Next time you may just point at the word and say, "Stay with it." "What could you try?" You may watch the reader go back and make a second try and then give a prompt to reinforce the work she did, and say, "You read through the whole word," and then say, "Nice."

A coaching conference can begin with the same kind of observation that one uses in a research-decide-compliment-teach conference, but the assessment may have been another day entirely. The goal is to intervene as lightly as possible while readers continue to move through text. The goal of coaching is partly to help readers develop unconscious habits. The coach is bypassing metacognition and trying to get good habits into the reader's system. When you coach the reader, you are trying to help the reader walk the walk, not talk the talk. Coaching moves are especially important when working with beginning readers who still need to develop a felt sense for moving through the text and when supporting readers with a difficult skill.

For this type of conference, it also might be possible that you already have the teaching point in mind, perhaps based on previous conferences or running record data. For example, if you noticed that a particular reader struggled with the literal comprehension questions on the running records, you'll have already made the decision that after you read with her, a teaching point on retelling or holding tight to the text will follow. Of course, you might also decide to focus on something you coached the reader on in the minutes prior.

Let's listen in on a coaching conference. Simone is a third-grader who has recently begun reading books that are at level N. Even before the teacher approaches her, she recalls her most recent running records and the results of Simone's performance preassessment. They suggested that Simone is growing ideas about the characters in her texts, discussing a character's traits, feelings, and motivations. She is considering how new parts of the text fit with parts she previously read. These assessments also suggested that when she encounters unfamiliar words and phrases in her texts, she often reads past them without pausing to think about what else those phrases might mean. When reading *My Name Is Maria Isabel*, for example, she might read quickly past the line, "The city seemed to be wrapped in silence" without trying to figure out the unfamiliar phrase. When the teacher pulls up next to Simone, she has just started a new book.

she read the words correctly, she has to do more work to determine their meaning. After Simone determines what the phrase means, rereading a little and thinking about the meaning of the whole text to do so, she continues reading. A few lines later, Simone reads the line "It will taste like a whole raft of lemons." The teacher gives her a prompt to stop and think, saying, "Think about that phrase." A bit later, Simone reads, "It will taste like a night on the sea," and she stops herself, saying, "That could mean that it tastes really salty, like sea water." The teacher gives her a prompt to reinforce the work she did. "You noticed a tricky phrase and thought about what it could mean."

Decide and Teach

As Simone begins reading *The Stories Julian Tells*, by Ann Cameron, the teacher reads alongside her, listening in to see if she is bringing all of her word-solving strategies to bear on the unfamiliar words and phrases she encounters in this new text. The teacher prepares to respond with prompts to support her in considering the meaning of these words or phrases while still listening closely to see if other coaching moves are more appropriate. With minimal expression, the teacher listens as Simone reads the lines, "My father is a big man with wild black hair. When he laughs, the sun laughs in the windowpanes." Then, she continues reading.

The line makes sense in the text, but the phrase itself is confusing. This confirms what the teacher had seen in the research phase, so she decides to prompt Simone to think about the meaning of the phrase, saying, "You read, 'When he laughs, the sun laughs in the windowpanes.' You read the words correctly, but it doesn't make sense. Will you think, 'Could this word or phrase mean something funny or special?' Reread if you need to." The teacher supports Simone with word solving by acknowledging that although

Link

As with most instruction, you'll want to wrap up the conference by reminding the reader of what you just taught. A conference usually ends with having the student go back to the text she just read and pointing out where she could have applied what she just learned. As with a minilesson link, you'll remind the reader that your teaching is something to be used not just on that day or in that text, but each day moving forward.

To do this, the teacher interrupts Simone's reading at this point to leave her with a teaching point. "Simone, you are the kind of reader who is working hard to ensure that every part of the book makes sense. When you read phrases that are tricky, you stop and think, 'Could this word or phrase mean something funny or special?' Then, you reread and think about what it could mean. This is important work for readers to do because authors often embed these funny phrases on purpose. Let me show you where you did that work by yourself." The teacher points out the part where Simone paused to consider the meaning of the phrase "taste like a night on the sea." Then she leaves Simone with some final words of encouragement. "Continue to do that careful reading work whenever you encounter tricky phrases, Simone!"

Chapter 8

Small-Group Work
Developing a Richer Repertoire of Methods

WHEN I WAS A YOUNG PROFESSIONAL, fresh on the scene, I was invited to be one of ten young women featured in a "Young Women to Watch" article in *Ladies' Home Journal*. I was asked to appear at a certain address downtown to have my photo taken. I spruced myself up—clean hair, new pink suit—and arrived at the appointed address, a New York City loft, my first time ever in one.

"Come, come, sit here," the people told me, and I sat in a chair, expecting to say "Cheeeese" and to be on my way. To my surprise, the chair on which I sat was suddenly cranked backward, and I found myself leaning so that my head was positioned over a sink, with a team of people surrounding me, one sending a stream of water over my already clean hair, another massaging shampoo into it. Once that process was completed, a man arrived with a suitcase. I wondered if this would be a new outfit to replace my new pink suit but no, the entire suitcase was filled with makeup. A full hour later, I was standing against an entire wall of cascading, shiny, white fabric, one foot slightly in front of the next, face cocked upward and turned to the side, chin up an inch—no, less, that's it. As I held that position, I felt someone's hands fumbling at my back, around the waistline of my skirt, and realized he was releasing the top button of my skirt so that it would ride a bit lower on my hips, then adding clothes pins to alter the drape of the skirt just so. "Head up again, eyes here," the photographer called. And then he said, "Just relax, be yourself."

There was, of course, no way under the sun I was going to "just relax" after having been subjected to these intensive efforts to remake me. And here's the point of my story: I think that many teachers have been subjected to equally intensive efforts to remake their small-group instruction so that it is "just so." There have been so many books written on how to lead small groups in the precisely right ways that too many teachers approach a little hub of readers, gripped by anxiety over doing this The Right Way. Meanwhile, the whole point is to be personal, to be responsive, and to channel kids to do some work while you observe and coach.

TO BE RESPONSIVE, THERE CAN'T BE JUST ONE WAY TO LEAD SMALL GROUPS

When I talk with teachers about leading reading workshops, there are always two topics around which anxiety runs especially high: time and small-group work. Often I sense that teachers have been schooled to lead one specific kind of small-group work (usually their district's version of guided reading), and they want to be sure that they can fit that small-group work into their reading workshop. Of course, my response to this question is that by all means they can do that. But I also encourage teachers to know that over time and with practice, they'll probably develop a more expansive repertoire of ways of working with small groups.

Some native Alaskans, lore has it, have twenty-six words for *snow*. They're such experts on snow that they don't think of all that white stuff as just one monolithic thing. And I'm convinced that with increasing expertise, teachers, too, come to realize that all our small-group work need not fit into one template or bear a single label.

To start, I suggest that you think about all the various ways you teach reading to your whole class, and consider whether each of those ways of teaching reading couldn't be done through small groups. Presumably, most teachers will spend a chunk of whole-class time reading aloud and engaging kids in accountable-talk conversations. Some kids will need extra support to learn how to participate well in that work. There will presumably also be time for the class to participate in either shared reading (where the class reads a text aloud in unison) or in whole-class close reading work. Presumably, that sort of instruction will have special payoffs for some students who could use intensive personalized doses of this sort of teaching. Hopefully, the class devotes some time to word study, which may center on vocabulary development or, depending on the ability levels of readers, on work with graphophonics. Again, it seems obvious that some students would profit from intensive intervention in those areas—and a little of this might make the whole-class work have more sticking power for them. My point is not to make you feel pressured to do it all, because there will never be enough time for everything. Instead, I want to help you imagine a wider repertoire of possibilities and to realize that you already know how to lead these sorts of small groups because you'd essentially be doing what you do with the whole class, only with small groups. My argument is that if these ways of working with texts are powerful enough

to use with a whole class, why would that sort of work not also be powerful when used with a small group?

Of course, there are many other ways that small groups could go—ways that are uniquely suited to small groups. Let me overview a few of these alternatives and encourage you to realize that each of the formats for small-group work that I describe could be adjusted to support a wide array of skill development.

Perhaps a group of kids are all reading a shared book, and you know the chapter they are approaching is a particularly complex and rich one. Maybe it advances some of the themes of the book, and you know you could teach interpretation by helping kids mine that chapter for all it is worth. You could suggest that the chapter merits being read aloud and discussed almost as if it was a whole-class read-aloud. You could start the group off doing this work by starting to read aloud, setting the kids up to listen for and signal when the text especially deserves thought. You could support that sort of listening even more by suggesting what might cue them to pause. One child could listen for repetition that felt significant, another for times when the author seems to be saying to readers, "This is a life lesson. Listen closely." Another child could listen for the presence of an object or a part of the setting that seems to mean more than at first meets the eye. In any case, students could listen to you and signal places when they'd like to halt your reading to reread and talk. You could respond to some but not all of their "Whoa!" signals. The first time you pause, you could simply engage kids in rereading closely, annotating (using Post-its), and talking. Another time you pause, you could teach readers a handful of questions that pay off to ask. You could also show kids the value of reading onward with possible theories in hand. After doing this work with children for a page and a half or so, you could suggest that one of them takes over reading aloud, with the listeners continuing to signal at pause-worthy spots, reminding them of the questions they might ask of the text. Once one group of kids has learned to do this work, you could send another group to watch them as researchers, studying what they are doing, and to try their hand at similar work. Over time, you could vary this by having readers pause not just for talking but also for jotting.

Perhaps a group of students are each reading different expository texts, and you want to teach them that readers read, thinking about the big points the text is making and the supporting examples that fit under each of those big points. You particularly want to show children that their lists of supportive points could grow very long and to encourage them to weigh those supportive points, choosing the most important ones. (For some reason, PARCC and SBAC both value a reader's ability to choose the most important supportive points, so this work will have extra payoff on those high-stakes assessments.) In this small group, you might return to an article that you already read aloud to the class and show students that you have already begun taking notes—you have recorded two main points that the article has made—and now you channel the kids to work together to reread and to choose the best supporting examples for each of those points. You leave children to do that work, then circle back once they are done and listen to their rationale for why they included some supportive examples and not others. Then you recap what the children have done and ask them to work in pairs, doing the much harder work of discerning both the most important main points *and* the best supportive details from the texts that two of them read (or reread) independently. Depending on how much support those youngsters need, you could make sure their texts are also ones you have read aloud to the class, or you could set them up to do this work first with videos or with texts that are especially well structured. As they work, you circle between them, making lean coaching comments. As part of your coaching, you could help students to note that sometimes authors clue readers into which examples are most important, using terms such as "most importantly." Again, once children became experts at this work, you could use them to teach others—including traveling to a younger grade to work one-to-one as reading buddies, helping those youngsters do this work with even more supportive texts. Your children's learning will be cemented in place if they not only have opportunities to do some important small-group work together, but if they also know that they will be called upon to function as maestros or professors on the topics they investigate.

Let's imagine another way that a small group could go. Imagine that your children have been learning to read nonfiction texts in such a way that they can summarize those texts effectively. They've been reading during independent reading time and writing short summaries of those texts. Now you gather a bunch of kids together and show them the learning progression for summarizing and ask them to work together to decide whether their summaries are at the third- , fourth-, or fifth-grade level and then to help each other revise those summaries so they are all at least at the fourth-grade level. You leave them with mentor texts—examples that you wrote of the same summary, written around the class's read-aloud text, written at each of those levels. You

FIG. 8–1

may stay and coach into students' work, or you may not. Either way, they'll learn tremendous amounts from the work. Obviously, this small-group format could be used to support any skill.

Here's another possibility. You want to teach students that when they predict, their predictions need to be based on the details of the text they have already read. You reread the last bit of the book you have read aloud to the class and show them that when they predict, they need to draw on details from earlier in the text. You do this just a bit, and then you get them to try it with the same book. Then you channel readers to read on in their books, and when they come to a spot where they can do some prediction, to stop and jot that prediction, remembering to do what you just demonstrated. As students work on this, you move from one to another, coaching into their work.

During reading time, you will sometimes lead guided reading groups. The term *guided reading* means remarkably different things to different people, and we encourage you to read Fountas and Pinnell's guided reading materials, which are foundational to the discipline. Generally, when my colleagues and I lead guided reading groups, we gather four or sometimes six children (usually two or three partnerships) and devote a minute or two to a book introduction that includes a summary of the book and supports readers in what we anticipate will be tricky aspects

of the book. The readers are usually holding the text while we do this, and we might have them point to or find a tricky part, just because their activity serves to highlight that item. Then children read, usually silently and not in sync with each other, while whomever is teaching rotates like the big hand on the clock from one reader to the next, tapping one at a time on the arm to signal, "Please read aloud, starting where you are in the text." If a child is in dire need, we are apt to say, "Can I take a turn?" and read to the child, figuring we didn't provide a supportive enough introduction or we put the reader into a too-hard text. After a child or two from the group finishes reading the selection and before the others have yet caught up, we often signal for those who have finished reading to reread or to find a favorite page or a tricky part (something like that). When everyone has finished, after no more than ten minutes, we engage the children in the briefest of conversations and then select a skill or strategy to teach, drawing on what we saw as a shared hard part. Often youngsters practice whatever has been taught, sometimes on the white board and sometimes by returning to the passage. Often we give a tiny text introduction for the upcoming section if we want children to continue reading on in the text after the guided reading session is over.

Guided reading is an especially powerful method to use in certain situations. For example, when working with English language learners, this is a way to scaffold their comprehension and vocabulary. When bringing readers to a new level of text difficulty, and especially when launching them into a new

series at the new level, this is a great way to provide extra training wheels for those readers. When we see children who seem to respond to trouble by forgetting meaning and relying only on letters and sounds in isolation, we find that strong book introductions make it much more likely that they'll draw on meaning as well as phonics when they encounter difficulty.

For your small-group teaching to be responsive, you need to outgrow any feeling that every small group proceeds in the same way. If you have been trained that every small group begins with a text introduction, followed by a time in which readers each read while you circle among them, listening to one child and then another and coaching into one individual's reading and then another's, with you ending the small group with a teensy book talk followed by a little teaching point, you need to understand that yes, indeed, that is one way that small groups can go. Many people refer to that format of instruction as guided reading. But other teachers do very different things under the name of guided reading; it is a term that has vastly different interpretations in one school and another. You would be in good company if you described any of the small groups I have detailed as "guided reading" if you felt the need to have just one term for all your small-group work. But ideally, you will not do the exact same thing with every small group, because different ways of working will be especially effective at accomplishing different goals.

The one thing we know for certain about young readers is that they are not all the same! At a conference at Teachers College, the reading researcher Richard Allington recently reported that most teachers have only one format for their small groups. The irony is that we work with small groups instead of the whole class precisely so that we can tailor our teaching to our students. So why think that The Right Way is to do the same thing in every small group? There are abundant ways you can work with small groups, and this is especially true because this is a format in which you will sometimes work in out-of-the-box ways, trying something bold that you have never tried before just on the off chance that it might help. After all, your small-group instruction will be your forum for working with students for whom in-the-box sorts of teaching may not have done the job.

PRINCIPLES TO GUIDE YOUR SMALL-GROUP WORK

The first and most important thing to say about small-group work is this: Do it! One of the reasons to lead a well-structured, streamlined reading workshop—one in which readers know how to carry on independently as readers—is that this provides a perfect context within which you can lead flexible small groups. While your kids are immersed in within-reach books that they have chosen, you can very easily pull together not just one but several small groups each day. You need to make leading a small group into no big deal.

Consider Shorter, More Frequent Small-Group Sessions, Decreasing Scaffolding over Time

Keep in mind that many of the Units of Study themselves set up small groups. At every grade level, there is at least one unit that supports book clubs, and most teachers add another book club unit to their year-long plans (using the units detailed in *If . . . Then . . . Curriculum*). These will be roughly homogeneous groupings of children working with multiple copies of the same book. Whenever you work with one of these book clubs, you will be leading small-group work. You can decide the format to use. Do you want to treat the book club as a guided reading group? You might start with an introduction to the book, then channel kids to read alongside each other while you coach into that reading. Or do you want to use the book club to teach a strategy lesson? Perhaps you show them how you do something (say, read with the lens of their current theory) and then watch and coach as readers try what you have taught? Be mindful, however, not to focus most of your book club instruction on the etiquette of conversation. Although kids do need to learn that—many twenty-first-century learning theorists think there needs to be far more teaching into collaboration because this will be a critically important life skill—you will want to take advantage of the fact that book clubs make small-group reading instruction very easy.

You will also find that many of the nonfiction units channel youngsters to work in research teams, and those teams can support small-group work. If two children in a research team have read one resource on the team's topic and two kids have read a different text, you have a perfect setup for teaching kids to extrapolate main ideas and supportive details, so that they will be able to teach each other about their texts and synthesize their knowledge.

In a typical day's reading workshop, you will probably aim toward working with two small groups and holding three or four conferences, some with individuals and some with partnerships. I can see you adding up the minutes, thinking, "Two small groups—that is thirty minutes right there, and three or four conferences . . . ," but remember that both conferences and small-group work can vary tremendously in length.

In general, though, small-group work will be more powerful if you do smaller bouts of it across time than if you have one gigantic small-group session every few weeks. It helps to work with a particular small group for around ten minutes, twice a week, for a sequence of three times, rather than working with that group one time for half an hour. The extra advantage of more frequent short meetings is that you can then ask (and expect) children to do some work related to the group between your meetings. This allows the group work to influence their reading for longer stretches of time.

A Sample Strategy Small Group

One of the small-group challenges that you may face is the planning time required. The Units of Study books will help with this, but for additional help, my colleagues and I—and especially my colleague Kathleen Tolan—have

developed a progression of small-group work that can be tweaked to support all sorts of skill development and that does not require a lot of planning. This progression has been embraced with great enthusiasm in many TCRWP schools.

Let's imagine that you want to convene a small group on envisioning because you have noticed that these readers, despite their different levels, are all having some difficulty discussing what they see happening in a story when they read. They are all reading different books. You decide you want to meet with these readers across a sequence of a few sessions. Here is one plan for how those sessions could go—a plan that would not require you to search for new materials or spend an extensive amount of time planning. This sequence is also replicable across any skill and designed to decrease the amount of scaffolding you provide, thus pushing students to more independence.

Possible Progression of Small Groups

Session 1:
Re-do a whole class minilesson (less time demonstrating) and coaching readers in their books

Session 2:
Scaffold with guided practice using your read aloud text and coaching readers in their books

Session 3:
Name the teaching point you have been working on and coaching readers in their books

FIG. 8–2 A sample strategy for small-group work

The first time you meet with this small group, you could basically redo a whole-class minilesson you taught on envisioning, only this time you spend less time demonstrating and give students more time to practice with your coaching support. You might tell the group why you have gathered them. You name the skill you plan to focus on working on with them and then remind them of what you demonstrated during the minilesson. ("Remember how we said he smoothed his hair back and his face probably looked so mean, there? So angry, right? And he probably took his fists and did what with them?") And meanwhile you are involving your readers in doing the same envisioning work as you are—in making the same faces you are and clenching their fists. This quick interactive reminder of the demonstration you did for the class should take only one or two minutes. Then you will want to quickly get your readers to open their own books and start reading while you go around to coach each child individually.

When you coach children, you want them to read a bit aloud to you, and you offer lean prompts and questions as they do so to coach into their thinking. One of the best ways to do this coaching is to think about the sorts of things you might say to your own child or niece or nephew if you were reading a bedtime story together. That is, think of what you would naturally say to a child as you read together. Sometimes just making exclamations ("Oh, wow!" "Oh, no!") or widening your eyes or gasping in reaction can help support a reader in doing stronger thinking work. Prompts such as "Oh, my gosh! Can you picture that? What else are you seeing?" will support envisioning work, in particular, but there are also lots of prompts you can use that are transferable to any kind of skill work, such as:

- "Say more."
- "What about . . . ?"
- "Oh, explain that to me."
- "Why does that seem important?"
- "So, what is that making you think?"
- "Can you find another part that fits with that idea?"

At times, I also tend to repeat what the reader just said and gesture for more information as a child is talking to me about his reading (and I can use all these moves during conferring, as well). The point is to coach into the student's thinking work so that he is doing more than he did before your

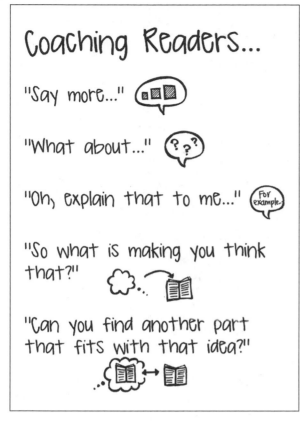

Coaching Readers...

"Say more..."

"What about..."

"Oh, explain that to me..." For example...

"So what is making you think that?"

"Can you find another part that fits with that idea?"

FIG. 8–3

coaching. And this structure also ensures that each student is getting some time to practice with your support, and when you are not coaching that child, the child is reading and practicing. You always want to make sure that your small groups offer the most time possible for your students to practice the work.

After you coach each reader, you'll want to call the group back together and highlight something you noticed. Then before sending them off, you'll want to give them a way to be accountable to this work (such as "Flag parts as you keep reading. Do this on a big pink Post-it."). Let the group know when you will all meet again and what you expect them to do in the meantime.

So, that first session required only for you to bring your read-aloud text and redo a bit of your demonstration. The rest of the group time was spent using students' materials and coaching into their work. Of course, coaching

can take a bit of practice to really get the hang of it, so you might jot down some of those transferable coaching moves I mentioned earlier and carry them with you until you feel more comfortable coaching on the run.

A day or so after that first session, you might work with a group member individually and glance over her Post-its to see how she is taking up the work of the group. You might listen in on two group members' partner talk as well to get more information about how they are doing. If your readers are still having difficulty with this work, you'll want to convene a second session. You might decide heavier scaffolding is needed, so you might reread a part of the read-aloud and involve the group in creating a shared envisioning (or prediction or inference about character). You might even do two of these if you feel it is needed. After a few minutes of that work, again channel children to pick up their books and try this work independently. You might even let the group carry on without you while you work with some other students, and then return a bit later to coach members of the group. After coaching one child, then another and another, each for a minute or so, you'll again want to talk to the group, highlighting something you noticed and giving an assignment for what students should do as they read until the group meets again.

During the third session, you might just name what the group has been working on and then have students open their books and read while you move to one, saying, "Tell me what you are envisioning," and then coach into that

work before doing the same with the next reader. This time you'll provide less scaffolding and more practice time. (Alternatively, of course, you might decide that based on the work students have done since the second session, they need another more heavily scaffolded session like the second one, using different parts of the read-aloud text.) Perhaps for the fourth session, each student brings a Post-it that shows an example of her best work in this area, and the students all practice self-assessing their work (with a partner) using a strand of the learning progression and revising that work to make it better. Suggest they use that revised Post-it as a mentor Post-it for their future work in this area. Session 5, if needed, might be similar, but you could push students to do this self-assessment and revision work with less coaching and more independence.

This sequence of small-group work is absolutely transferable to any skill. It will allow you to put your focus on leading the groups and spend less time planning them. And it will move your readers in ways that you can see. Across the sessions, you decrease your scaffolding so that your students can assume more independence. This is just one possible sequence, but my point is that small-group work does not always have to mean multiple extra materials and planning hours.

A Sample Guided Reading Small Group

In addition to the sort of strategy group just described above, it is especially important for you to organize your small-group work so that you lead a sequence of guided reading sessions, working with the same group of children perhaps three times in a week or so to help them to handle texts that are a notch more difficult than what they are reading now. In these sessions, you want to make sure that you are gathering texts that will offer the appropriate challenges for those readers and that you spend a little bit of time planning out what you'll say when introducing the text, so that you can help readers with some of the challenges this kind of text poses.

Plan these sessions so that you lighten your scaffolds across the three sessions. For your first session, you may tell readers that you believe they are ready to handle texts that are a notch harder than those they have been reading, and you may then give a text introduction to whatever they will be reading in sync with each other. Let's imagine it is an article. In your text introduction, instead of simply telling them about the article they'll read, you will want to do so in ways that show them how to orient themselves to future

FIG. 8–4

articles. So you'll say, "Let's preview this article, as readers do, to get ready to read." Then you might say, "I usually look first to see if there are headings and introductory comments, don't you? Let's look." In that way, you walk kids through the sources of whatever orienting comments you will give them. You might then say, "The other thing I do before I read is think about some of the challenging words I'm apt to encounter," and you could show kids how you skim for those words, and that would then set you up to explain a few of them. Your introduction will obviously provide more information than the readers could have extrapolated themselves, but my point is that you do this work in a way that sets them up to do it themselves. You will probably also want to let the readers know about a way the texts they are tending to read these days will pose challenges, and help them with one or two of those challenges.

Maybe, for example, you'll want to help them to integrate the text boxes and illustrations into their reading of the paragraphs. Then the kids can get started reading while you either listen to one child after another, coaching into their reading, or while you check the rest of the class.

In any case, the next day when you reconvene this group, you will not want to provide as much scaffolding. You might instead ask the kids to preview the text themselves, constructing their own approximation of a text introduction, with you chiming in to coach or to help as needed. By the third session, you might set readers up to do this work individually, on their own, and then to teach each other what they noticed, with you again coaching in. In that sort of a way, you go from heavily supported to more lightly supported guided reading.

Plan with Learning Pathways in Mind

It is helpful to approach a small group with a sense for the developmental pathway readers progress along when learning the skill you hope to teach. This way, if you have a sense for what beginning, intermediate, and proficient work with the skill entails, then you can see where a particular learner is in that progression and be able to help that learner go from where he is to where you hope he will go. You'll rely on the learning progressions.

For example, you may work with a small group of readers to support their efforts to preview nonfiction texts. You could ask one reader to preview an article, thinking aloud as he does that, and you could suggest to the other members of the group that they watch his work, learning progression in hand, and note if there is evidence that he is doing the previewing work expected of third-graders or fourth-graders or fifth-graders. You can tell the observing children that after watching for a bit, you'll pass the baton to any one of them and see if that reader can ratchet up the level of previewing.

As you and the children watch the one reader preview, you might note that he checks the front cover, back blurb, headings, and introductions and that he thinks about whether the text is organized in an expository way or as narrative nonfiction. But you and the observing children might note that the reader doesn't check the topic sentences of paragraphs or the transition words to get further information about how the text might go. Congratulating the first reader on doing a lot of important previewing, the next reader can take over and essentially do the work detailed in the fourth-grade learning progression. You could then ask all the observing kids to talk together about how the

previewing could be done in an even more sophisticated way, and you could take over, doing as they instruct you to do.

Of course, this skill is one of many that are supported in the learning progressions, and you can use any one of the progressions to lift the level of what students do.

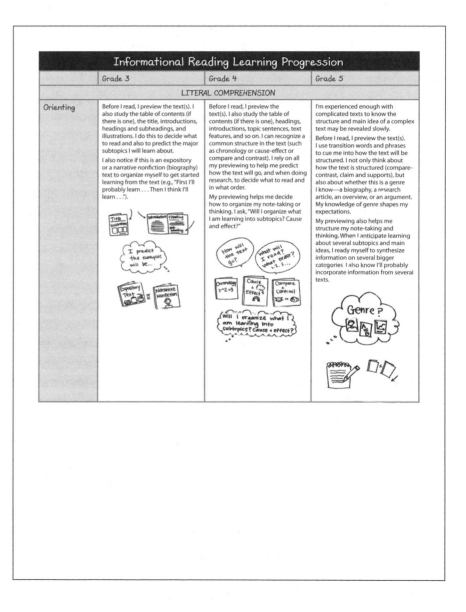

Plan to Gradually Decrease Scaffolding, and Vary Scaffolding for Each Learner

As you plan your small groups, it is also helpful to anticipate using the gradual release of responsibility model to progress from heavy scaffolding to light scaffolding as learners become more proficient in the strategy you are teaching. The concept of scaffolded instruction was first used by Wood et al. (1976) to talk about children's language development. Referring to the temporary structures that are installed and eventually removed from around a building under construction, they suggested that with varying amounts of scaffolding, learners can be successful. This can become an important principle of teaching. Teachers provide learners with maximum support for something that is just beyond their reach and then gradually remove that support so learners can function with increasing autonomy (Pearson and Gallagher 1983).

When I'm planning a sequence of small-group work designed to help a cluster of readers extend their skills, I know that I will move from more to less scaffolding and that I'll vary the amount of scaffolding I provide different learners based on my on-the-run assessments as I work with individuals in the group. Always, the goal will be to teach toward independence, so as a cycle of small-group work ends, I try to make sure that before I send readers forth into the world, they have begun incorporating whatever I've taught them into their independent work.

It is always important to ask yourself, "Who's working the hardest here?" and to remember that children benefit from their hard work—and not so much from yours! When I watch small groups that are not working, almost always what I see is that the problem literally is that the group is not working: the teacher is talking and talking. Limit yourself to two minutes of talk up front; then mobilize the kids to get started on the work, and shift into lean coaching. That coaching will involve a minute of watching, ten seconds of a prompt, another half minute of watching, and another ten-second prompt. That is, small groups need to provide kids time to work and you time to watch and coach.

AN EXAMPLE OF RESPONSIVE SMALL-GROUP COACHING

Recently, I decided to work with a small group to help them see that details that occur on one page of a text pertain to the larger text. I came up with this goal after being flabbergasted at how many readers of Patricia MacLachlan's

FIG. 8–5

Skylark read that a ravaged coyote approached the house and yet missed the connection between that detail and the drought that had brought life on the prairie to a standstill. For too many readers, the coyote was just a coyote, and its presence had no connection to the drought or its consequences, including the fact that yet another set of neighbors had just packed up and moved away.

I convened a group of four readers in hopes of reminding them not to read as if they have on blinders—that what happens on one page in a book is utterly linked to what happens on other pages. I knew I'd want to begin by spending a minute or two telling them why I'd convened the group and what I hoped to teach them. I then planned to do some teaching and then provide them with guided practice.

Choose what and how to teach.

As teachers, we always have the choice of not only what we will teach, but also how we will teach. In this instance, I could have decided to teach readers by using a read-aloud as a small-group strategy. I could have said to this group, "Can I read this with you? I want to show you the way we can think about passages that seem important." Then, as I read a bit of the book aloud to the group, I could say things like "This seems really important. Let's slow down and think, right?" Or "Oh my gosh, this goes with what we were talking about earlier in the book, doesn't it? Lots of times, important passages set us thinking about earlier parts of the book, don't they?" I could say, "Huh? I'm trying to figure why he did that. Let's look back, because usually the answer's there. It just takes a second to see it." Of course, throughout the read-aloud I could progress from demonstrating to scaffolding, so that after a few minutes I'd say, "So what are you thinking now? Turn and talk." And then after they talked, I could say, "I loved the way so many of you were thinking, 'How does this part fit the earlier parts of the book?' That's such a smart question to ask." In time, I might pass the read-aloud baton to kids, letting them know that just as I sometimes read to them, they can read to each other. And I could point out that when something important happens in a story, it sometimes helps to pause and to think, "How does that connect with what I've already read?" The child who had agreed to read aloud to the others in the small group could now determine places in the text that were suited to pausing and synthesizing.

Of course, there is nothing magical about using reading aloud as a method of instruction for a small group. It is just as possible for me to adopt and adapt any other method that I use in minilessons, tweaking the method so it fits the new format. Later, I'll show how the same teaching point could have been taught differently. Whatever method you choose, teaching almost always begins with you naming what it is you want to teach, just as you name your teaching point in a minilesson. Letting kids know why you've convened them is common sense.

Keep teaching short so that small-group time can mostly be for guided practice and coaching.

After saying, "I pulled you together because I'd like to teach you . . . ," I often demonstrate whatever it is I hope children will learn. Any demonstration I do while leading small groups will always be quick, because the structure of small-group work is especially conducive to a teacher observing, scaffolding, and supporting individual readers. If I am going to do a long demonstration, I might as well do this within the minilesson, with the whole class benefiting. If I've cordoned myself off with just a little group of four readers, I want to spend most of my time seeing what each can do and then teaching in response

to what I see. So I start off expecting that at least 80% of my time with any small group will be time when the kids are actively engaged in their reading work and I am watching and supporting what they do.

Use familiar texts when demonstrating.

Because I want my demonstrations to be two or three minutes long, I am apt to return to a text the readers know well, because I don't need to explain the story's content. Working with familiar texts allows me to zoom in on a page smack in the middle of the text, one that is conducive to what I want to teach, without the kids being disoriented. I'm apt to teach into students' own independent reading texts most of the time when coaching, but sometimes I give all members of the group copies of a text I've chosen.

Condense, but keep, all the parts of an effective demonstration: name the teaching point, enact it, and name what you hope they've seen.

So on this day, because I had read *Stone Fox* aloud earlier in the year (in Unit 1), I brought that book with me to the small group. "Today I want to remind you that when I'm reading a page, sometimes stop to think, 'How does this part fit with what went earlier?'" I said, naming a teaching point. "So watch." And then I read three or four sentences from a page—sentences that told that even though the potato crop is turning out to be a good one, Grandfather is still really depressed. I wanted to show children that first I read and then I paused to do the work I was asking them to do. After pausing, I articulated what I was thinking, trying to do this in ways that were somewhat transferable to other books. "I'm just trying to think how this part connects to stuff that has happened earlier," I mused as if I was thinking aloud. "Oh yes, I'm remembering that yesterday we read about how the grandpa owes a ton of money! So that part that we read yesterday may connect to this passage, where the grandpa doesn't cheer up, not even when he hears the potato crop is going to be good. Wow! Now I understand this part about Grandpa still being upset, because now I'm remembering that Grandpa owes a ton of money. That may explain why he isn't jovial now. One good crop probably isn't enough money."

By this point, the demonstration was over, and I needed to name what I had done just as I do in minilesson. "I'm hoping you see that when I'm reading one part—especially a part that feels important—I pause and think to myself, 'How does this part go with things that happened before? How does the part clear up questions or add to thoughts we were having earlier?'"

Use a rhythm of guided practice or coaching—one that allows space and time for readers to work in front of you.

Now I wanted to let the members of the small group try this. I might have decided to have them try this first with another section of *Stone Fox*, in which case I would have again read aloud and gotten them started doing this sort of thinking, exactly as I would have done in a minilesson. But I tend to want to focus more on kids' own work during our fleeting small groups, so I said, "Now pick up your book and begin reading where you left off, but as you read, do what readers do and ask, 'What information am I learning that clears up questions or adds on to something I learned earlier?'" In small-group work as in any other teaching, I trust repetition, and I often repeat anything I hope students will internalize.

Intervene in ways that lift the level of the work each child is doing, differentiating according to the child.

As children began their quiet reading, I circled among them, turning like the hands of a clock to the children who are sitting at 12:00, 3:00, 6:00, and 9:00. To one child I said, "First, what you just read right here, does it fit with the last chapter? Tell me about that."

I wanted to make this work easier for the next child, so I rephrased that question, asking, "What are the things you are noticing that are continuing from earlier in the book?" One child was reading *Number the Stars*, so I said, "In the last chapter you read, you told me about how there is a list of Jewish people at the synagogue, and now you are finding that the community has been talking. Is the fact that they are meeting to talk related to the list that contains everyone's names?"

If I had wanted to prompt this child in ways that were more challenging than either of these ways, I might have said, "Can you tell me some of things your character is doing that make you wonder, 'Why might she do this or he do this?'" Then I could have

added, for transparency's sake, "I'm asking because usually the causes—the reasons—are earlier in the book. Asking 'Why might she be doing this?' is a way that helps readers realize that the beginnings of our books connect to the middles and to the ends and so forth."

Of course, if the reader struggled with a question, then I might have decided I needed to provide scaffolding, and I might, in that instance, have stepped in and asked more targeted questions. "Have you thought of why she is doing this? Might it be because she thinks it is her responsibility to protect Ellen?" If I essentially end up doing the work for the reader, then I need to channel the reader to do the next bit of work. For example, in this instance, had I felt that I needed to provide the reader with a lot of help, I might then have suggested, "You could read on to confirm or to get new information." In this way, then, I worked with each reader in the group for a minute or two, scaffolding them to attempt work that felt within reach.

Make an appointment to check in again on this ongoing work that they will continue.

At the end of this small group, I suggested we meet again in two days and that until then they take some time to do this sort of thinking, asking, "How does what I am reading go with earlier parts in the book?" I asked them to use purple Post-its when they did this work over the next few days so that I could

quickly ascertain how many of them were doing this and how much they were doing. Over the next two days, I nudged the one child who did not have many purple Post-its to remember to do this work.

Follow up with the group and help the members take next steps.

A couple of days later, when I reconvened the group, the first thing I did was to suggest the children work with their partners within the small group, telling each other about the instances when they'd done this work and talking about their purple Post-its. I also asked them to start with the part they were reading and then to show how they looped back to an earlier part in their mind as they read that part. For the reader who needed more clear scaffolding, I gave her a sheet of paper that said:

What I just learned here is _____,

and that goes with _____,

and kind of goes with this _____.

As I coached on this day, I nudged children to see that the one passage they were reading linked not just to one thing, but to many things. "What else does this connect with?" I asked. "Is there a possibility that this might fit with something earlier? Okay, then read on and see." After a few days of supporting this sort of work, I pointed out to readers that what they had been doing is called synthesis, and that readers needn't stop other skill work to synthesize. For example, readers can predict by first synthesizing lots of passages across the whole book.

Approach your small-group work as an ongoing research project. You are continually researching the children, their needs, and their response to your instruction. Bringing a research stance and a sense of innovation to your small groups will ensure they are joyful, energetic parts of your children's reading lives and your teaching days.

It is my hope that by building your repertoire of methods—trying out one type of small group and then another—you'll find what types of small-group work are best suited for your children. You'll also come to view this time in your teaching not with anxiety but with excitement, knowing that it is some of the most powerful time you have to help your readers to grow.

Chapter 9

Resources to Draw Upon When Conferring and Leading Strategy Lessons

I MAGINE THIS: you draw a chair alongside a reader and ask, "How's it going?" The child shrugs and answers, "Good. It's a good book." The child is sitting there, holding a 200-page book that you only vaguely remember. What do you say next? You can elicit from the child what will probably be a somewhat jumbled and unclear summary of the book, but you're not sure that doing so will pay off. And other than that, you are not sure how to get a footing so that the conversation has traction, so that your teaching is worth taking the child away from his reading.

Or imagine this. You look over your classroom. Kids' noses are generally in their books. You see the pages turn, an occasional yawn. You know you are supposed to lead small-group instruction. But what do you say once they are all sitting around you, ready for you to deliver your brilliant tip? What could you possibly say that will be helpful—and especially, that will be helpful to a group of them? It would be one thing if you knew the books they were reading backward and forward. Then you could quiz them on whether they saw the symbols you saw, noted the gaps in time that you noted. But their books are only vaguely familiar to you. Why stop their reading when you have nothing, really, in mind to teach anyhow? As the saying goes, "Let sleeping dogs lie."

If you have found yourself feeling felt empty-handed when you go to confer or lead a small-group strategy lesson, you need to know, first of all, that you are in good company. This is one of the rather unique challenges inherent in teaching reading to kids once they can read with some proficiency. Because reading happens largely within the black box of the mind, it is not easy to know how to ruffle the surface of "they're just reading."

This chapter will help you know resources to draw upon so that you can teach from an abundance of possibilities. But before launching into that discussion, I want to offer one caution. It is often tempting *not* to tackle the challenges inherent in teaching reading by instead teaching something that is not reading but a substitute for it.

Follow my argument for a minute, because this is important. When you look over the class and see eyes on print and wonder how (or why) you should disrupt that reading to teach reading, it is tempting to channel students into spending reading time making their thinking visible to you. Sometimes in classrooms of second- and third-graders, I will see most of the children running a finger under the words and whispering to themselves as they read. In those instances, I know that the teacher has (probably inadvertently) channeled students to make their reading visible so she can trust the child *is* reading. This is understandable, but it is not helpful: once a child is reading books at approximately level H, readers should not voice or point unless they are encountering special difficulty. They may need to sit on their hands to stop themselves!

As readers become more proficient, ways of making reading visible change. It is not uncommon for me to visit a reading workshop and to look around the room and see that almost no child is reading because, instead, everyone is writing about their reading. Although a little writing about reading can be a potent lever to lift the level of students' reading, ultimately, readers learn to read from *reading*. It is a big problem if kids spend all their time writing about reading (or answering questions about reading, annotating texts, even talking about reading) and don't, therefore, get extensive time for eyes-on-print reading.

Another way that teachers get around the challenges of teaching reading by teaching a substitute for reading is that sometimes teachers decide to teach the text, not the reader. This happens all the time in high school. The teacher has studied the *The Scarlet Letter* in college and has notebooks full of notes on the historical context for the book, the author's life and times, the symbols and their meaning, the characters and their significance, the key scenes, the plot outline, the use of figurative language—the works. "In the third chapter, what is the significance of the weather?" the teacher asks, and then leads students to see the answer in her spiral notebook from her college literature course. Of course, that's an extreme example. But you may find yourself longing to keep your kids in books you know well. After all, if they are all reading *Skylark* and you have taught that book for the past few years, you can point out the four references to summer heat and dryness in the first two pages and emphasize that Patricia MacLachlan deliberately highlighted the drought because it will be central to the story. Then you could point out all the references to people leaving the prairie for other places and explain that this is foreshadowing, and onward you could go, page by page through that book, finding things on every page that you could teach.

Clearly, there is a place for instruction that is grounded in a specific book. There's so much to notice in a book and so many opportunities to teach! This is why we teach through interactive read-alouds and why we thread a book through minilessons. But the power of a minilesson is that the structure is designed so that we use a shared book to teach kids reading strategies that they can transfer to other texts. The structure of minilessons reminds us that ultimately it doesn't matter whether kids see the exact example we saw of foreshadowing. What matters is that kids bring that alertness to all the books they ever read, on their own. That is, the structure of a minilesson saves us from the temptation to function as tour guides, pointing out all that we see in a book that students might miss, rather than functioning as teachers, teaching students work they can do on their own when we are not with them.

That doesn't mean that helping kids to see more in texts that we know well doesn't have enormous value. It does, and that is work we can do in book clubs as well as in minilessons. But often, your conferences and small-group strategy lessons will be designed to teach reading when you don't know the book well, and learning to do that kind of teaching is important. You know the importance of this. After all, if I were to ask each of you, "What is your real goal as a teacher of reading?" most of you would say that you want to help the young people read their own books with increasing engagement, discernment, power, and responsiveness. My point is that if one of your ultimate goals is to support kids' own reading, then you need to make sure that a fair percentage of your teaching time puts you face to face with kids' own reading. And that is what happens when you pull a chair alongside a reader during reading time or gather a small group of kids who are each reading different books. The work you do with those readers supports independent reading. Even if you are not as adept as you'd like to be at doing this work, kids notice what you notice. If you care about their independent reading, they'll care about it. And then, too, as you do this conferring, you learn to do it, and you become skilled at this, just as you may already be skilled at other aspects of teaching reading.

But also, it is important to help children use all you've been teaching as they read independently, because your attentiveness to the extent to which students transfer and apply your teaching makes it more likely that your teaching will be in the service of independent reading. If you are working with one child and another and another, and you see that most of your kids are starting and abandoning books or are not getting engaged in the through-line of the story when reading independently, you're going to think twice before making your minilesson focus on teaching readers to notice the repetition of drought images in *Skylark*. Instead, you'll look at Skylark with your kids' independent reading in mind and think, "How can I find in this book—or in some place other than this book—some lessons that are actually going to pay off for the kids I have, not the kids I wish I had?"

I hope I have been persuasive enough that you are convinced that it is critically important to confer and lead small-group strategy lessons that lift the level of your students' independent reading. The issue remains that sometimes, when you pull a chair alongside the child and ask, "How's it going?" and hear in response, "Fine," you don't know what to say. Sometimes you don't convene a small group of kids because you aren't sure what to teach that small group. It is easy as a teacher of reading to sometimes feel empty-handed. In the upcoming portion of this chapter, I'll help you feel less empty-handed.

RESOURCES TO DRAW UPON FOR CONFERENCES AND SMALL-GROUP STRATEGY LESSONS

I always know that I'm working with a strong teacher if he asks me, "How do I know what to teach when I confer with a young reader or lead a small-group strategy lesson? I always feel sort of at a loss." The teacher who asks that question has made the enormous leap required to understand that when we work with kids one to one or in small groups during the workshop, we are not simply helping readers implement the minilesson. Conferences and strategy lessons are not little personalized reiterations of the minilesson! Instead, these are opportunities for new teaching, and often that teaching will not relate to the minilesson as much as it relates to a student's ongoing direction as a reader, to the skills with which the child is and is not yet proficient, and to the work that the texts that reader is working with ask of a reader.

There will never be an answer to the question "How do I know what to teach?" because there are always a zillion possible teaching points. But there certainly are resources that you can draw upon to imagine possibilities. In addition to drawing on the current unit of study and the minilessons in it, you can draw upon these resources (and others) when conferring:

- Previous conferences and small-group work, as recorded in your records
- The genre and the work that the particular genre asks readers to do
- Patterns in the reader's behaviors and responses to text, as evidenced in recent running records

- The band of text complexity within which the reader is working (or the readers are working) and the work that books in that band of text complexity tend to ask readers to do
- The child's readerly life—and the opportunity to glean evidence of that from the reading log and elsewhere
- The child's thinking and writing about reading, as evidenced by Post-its, entries, and notes

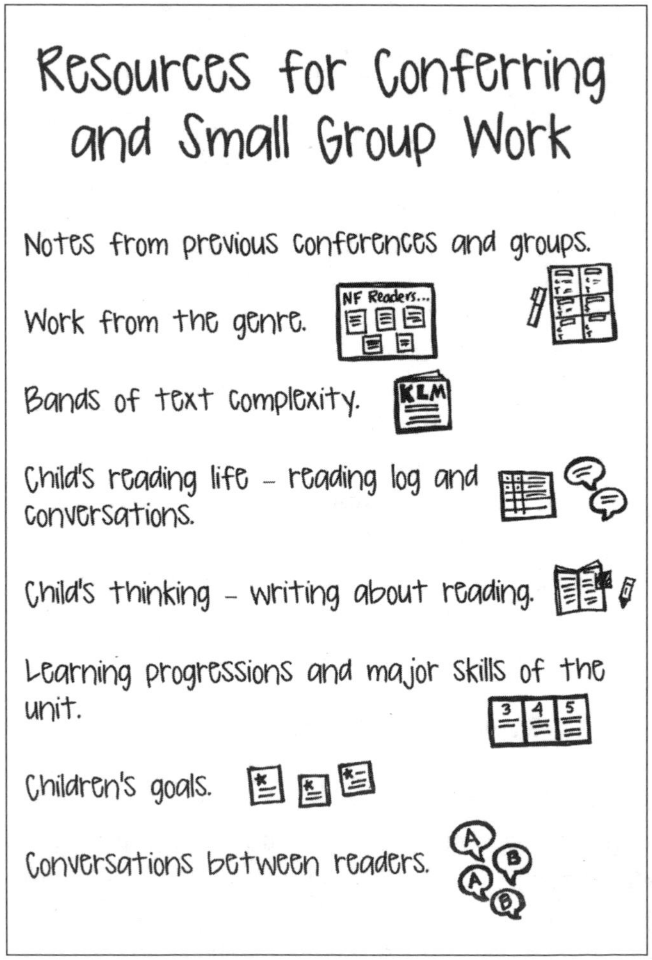

Resources for Conferring and Small Group Work

Notes from previous conferences and groups.

Work from the genre.

Bands of text complexity.

Child's reading life – reading log and conversations.

Child's thinking – writing about reading.

Learning progressions and major skills of the unit.

Children's goals.

Conversations between readers.

FIG. 9–1

- The child's place along the learning progression of the major skills that either you are teaching in the unit or that you and the child have identified as goals
- The child's conversation (or otherwise, the child's work) with a partner about her reading

Your Records of Previous Conferences and Small Groups

Records of reading are vastly more important than records of writing, because when you work with writers, their writing is right there, in front of them and you. So the records are helpful, but the writing also speaks for itself. But when working with readers, the reading can't be there, on the table between you and your student. The book, even the book with the Post-its stuck onto it and accompanied by a reading log, doesn't add up to being the child's reading. How important it is, therefore, that you collect records of your observations, assessments, conferences, and small-group work to draw on when you confer. If, for example, when conducting running records, you see that the reader could read accurately far beyond the level at which she could comprehend, then that note will be enormously helpful to you. And if the reader didn't seem to have trouble with literal questions, but rather with inferential ones, that'd be important to keep in mind. These records won't actually tell you what to teach, in that almost any skill can be done at a literal or an inferential level, but still, it is helpful. And if you also know that on an informal assessment, you saw that the child tends to notice who did what, in large sweeping steps, then this can get you started on a direction for a conference. The records alone won't guide you, but this in combination with any of the below will be critical.

The records are important for another reason. It is all too easy for kids to "just read." A good part of teaching reading to kids who are proficient at processing texts involves encouraging those kids to aim to think in new ways as they read, to bring new lenses to a text, and to work with deliberateness toward new goals. Having launched a reader on some work that the two of you decide is important, it is absolutely critical that the child know the conference or the small group wasn't just blow-in-the-wind words. After you and the child spend five minutes coming to a work plan, making a shared decision about the next steps for that reader, you absolutely do not expect the child to let your instruction roll off as if the child was made of Teflon. So, yes, it is important for you to approach a child who is reading and to say, "Can I interrupt for a bit? Last week we talked about how you were going to pay a lot more attention to the minor characters in your book. Can you walk me through the work you have done to accomplish that goal and give me a sense of your evaluation of that work?"

Your Knowledge of the Genre and the Work It Asks Readers to Do

If you do not know the book that the reader is reading, but you know the genre, then you can draw on your knowledge of that genre to ask wise questions and to gauge a reader's response. If this is a fiction book, you can ask, "Who is the main character? What does this character seem to really, really want?" Of course, that sort of question merits a follow-up. "Why does the character want this? How does this fit into what you know of the character's traits? What do you think might stand in the character's way of getting this?" Knowing that a child is reading a fiction book can lead you to scores of other lines of inquiry. You could, for example, ask about the minor characters. What role might these play in the book? You could ask about the setting—and whether the book might be different had it taken place in another setting. How does the setting influence the story? Of course, if you know the book is a particular kind of fiction text, that can steer your conference or strategy lesson as well. If this is historical fiction, you might wonder if the child can talk about the unfolding time line of the historical setting, and then, once you learn about some of the events that are occurring in history, you could inquire with the reader about whether different characters respond differently to events in the story. Do their different responses reflect not just their personalities, but also the groups to which they belong? When the child in the book is all excited that the pool that has been segregated for so long will now be open to all and the mother is weary, the reader needs to know that this might not reflect simply their different personalities; it might also reflect the groups to which they belong. If, on the other hand, the student is reading a mystery, you can draw on your knowledge of that genre to ask whether he has found some parts of the book that make him suspicious. What are the clues he has gathered so far? Do any seem to be red herrings?

Of course, all of these questions, in any genre, will require follow-up work, and typically this will involve us saying, "Take me to that part," and "Can you read this to me?" It is important to instruct kids to look over a text before they begin reading it, to notice the genre, and to think about the sort of work that readers of that genre need to do—and this instruction can easily be given to a group of readers who are reading diverse books at diverse levels.

Patterns in the Reader's Behaviors and Responses to Text, as Evidenced in Running Records

The data gleaned from running records reaches far beyond matching the student to a level. When you look through running records carefully, not so much for the level, but more for the patterns that crop up in students' reading, you will discover where each reader's strengths and weaknesses lie.

Note that if you are looking at running records at an independent reading level, this information will be difficult to find. You will need to study what readers do in their reading when faced with a challenge. You'll need to study what students do when they are reading at an instructional or even a frustration level to discover this information. Look for the student's ceiling. A running record without miscues leaves you nothing to study!

As you analyze the miscues in your student's reading, remember to approach the work with a sense of curiosity. Unlike writing, where we can study what a child has put on the page, reading is an invisible process; the child's thinking is tucked inside the mind and out of reach. Analyzing a running record or listening to a child read is your chance to make this process visible, to peek inside the mind and try to figure out how the child is making sense of one of the most complex things children will ever learn to do.

As you study running records, remember to ask yourself:

- What are my students doing when they encounter trouble?
- Do they make attempts?
- Do they check their attempts?
- Do they make multiple attempts?
- What sources of information do they use?
- Do they use meaning, structure, and visual information equally, or do they lean more heavily on one information source?
- How effectively do they use sources of information?

As kids are reading, they need to practice using all available sources of information in an integrated, reciprocal way: the meaning (semantic),

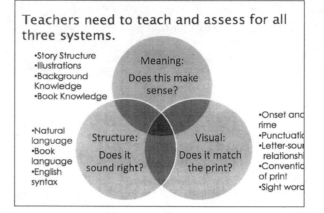

FIG. 9–2   Diagram of an effective reader's MSV Processing

structure (syntactic), and visual (graphophonic) cueing systems. If a child neglects to use or overuses one source of information, you need to teach him to integrate his cueing systems more effectively. A successful reader draws upon all three sources of information.

For example, imagine that you notice the student consistently goes to the print whenever he encounters an unfamiliar word, rather than attempting to use context clues to figure out a word that might make sense. If this happens repeatedly, you'll probably have a pretty good clue that this is what this particular reader does when encountering unfamiliar words. This lets you know that you will want to teach this student strategies for using meaning and syntax, in combination with the print, to solve new words. This also indicates that the student may need some strategies for learning new vocabulary.

Imagine that another student, a more advanced reader, reads accurately and fluently—in fact is very expressive. But then you are surprised to discover that when prompted, she cannot retell or discuss what she just read. This is only a problem once you ask her to read at a level or two higher than what she usually reads on her own. Although this reader has gained enormous automaticity and fluency in her reading, things are starting to break down when she encounters a more complex text. When the text gets more complicated, all her energy goes into decoding and saying the words. You'll need to support her in self-monitoring, stopping to reread when she doesn't have a picture in her mind, pausing to recap what has happened so far before continuing on, and going back when she's not so sure. She'll likely need support with keeping track of how characters feel and inference in general, because just holding onto the literal events will not be enough in longer, more complicated books.

As you do this work, remember to work from a strength-based model, notice what each child *can* do, and then think about what their next steps might be. Often we are so eager to decide what to teach next that we skip right over what it is children are already doing. Take time to notice their strengths and use this as a jumping-off point for your next teaching.

The Level of Text Complexity and the Work that Books at that Level Ask Readers to Do

In *Reading Pathways*, you will learn that the Teachers College Reading and Writing Project has found it fruitful to think about levels of text difficulty as falling within bands, and those bands as having a few shared characteristics. For reasons I describe in that book, we do not think it is helpful to try to keep in mind fifteen characteristics for each discrete level of text difficulty. However, it is enormously powerful to be able to look at the book a child is reading, notice the level of that text, and then approach the child already anticipating some of the new work that she will need to be doing once she progresses from one band of text difficulty into the next. For example, if this is a small-group strategy lesson, you could suggest that the group members read in same-book partnerships as they progress into level N books, and explain that they need to help each other with some of the new work that books in that N–Q band of text difficulty will be asking them to do. You could point out that whereas in the books those readers have been reading over the last few months, characters tended to have two or three dominant and crystal clear traits that endured across those books, in the books they'll be starting to read, the characters are often more complex, even ambivalent, and they are apt to change across the text.

A week later, when you confer with one of these readers (or convene the group of them into another strategy lesson), you could say, "Remember that earlier we talked about how books in this band of text difficulty often have characters with complicated feelings. Have you noticed that?" You could ask the readers to consider whether the characters' personalities even seem different in one setting versus another, in one relationship versus another. Might one of their characters have ambivalent feelings—feeling partly one way, partly another way? Perhaps a character partly likes a person, partly doesn't, for example, or partly likes to do something and partly doesn't. You could

explain, "I'm asking because books that are as challenging as the ones you are reading tend to have really complicated characters. The main characters usually aren't just one way. Instead, they are more like you. You are outgoing some of the time, but sometimes I notice you get sort of shy. Is the character in your book complicated in the same sort of a way?"

Of course, there are at least half a dozen other traits that pertain to books at this band of text difficulty—and this is just one band of text difficulty. My point is that if you look over your class of children and see they are all nose deep in their books, you could pull together a group of kids who are reading within the same band of text difficulty, and even without knowing the particular books that the kids are reading, if you know the band of text difficulty, that knowledge can direct you to lines of inquiry that are sure to pay off. If a child is reading a level U book, then chances are really good that the characters advance the theme of the book. The issue that the protagonist struggles with is probably an issue that people the world over struggle with, and readers might think, "How does the character's way of responding to this issue relate to the life lessons this text is teaching me?" The powerful thing about this teaching, of course, is that you'll be addressing work that readers need to do not just in the book a student is holding at that moment, but in lots of books.

This line of thinking also holds true for nonfiction. In Chapter 13, I write about ways nonfiction texts become more complex. For example, more challenging nonfiction texts forward more than one main idea. Those ideas also become more implicit; the headings and subheadings that guide readers in the third grade are often not present in the nonfiction texts that fifth-graders read. Of course, as students become more proficient as readers of nonfiction texts, they are more apt to encounter technical vocabulary—and even the definitions of those words contain hard, technical words!

The Child's Readerly Life: Evidence from the Reading Log

Stephen Covey, in his important books on leadership, cajoles all of us to remember "first things first." It is important as a teacher to have priorities, and for those of us who are responsible for a child's growth in reading, few things are more important than keeping an eye on the actual amount of reading that a child is doing. So plan to look at the child's reading log. Notice even just the record of the reading that has occurred the day of your conference. If the child has had eleven minutes so far today to read, has the child read at least seven or eight pages? If not, then you'll want to research the patterns in the child's reading log, looking for whether, on the whole, the child reads at least three-quarters of a page in a minute. That's a rough rule of thumb, and sometimes it proves problematic, but most of the time if a child hasn't been reading at that rate, something is amiss. So talk to the child. Say, "When I sit with you and look over your reading, one thing I notice is whether you are reading about seven pages in ten minutes. Usually (but not always) if a reader is reading less than that, something's going on that is not quite perfect." Then, of course, you'll want the child to read aloud so you can listen for fluency and so you can make sure he isn't being stumped by tricky words every other minute. You'll want to examine whether he might be doing too much writing about reading. Is he interested in the text? Of course, this is just one of many things you can study. You might notice the amount of reading the child is doing at home. If he seems not to get to reading very often, you'll want to make a gigantic point of celebrating that he has kept accurate records that reflect this lack of reading. He's like a true scientist, collecting real data. That is so key. Then, with all the support in the world (so you don't lead kids to falsify their logs) you will want to talk about what gets in the way of doing more reading and what ideas the child might have for remedying this. You might notice that he seems to read the assigned amount each night but never gets lost in a text and reads beyond that amount. Take that up, then. Or you might notice that his reading volume escalated when reading a particular author or genre. Again, take that up as well.

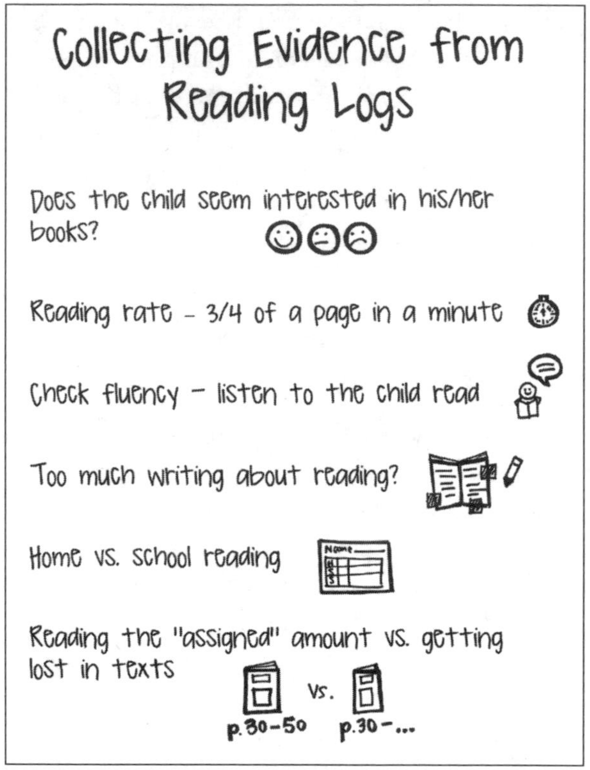

FIG. 9–4

Of course, there are other aspects of the youngster's readerly life that you might focus on in a conference or, conceivably, in a small group. You could talk about the child's social life around books. People who are great readers find ways to bring books into their conversations and their relationships. They have friends who give them book recommendations. They swap books with other readers and talk over their responses. Then, too, people who are avid readers bring reading into their hobbies and passions. If they are fans of a sports' team, they read websites and blogs and newspaper articles related to their team. They do the same with authors they love—joining their fan clubs, reading about upcoming books long before others even know the books are coming.

Children who do not grow up in families that are richly literate won't have a clue that this is what avid readers do. It's up to you to teach this to kids. And think what a difference such a conference or strategy lesson could make!

FIG. 9–3

The Patterns of a Child's Ways of Responding to Reading: Evidence from Post-its and Entries

One of my favorite ways to confer is this: I sit beside the reader and say, "Will you walk me through the thinking you've been doing as you read?" and then gesture to the child's Post-its or entries in her reader's notebook, as if clearly they are abbreviated markers of the child's thinking. The important thing for me is that I want to start earlier in the book and tour the progression of the reader's thinking. I do not read every Post-it with great care, but instead I graze through them, thinking, "What patterns do I see in this reader's ways of responding to a text?"

Most readers have a fairly limited repertoire of ways to think about books. Some people are always reading on the edge of their seats, in a plot-driven and active way, anticipating what will soon transpire in the story and hoping and worrying about it. Other people read as writers, noticing the decisions an author has made and wondering at the author's reasons for those decisions, thinking about how the text would be different had the author made other choices. Some readers read with pen in hand, recording the important points to take away from a text. I find it is helpful to say back to a reader what it is that the reader tends to do a lot.

In life, it is a gift when someone helps us see what our characteristic ways of engaging tend to be, and I think it is a gift to do this for a reader, too. I then make a point of trying to build upon whatever the child is already doing. (My instinct is to take the child to whatever she is not doing, but I know better than to let my knee-jerk deficit thinking actually control what I do.) I can often suggest that if this reader could work on becoming even better at whatever it is she often does, then maybe she could teach others in the class how to do this. You won't be surprised to hear that after making a fuss about what the child tends to do as a reader, I do often suggest that it is also helpful to expand the reader's repertoire and to deliberately take on a way of responding that isn't second nature to that reader.

The Child's Place along the Learning Pathways of the Major Skills You Are Teaching in the Unit

Skills are pathways, not end points. When you are teaching a skill, you are helping readers to move along a learning progression (or pathway), becoming more adept at that skill. This means that it is helpful to look at the skills that

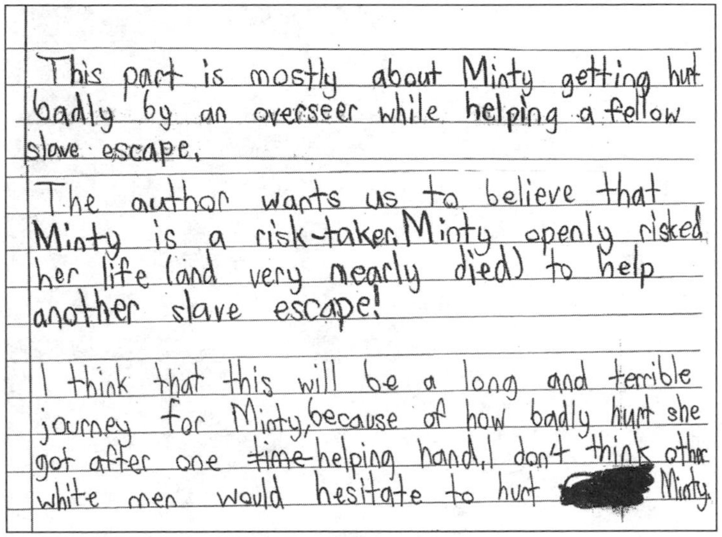

This part is mostly about Minty getting hurt badly by an overseer while helping a fellow slave escape.

The author wants us to believe that Minty is a risk-taker. Minty openly risked her life (and very nearly died) to help another slave escape!

I think that this will be a long and terrible journey for Minty, because of how badly hurt she got after one ~~time~~ helping hand. I don't think other white men would hesitate to hurt ██ Minty.

FIG. 9–5 Student's thinking leads to prediction.

a child is using as he reads and then to think, for at least the most dominant skills, "What would be required for the child to progress a bit farther along the pathway of this skill?"

For example, imagine that a child either tells you or shows you (through Post-its and entries) that she fairly often notices a small point in a book and then says, "This reminds me of . . ." and then makes a personal connection. As far as you can see, that work—drawing a line between a detail in the book the child is reading and a detail in her own life—is what the child does when making a personal connection. You, then, will want to think, "What might it mean to make personal connections in a more advanced way?" That is, you need to have in mind a progression (or learning pathway) that will help you know what you might teach next. In this instance, I'd probably want to help the reader know that once a reader says, "This reminds me of . . . ," then the reader mines that personal connection for all sorts of help. If a character in the book is going to the dentist and worries tremendously about it, and the reader says, "This reminds me of when my brother was scared to go to the dentist," you'd want to help that reader to know that that personal connection enables her to predict what might happen next. The personal connection also allows the reader to fill in details from her image of what's happening. She can draw on all the dentist chairs she's ever sat in when imagining the scene. So one

My bigger point is that when teaching reading, it always helps to have in mind the learning pathways along which children are traveling so that you can be diagnostic teachers, thinking, "If . . . , then. . . ."

The Child's Conversation (or Otherwise, the Child's Work) with a Partner about His or Her Reading

Imagine that a child is reading quietly. You want to get a sense of her thinking about her book. One option is to say to her, "I know this is quiet reading time, but while I'm here, would you and your partner mind talking about your book as you usually do during partner time? I tend to miss out on hearing how you talk together, and I'm dying to get a sense of it." Then you can listen as the two readers externalize their reading, and you can decide whether you want to work with just one child or both and whether you want to work on the reading itself or on the ways of talking that the partnership seems to have established. For example, you might hear that a child has a ton of random little one-sentence-long thoughts about a book, and you could take that up as an individual matter and confer with the child to suggest she snowball her ideas a bit more, staying with them longer, almost having conversations in her mind about them. Or, alternatively, you could address this as the work of the partnership and show the readers how they can help each other to develop their wonderful but undeveloped ideas, turning sentences of thought into passages of thought.

possible next teaching point might be to help readers know that saying, "This reminds me of . . ." is the start, not the end, to a reader's thinking.

Then again, if the reader seemed to make personal connections about extraneous details in the text, the more immediate goal might be to teach him that it can be distracting to think, "What have I experienced that reminds me of this?" for every little detail in a text. It's more important to follow the trail of a story than to constantly be leaving the story to rope in every parallel experience imaginable.

Chapter 10

Writing about Reading

THE TOPIC of writing about reading has been on my mind lately—and chances are, it has been on your mind as well. After all, it's omnipresent in classrooms these days! Will you think for a moment about the writing about reading that is going on in your school? To do this, imagine that you drew a giant net through your school, combing out all the writing about reading that students have done over the past month. Your net pulled Post-its from books, gathered up homework assignments, and collected answers to questions, as well as notebook entries and essays—the works. Now imagine that entire haul was dumped in front of you. You sort through it, dividing the writing into piles according to the work you see. What will your piles contain?

When I've asked teachers to imagine themselves doing this, they've told me that they will have a pile of writing that recaps a chapter. They'll have a pile of entries about favorite lines and about characters that readers do or do not like, as well as entries containing an assortment of comments about this or that part of a book. There is also writing about reading in which the reader has answered questions someone else generated about a text.

Here is the really important question. Is that writing about reading doing more good than harm? Remember that every minute in which kids are writing about their reading is a minute when they are not *reading*—and remember, in the classrooms of truly proficient teachers, kids read ten times as much as in other classrooms. Remember, too, that the time spent writing about reading probably detracts from kids' appreciation for reading. How many of you would choose to read if you knew you had to write at the end of every chapter? Given that your students' volume of reading and engagement in reading are big deals, I ask you to look again at the quality of the writing about reading in that imaginary pile in front of you and weigh the costs and benefits. Is that writing such a potent force for good that it's adding more than it is taking away?

I'd argue that a good deal of the writing about reading that occurs in schools today is *not* worth the trade-off. But here is the important thing: it could be. I'll go farther and say that there are efficient, easy ways to dramatically lift the power of your students' writing about reading. And doing so can dramatically improve the education your children receive.

CONSIDER HOW YOU DO—AND DO NOT— SUPPORT WRITING ABOUT READING

I write this chapter knowing from the start that the question can't be "How could your students' writing about reading improve if you had hours and hours each week to invest in it?" I assume from the start that you don't have that time. So instead, I offer some easy, accessible, no-big-deal ways you can increase the potency of the writing about reading that your students are doing.

To start, think for a moment about how you treat your students' writing in *writing* workshop, compared to how you treat their writing in *reading* workshop? Try not to get defensive as you do this thinking. This is not an individual matter; this is endemic across most schools. Start with the issue of audience. During the writing workshop, your students' writing is presumably brought out into the world, celebrated with pomp and circumstance. Great writing done in the writing workshop is displayed, saved, and sent home with fanfare. During the writing workshop, you show students mentor texts that exemplify what you hope they do. You, yourself, produce texts that provide goals to work toward. You confer, with mentor texts tucked under your arm, explaining ways your children's writing *is* like those mentor texts and ways *it could be* like them. You channel kids to spend time annotating the mentor texts, and you ask them to keep those mentor texts close as they work on their own writing. You and your students develop a whole language for talking about exemplar writing. They know that studying and emulating exemplars of good writing is serious, grown-up work that famous authors as well as kids do.

We'll come to the ways you celebrate the writing done during reading time—the Post-its, the entries—in a moment.

For now, keep thinking about how you treat writing during the writing workshop. Chances are good that you teach kids to reread, assess, and revise their own writing. You give them feedback and set up structures in the classroom so others give them feedback too, and you let students know the importance of using that feedback to improve their rough draft work. They have tools and strategies for revising their writing: they add flaps to insert more detailed information, they cut the draft apart and add a blank page into the middle of it to expand the heart of the story, they divide a chaotic chapter up into three chapters so that information is sorted into categories. Those strategies are named all over the room on anchor charts.

Think, too, about the attention you give to students' progress over time. You and your students often look back to the work they did earlier in the year,

and you talk and think about ways their work is getting better now. You watch over that progress and teach them to do so as well, and both you and your students have a clear sense of what progress looks like.

We could go on, but I suspect the point has been made. If that is how you support writing done within the *writing* workshop, how do you support writing when it is done during the *reading* workshop? My hunch is that the writing students do as they read receives very little of that support. And the simplest way to improve students' writing about reading is to provide the same conditions to support that work that you've already determined are essential to supporting writing within the writing workshop:

Ways to Lift the Level of Writing about Reading
- Provide the conditions that support writing
  - Give an audience to writing about reading
  - Provide students with exemplars
  - Encourage revision
- Broaden the topics students address
- Teach students to write and think more analytically
  - Partitioning
  - Ranking
  - Comparing and contrasting
- Read differently, letting the intention to write provide a lens

These are all simple, efficient ways that you can significantly lift your students' writing about reading. I'll explain each of these topics in more depth in the following sections.

EFFICIENTLY PROVIDE THE CONDITIONS THAT SUPPORT WRITING DEVELOPMENT IN THE READING WORKSHOP

To lift the level of your students' writing about reading, you need to find doable, accessible, no-big-deal ways to provide more support for your students' writing about reading. You already know the ways to support writing, because those are the ways you support the writing students do during the writing workshop. The question is, how can you bring some of that into reading, without it requiring a lot of time and energy from you?

Start with the question of audience. In most classrooms, students write about reading repeatedly, over and over, with no anticipation that they will ever have an audience for that writing. If someone reads that writing, it usually is the teacher, who reads to assess, not reading to learn from the writer's ideas, to follow the writer's argument. That, for a start, is easily changed. Here are a few ways to give students' more audiences for their writing about reading.

During Writing Time, Give an Audience to Writing about Reading

Students can regularly reread the writing about reading they have done during the reading workshop or at home to select an especially thoughtful bit that is then read aloud—or exchanged for people to read silently—as the starting move in a book talk with partners or in clubs or research teams.

As a change of pace, all students can be asked to display their writing about reading, laying it out at their work spot, and the class can do a gallery walk, moving among the work to see the writing their classmates have done. The viewers can be asked to be absolutely silent, leaving Post-it notes or flags beside passages others have written that are particularly provocative ideas, or they can be asked to talk among themselves about the ideas as they read them.

Students can be asked to be anthropologists, studying their own or another person's writing about reading to notice things about that work. What kinds of thinking about reading is the reader doing (and not doing)? If the writing responds to nonfiction reading, for example, is the reader taking notes? Are those notes organized? How? Do they include quotes? The writer's own thoughts? Arrows or other ways to signal cross-connections? Students can compare and contrast the work two students have done, noting how it is similar and how it is different. People can come to new goals.

Students can be asked to select their best examples of a certain kind of writing about reading they have done. Perhaps a bulletin board is being made titled "Readers Notice the Techniques Nonfiction Authors Use," and students select entries they've written in which they do that work. Perhaps those entries are annotated by the author or by another student so a language begins to develop about effective writing about reading. Perhaps those exemplars are not displayed on a bulletin board but are instead distributed to others (within that class or in classes of younger students) as exemplars to be emulated.

Students are asked to look back at the writing about reading they did early in the year and the writing about reading they have done recently and

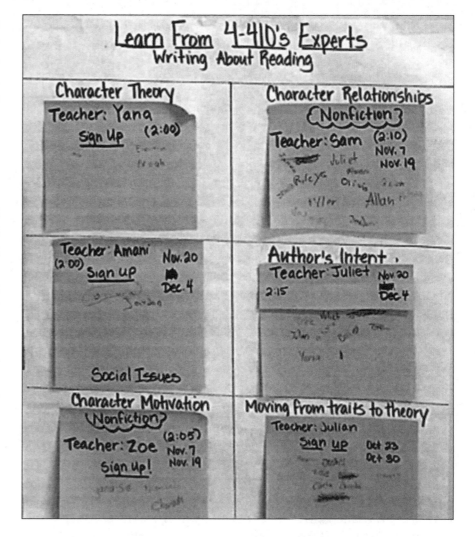

to make a display of "I used to write about reading like this . . . Now I write about reading like this . . ."

Students can think about what they do best as writers about reading and set out to do that work even better. They can get together with others who have a similar specialty as writers about reading, and they can talk and think about how to do that sort of writing especially well. They can give each other feedback. Once the students think their work is especially strong, they can lead student groups and mini-courses to help others do similarly strong work (while they also attend such courses led by others).

During Writing Time, You Provide Students with Exemplars of Writing about Reading

If we return to the list of ways writing is often supported in the writing workshop and not supported in the reading workshop, you'll quickly find other ways to lift the level of students' writing about reading. For example, if you will recall, I mentioned that during the writing workshop, students are explicitly taught the qualities of strong narrative writing, strong information writing, and strong essay writing. Students study exemplar texts that illustrate those qualities, carrying those exemplar texts around, talking about them with others, keeping them close as they do their own approximations of that work.

How hard would it be to provide students with texts that illustrate your image of powerful writing about reading? Let's think, for example, about the sort of note-taking you hope students do as they read a nonfiction text. There presumably is no one way you expect students to take notes. But what are qualities you look for? I, for one, am pleased if the notes are layered. That is, I am glad when I can see that a student seems to have returned to earlier notes to add in information that he learned later, because that shows me the student is synthesizing as he reads. I also like to see evidence that the student sees that two parts of his notes are connected to each other. Perhaps he is studying volcanoes and he notices ways that the second volcano seems to be different from the first, and his notes show he is doing that sort of thinking. I'm glad if I see evidence in his notes that he returns to them to record questions. My point is not that this is a quality of good note-taking. Instead, my point is that if I want students to do that work, I would be wise to provide examples that illustrate this.

During Writing Time, You Encourage Revision to Support Thinking and Writing about Reading

Earlier, I mentioned that when students write during the writing workshop, there are a lot of supports to help them reread, assess, and revise their first draft writing. The message is that the best way for students to lift the level of their writing is for them to return to a draft and to roll up their sleeves, working to make that draft better.

Granted, revision will seem more important when the goal is to produce publishable work rather than to grow ideas about a text. The writing that students do during a reading workshop isn't meant to yield masterpieces. Still,

people revise to ratchet up the level of their work. The young trombonist plays the same tune over and over without any plan to perform at Carnegie Hall! That sort of revision is done in support of learning. It would be wise for young readers to do more of this. And if you think about it, chances are good that in entry after entry (or Post-it after Post-it), students are probably doing similar work with one text after another. Why *not* teach a reader to look back at an entry about a book and to think, "How'd I do?" and then to revise that writing?

Say, for example, that your students tend to take notes on the subjects they're researching without paying attention to the author of the sources. They also tend not to notice the various perspectives of the authors or to weigh the knowledge bases or perspectives of an author. They tend to accept all sources as similarly authoritative and to read by drawing information from hither and yon into their mental model of the topic. That way of learning from sources will have worked perfectly for students as third-graders, but by the time they are fifth-graders, you will want them to begin to be more aware of the sources of the research they read. You'll want them to note the perspectives of the different authors. To help students learn that next step, wouldn't it be advisable for them to revise their entries to acknowledge the missing perspectives?

We have found that asking students to revise even just their Post-its has provided an unbelievably powerful engine for lifting the level of students' thinking about reading. Usually this work, for us, has been done around the learning progressions, and you can read a lot more about it in *Reading Pathways*. For now, say we want to teach students to predict better. We pause in the read-aloud book to get students to join us in predicting. "What do you think will happen next?" we ask, and we record a rather low-level prediction that we hear one child in the group say. Perhaps that prediction goes something like "I think he'll win the prize in the end." Then we tell students that there is research on skillful predictions and that research suggests that predictions are better if the reader predicts not just the end point, but the journey there. The class revises that initial prediction. Then we teach a few more tips: better predictions include not just what will happen, but *how* it will happen. Better predictions draw on specific details from early in the text. Better predictions reflect a knowledge of the genre. As more qualities are added, the initial prediction goes through more revisions, and soon the class has coproduced a ladder of predictions. Then the call can be given. "Work with a partner to look over one of *your* predictions from your independent reading book (or club book). Try to revise your predictions in similar ways." That day, as kids go off to read, they can keep their one best prediction out on the desk as a mentor prediction, and they can aim to predict in equally potent ways. During the share, four readers can get together, share their best prediction, and rank what they have done, detailing why the one reader's prediction is the best of them all. They can help each other revise so each of them has equally good work to show.

All of this discussion, so far, has come from one question: what are some doable, practical, no-big-deal ways you can provide some of the support that you provide for writing within the writing workshop to your students' writing about reading. Let's turn now to consider other ways you can lift the level of your students' writing about reading.

BROADEN THE TOPICS STUDENTS ADDRESS

This is an easy way to improve your students' writing about reading. To consider this topic, join me for a moment in listing all the sorts of things that readers think and talk about when discussing texts. Do that for fiction texts and do it also for nonfiction texts. For fiction, your list will contain these and many other elements:

Elements that Are Often Discussed by Fiction Readers

Character	Structure
Traits	Chronology
Relationships	Passage of time
Feelings	Flashback/flash-forward
Changes	Theme, message
Motivations/pressures	Setting/place
Lessons/changes	Tone, mood
Voice	Patterns
Power	Author's craft
Point of view	Lead
Important objects	Ending
Symbols	Repetition
Language choices	Elaboration
Metaphor, simile, personification	

The nonfiction list will have many of the same elements, although some are specific to nonfiction:

Elements that Are Often Discussed by Nonfiction Readers

Main idea and supporting details	Chronology
Cause and effect	Passage of time
Character	Flashback/flash-forward
Traits	Theme, message
Relationships	Setting/place
Changes	Tone, mood
Motivations/pressures	Patterns
Lessons/changes	Author's craft
Power	Lead
Point of view	Ending
Language choices	Repetition
Structure	Elaboration

Here is my question. Think about your students' writing about reading. Which of all these elements do they tend to address? Which don't they address?

If your students are anything like those I know best, they have a very limited repertoire of topics they take up when writing and talking (and dare I say, when thinking) about texts. Give them this list. Ask them to do an inventory of the elements they incorporate into their writing about reading. Then ask them to set New Year's resolutions to dramatically expand their repertoire. If that leads your fiction readers to think and write about characters who have and do not have power, about the passage of time in a text, about the language choices writers have made—right there, you will have dramatically lifted the level of work that writing about reading does. If it leads your nonfiction readers to think about the causes and effects of historical events or the relationship between animals and their habitats or the point of view of a newspaper article or the changes that humans have made on the environment—imagine the intellectual payoff!

TEACH STUDENTS TO READ AND WRITE MORE ANALYTICALLY

This is a thought that has become important to me. I contend that if you simply ask students to turn and talk or to stop and jot or to write about whatever they just read, and you do not either channel them or teach them otherwise, then the strong students will think analytically and the less strong will not.

Imagine that your students have just read a few pieces about the debate around cell phones in schools. They know they are expected to write after they read, so when they come to the end of those articles, they pick up their pens to write. What sorts of things are they apt to write?

I suspect that a lot of students will repeat what an article said, add personal preferences, and write free associations. A lot of their writing will go like this: "I like how so-and-so said . . . That's true for me too! When I brought my cellphone . . . I think all schools should . . ." Think about the kinds of thinking that those students will have just done. They'll have simply reacted to what they read, added in their opinions, and connected personally to the general topic. They will have responded to those texts the way they presumably respond to news they hear around town. That's about it. And chances are good that this will be the way their writing goes, whether the original text is nonfiction or is literature. They repeat information. They write about their preferences—a character or a book or a part of a text that they like or do not like. They cite personal connections. They associate.

Meanwhile, however, the strong students will have reacted differently to the articles about cellphones. They may have compared the several different texts, noting how they are similar and different from each other. They may have categorized them (two are somewhat similar, one is quite different). They'll think about why the texts that are different are that way (they were written by people with different roles, different viewpoints). They may rank the texts (which is more persuasive and why, or which part of a text is especially persuasive and why).

In similar ways, when strong students write about a story, they might rank, select, question, categorize, and compare. Which is the most important scene? Where does the turning point come? How is this relationship or decision or place like and unlike that one? How would the text have been different had this or that not occurred? How does this or that connect to what came earlier? Why did the author add this part, end this way, use that metaphor?

This is a big deal. It suggests that day in and day out across a year, students who think analytically are doing different work than the students who do not. That is true of their writing about reading, their talking about reading, and, presumably, their thinking about reading. For the students who think analytically, when you give them free choice over what to write or talk about, you are inviting them to flex their mental muscles in ways that respond to their particular text. But when you give free choice to students who do not think analytically, they are doing a sort of thinking that may not pay off in the end. Students who do not naturally think analytically need to be given either tasks and assignments that channel them toward thinking analytically or instruction in doing so.

But that doesn't mean you should take over responsibility for deciding what students talk and write about as they read (although there are advantages to and times for doing that). In the end, students need to be able to initiate their own analytic thinking about a text, and the key is for you to teach them to do that on their own, without you. To start, think about what analytic thinking entails and make sure that *you* are apt to do this sort of thinking.

It helps to try this sort of thinking around a concrete subject, not a text, for starters. Let's take the reading workshop, because it is a subject we have in common. I'm going to talk to you about what analytic thinking entails and then ask you to try this sort of thinking in relation to the reading workshop.

One way to think analytically is to divide a topic into parts. In your mind, do that for the reading workshop.

You may be thinking minilessons, workshop, share, but there are many ways to divide any topic. You could divide reading workshop into whole group, small group, and one to one or into fiction and nonfiction or reading, writing, and talking or any of a number of other ways. Doing this work, alone, may not yield much, but

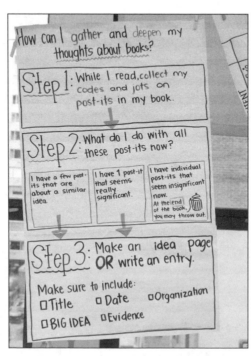

if your thinking about the topic begins with you dividing it into parts, that step alone will lift the level of your work. The good news, however, is that it is easy to layer one form of analytic thinking onto another.

Next, let's try ranking, and because we've just divided the topic into parts, try ranking the parts—perhaps by which is most important and least important and, of course, by thinking why.

Where does that trail of thought lead you? What are you realizing?

Return to ranking, and this time, rank which part of reading workshop seems to you to be most important, next most important, and least important.

Now do the same thing for me. Which part do you think I believe is most important? Next most? Least? What about the kids? Where will their thinking about this go? Why?

Of course, the point really is to let any of this spark you to talk and think long about whatever surfaces in your mind.

There are other ways to think analytically. Let's go back to the original topic of the reading workshop and, for now, try connecting the reading workshop to other parts of your teaching or your life. What feels similar to the reading workshop, and in what ways? Then again, you could try another sort of connecting. When you were little, what part of your life was like a reading workshop?

Analytic thinking can also involve categorizing. Think of ways you can categorize the main challenges you face when teaching reading. Or categorize anything related to the reading workshop: the ways you teach during the reading workshop. Of course, categorizing will probably lead you to want to compare. How are those ways of teaching like and unlike ways you teach during, say, science? Then again, this sort of thinking could lead you to want to rank. Which of those categories is the most dominant?

Next, let's think about comparing and contrasting. How is the reading workshop like and unlike other parts of your teaching? How about the writing workshop? If you teach that structure as well, how is the reading workshop the same? Different?

I hope my point is abundantly clear. There are ways of thinking—ways some people refer to as analytic thinking—that involve higher-order mental processes such as ranking, selecting, partitioning, categorizing, and comparing and contrasting. If a person thinks in those ways about any subject, and if a reader thinks in those ways about texts, that person is apt to spark insights and to develop ideas that are fresh, provocative, and significant. The thinking that results will tend to be qualitatively better than the thinking that comes from merely making personal connections, commenting loosely on a topic, or adding on an associated thought.

You'll have to decide whether you want to teach students that analytic writing and thinking is a choice, always, across all of life. I would probably start by doing an exercise like what I just did with you, only on a topic the class knows well, such as recess time. I would start by giving time for students to jot their thoughts about recess. Later, at the end of the sequence of instruction, I'd suggest they compare their original thoughts with those they came to after working to think more analytically.

It is entirely possible that this metacognitive discussion is better for teachers than for kids. Marie Clay always cautioned against too much of an emphasis on metacognition, saying to me, "They don't need to be able to talk about their strategies. They just need to be able to do them." Your goal may just be to get students doing this sort of thinking rather than bringing this to the forefront of their consciousness.

Students Can Learn to Partition Texts They Read

Let's start as we did when thinking about the reading workshop, and this time, let's think about texts. You'll recall that we said that one way to think analytically is to divide a topic into parts. Our goal now is to give students ways to proceed that will pay off when they read.

You might suggest that after reading a text, students could make a diagram of it and label the parts. So, for example, after reading any story (or part of one), the reader could map the plotline of the story and label the parts.

Partitioning Literature

I recently led a workshop on this for teachers, and we used the fascinating story "A Pet," from Cynthia Rylant's *Every Living Thing*, as our fiction text. I strongly encourage you to get out "A Pet" and to read it—it will take five minutes to do so—before proceeding.

Imagine, if you have read "A Pet," how you would map the plotline of the story, labeling these parts:

Setting/contextual information

Character motivation

Problem

Rising trouble/ways character responds to trouble

Crisis/turning point

Solution/resolution

There are, of course, a handful of other important labels that a reader could use (or not use) depending on the story. These include:

Gaps in the passage of time; flashback, flash-forward

Subplot

Causes of an action, consequences or effects of an action

Earlier, when you divided the reading workshop into parts (whole group, small group, one-to-one, for example), you then thought about those parts. You probably want to teach your readers that mapping the way a story goes and labeling its parts can spark important thinking. Readers might think about these or other questions:

- How does one (or more) of these moments connect to the larger messages or themes of the text?

- How do different characters respond differently to the moment you are analyzing (or how might they have responded differently had they been there, knowing what you know about them and their roles)? What from earlier in the story explains the character's response?

- It is important to see parts of the story as connected. Draw arrows between parts that seem connected to you, and push your mind to see connections that you might not at first see.

- Star moments in the story that seem especially key. Think about any one of those moments. Think big: How does this moment contribute to the whole story? Think small: What are the key details that are present in that moment. Those details are there on purpose. Why did the author choose that particular detail? How might that detail help forward the central meanings in the text?

Partitioning Information Texts

Just as you asked students to make a diagram of a text, label its parts, and then think about those parts, that same work can be done in an information or argument text. Readers could learn to create a model of the text as they read it and to label (or at least be able to label) the parts of that text using terms such as these to do so:

Thinking Analytically about the Parts of a Nonfiction Text

Parts
- What are the major chunks or categories in the text?
- What are some of the subpoints?

Idea/Point/Claim
- Where does the author forward his or her idea/point/claim?
- Are there two of the above?
- Does one chunk of text support one idea/claim and another chunk, the other, or are the ideas/claims threaded throughout? Which is most important?

Elaboration/Evidence
- Does the writer support the claim/idea/point with a story?
- With a description?
- With a definition?
- With a comparison?

Transitions/Relationships/Logical Order
- Is this organized chronologically? Sequentially (first, next)?
- Is this organized as causes/effects or results?
- Is this organized by priority (least to most)?

Of course, when reading nonfiction, as when reading fiction, there are key parts that merit attention. In nonfiction, the key parts are often just before and in places where the text shifts in focus and structure. Readers can think carefully about those parts and write to think about some generic questions:

- How does this one part connect to the larger message or idea(s) of the text? What other parts support this idea?

- Why is this example, illustration, or anecdote here? What does it highlight? How does it fit with what comes before?

- Does this extend or illustrate what I just learned? Is this the beginning of a new point? Does this offer a conflicting perspective?

- What details has the author used in this key part of the text? Why might the author have chosen to include those details?

Students Can Learn to Rank Ideas/Claims/Evidence

Once you have divided a subject into parts, it's quite a natural extension to rank those parts, and to do so in ways that reflect whatever it is you are especially interested in. The recent release of PARCC, SBAC, and other high-stakes assessments aligned to global standards reveals that a large number of questions on these assessments ask students to rank. "Which of the following details best supports the claim that . . . ?" "Which of the following theme is most important in the story?" "Which of the following sentences best supports the main idea of . . . ?"

Generally, in those questions, most of the details *do* support the claim, most of the themes *can* be located in the story, and the challenge is, indeed, to rank possible candidates. One can assume these questions are included on high-stakes tests because they are test-makers' ways to put higher-level thinking skills into a multiple-choice framework, and the constraint of needing things to fit into a multiple-choice framework needn't restrict the work you do all year long in your classroom. But for readers to be able to decide which evidence best supports a claim, they need to do important and challenging work weighing and measuring evidence and linking that evidence to the claim. Being able to judge well is no small deal. In fact, in his book *Blink*, Malcolm Gladwell (2005) suggests that one of the key identifiers of expertise is that a person is able to judge in the blink of the eye. He goes on to suggest that one reason an expert can do this is that he has internalized the criterion that matters and can weigh the choices against that criterion.

It makes sense, then, that when students are writing about reading in your classroom, you teach them that there is a set of ranking questions that can be asked of almost any text. Teach them to ask those questions as they read

and to become skilled at responding to them. These are just a few of those questions:

- Which is the most significant theme in this story?

- Which line best captures the theme/central idea of the text?

- Which is the most important central idea in this article?

- Which details best support that theme/claim/central idea?

- What moment best shows the character's motivation?

- Which detail best captures the contribution this person/thing made to history?

Students Can Learn to Compare and Contrast Texts

If you spend a lot of time listening to readers share their ideas about texts, you begin over time to sort out the qualities that separate the sheep from the goats. Some students think in ways that reflect a rich background in reading; some do not. Readers who come across as more literate read one text, thinking about other texts. When discussing one text, the reader refers to others that are similar in some ways and different in other ways. It is as if thinking

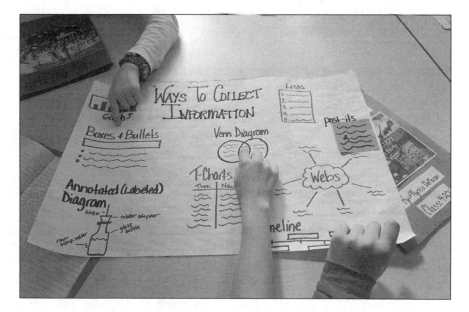

between texts is what allows these readers to sharpen their ideas. So if two texts both discuss the intelligence of octopus, how do they do that differently? Are they written from different perspectives? Do they highlight different points? Is their audience different? And how are they the same?

The Larger Work of Becoming Someone Who Thinks, Writes, and Talks Analytically

This list of ways students can think analytically is only partial, and you can easily extend it yourself. I'm reluctant to do so because I think the real point is not for students to have an ever broader repertoire of ways to think analytically, but rather for them to realize that when they have a moment to think, write, or talk about a text, it is valuable to take just a second at the start of that work to make a quick choice about an avenue into this work. If rehearsal is critical to the writing that students do during the writing workshop and that scholars do at their desks, then even sixty seconds of rehearsal would be valuable before a writer jots a Post-it response to reading or initiates a bit of angled reading in pursuit of a question.

Then, too, I think that it is advantageous if students become accustomed to doing a kind of analytic thinking repeatedly, so that the student can become increasingly skilled at that work. Any of the kinds of thinking I have described so far can be done modestly or can be done well, and for students to think carefully about how to achieve maximum insight and power from one of these ways of thinking would be valuable.

Students need to anticipate writing about reading, so the intention to write provides a lens that lifts the level of reading.

Oftentimes writing about reading happens like this: a student reads a chunk of text. Upon reaching the end of that text or of the time set aside for reading, the reader puts down the page. Then the reader remembers, "That's right. I'm supposed to do some writing about what I just read," so the student picks up the pen or opens the computer, searches her mind for something to say, and writes.

When writing about reading fits into a sequence like that, it is reasonable to wonder whether that writing lifts the level of that reading. After all, the reading was already completed when the student turned her mind to the prospect of writing. So the writing only lifts the level of the reading if one defines reading broadly to include what occurs as the student talks or writes about the text.

It is relatively easy to alter this, and probably it is important to do so. One way is for readers to be given a task prior to reading time. "Today, read your text and think about . . . Prepare to write . . ." When this is done, the obvious source of texts is the whole-class shared unit. For example, third-graders could be told, "Today, look over your books about your animal to find some topics that are written about again and again. Choose one such topic and read a few of the texts that teach about that topic. As you read, think, 'Does this say more than what I already knew?' If so, mark that part."

You can alter this by teaching students to think, before they read, "What is the work I want to try to do today as I read?" Students can draw on their knowledge of the learning progressions, their self-assessments, or their prior thinking to generate this. For example, if a student is not accustomed to organizing notes as he reads nonfiction, he would be wise to give himself goals to do so. Before he reads, he'll want to do some careful text orientation and to look especially at the organizational structure of the text he plans to read. As he reads, he'll want to pause at places in the text's structure that seem like stopping spots and to take notes that reflect how the part of the text he has just read fits into the larger text.

Of course, another way to make sure that writing lifts the level of students' reading is to ask them to think about their writing not as a one-shot patch of thought, but as the result of reading with a lens. If readers are thinking about a text by especially noting the author's craft, for example, and ways the author uses craft to highlight the importance of some ideas, then the writing a student does after reading two pages is also writing before reading the upcoming pages.

One way to help readers set themselves up to read with a lens, reading differently because they anticipate writing, is to make sure that before they begin reading a text, they take time to orient themselves to what they will read, thinking, "What kind of text does this appear to be, and what does that suggest I should be attentive to?" Certain kinds of texts require certain kinds of reading work. So, for example, if this is an editorial page or an op-ed column, the reader should consider approaching the text by noticing the claims and the supports. Depending on the reader's skill level, she might also notice the axe grinding behind the text, looking at the author's biography and at the sources of information cited for clues about the author's bias and perspective. On the other hand, when reading historical fiction, the reader will want to begin reading, alert for information about the historical context, looking to see if trouble is brewing. The reader will be aware from the start that the characters are apt to represent different social groups or different perspectives, and their varying reactions to the events will reveal some of the tensions of the day.

There are lots of other kinds of texts that, like editorials and historical fiction, are written in ways that ask readers to read, think, and perhaps write with particular slants, and students would be wise to note the kind of text they will be reading and to consider what that kind of text is asking of the reader.

One way or another, it will be a good thing if oftentimes your students read texts with a lens in hand, intending to think about a particular topic and thinking about that topic (or extensions of it) across a long stretch of reading. Having said this, it is also important for students to know that part of their job as they work to write, talk, and think well about reading is to notice places in a text that merit attentive response. These might be places that relate to the student's chosen lens, but they could also be places that call out for attention related to other lenses, other ways of reading.

If a reader reads straight through places where the text detours dramatically or includes a contrary perspective or foreshadows, and the reader just races on, eyes fixed forward, intent on finding out what happens next or on supporting the big idea, there is little chance that the reader will theorize about the overlooked textual moves. This means that just as it is crucial for a young child to monitor for comprehension and note where the text is not making sense, because the child will only reach for fix-up strategies if he notices meaning breaking down in the first place, it is equally important for students to note signs that something has happened in a text that is pause-worthy. That sense of "Whoa!" is a precondition to the reader using not just fix-up strategies but also higher-level comprehension strategies.

Because learning to note, to pause, is important, it is worthwhile to encourage students to read with little flags in hand, taking note without necessarily making long responses. The book *Notice and Note*, by Kylene Beers and Robert E. Probst (2012), is a helpful resource on this.

Students need to write text-based responses, citing evidence from the text.

The final way I'm going to suggest you can help students lift the level of their writing about reading is by helping them to really understand and embrace today's call for more text-based writing about reading. What we have found is that even after teachers encourage students to cite evidence from the text, very few students seem to really grasp how and why to do that. Their efforts at doing this often leave much to be desired.

Say that a student wants to show that the Battle of Gettysburg—which historians describe as a turning point in the Civil War—was a costly one. That student has found a passage in Jennifer L. Weber's *Summer's Bloodiest Days: The Battle of Gettysburg as Told From All Sides* that provides evidence. What we see a lot is that the student will go to the passage and attempt to retell the gist of it, writing like this:

The battle was very bloody and hurtful to both sides. Many died. After the battle, all the barns were turned into hospitals and were full of injured soldiers. Hundreds of other soldiers wandered around looking for hospitals. There were 9,000 casualties.

It is important for you to help students know that what they have done, writing like that, is not that different than writing about a mountain climb by writing four sentences that essentially recap the drive to the mountain, the trip up it, the view, and the trip down. In the narrative writing workshop, students learn to focus in on small moments that become emblematic of larger meanings, and they need to focus in similar ways when referencing the text. It is fine to write a summary, to say something general, but then the student would be wise to ask, "What specific lines, details, images best make my point?" and to include those.

When including those chosen specifics, it is usually best to actually cite the text, and especially to do so if there are parts of the text that are as close as possible to the topic. So if this is history and the text includes some accounts from people who participated in that bit of history, those would be important bits to actually quote. In contrast to the basic retelling of the Battle of Gettysburg above, this rewrite cites meaningful evidence:

The Battle of Gettysburg was especially brutal. Lieutenant George Grenville Benedict of the 12th Vermont Regiment describes the scene in barns. He writes, "Each of them was a field hospital; its floor covered with mutilated soldiers, and surgeons busy at lantern-lighted operating tables. By the door of one of them was a ghastly pile of amputated arms and legs, and around each of them lay multitudes of wounded men. . . . It seemed to me as if every square yard, for many square miles, must have its blood stain."

To do this work, students need to identify parts of the text that are most relevant to whatever they are thinking. You'll want to encourage them to actually frame those bits—perhaps making a little frame by cutting a window from a page of notebook paper or by using torn bits of Post-its to set apart the chosen lines. Become accustomed to saying to students, "What specific sentences make the point you are trying to make?"

The challenge for students is not just to grasp that actually citing the text matters and not just to locate passages that do the job, but also to make the transitions from paraphrasing to citing. Teach them to use these and other transitional phrases:

- For example, the text (or a character/author) says . . .

- For example, according to the text (the character) . . .

- For example, early in the text, readers learn that . . .

- For example, in the beginning, we hear that . . .

- So-and-so claims . . .

- So-and-so writes . . .

- So-and-so describes this, saying . . .

- One thing to note is that, toward the end of the text, readers learn that . . .

- Readers learn, early on, that . . .

It can sometimes help to support students in citing texts when talking about them, even before fretting about whether they cite texts when writing about them. We often ask partners to keep cue cards close by and to use them to help them to shift between discussing, paraphrasing, and citing.

When writing text-based responses, students need not only to cite the text, but also to analyze it. Again, you will want to teach students to do this, realizing that mostly, they think they are doing this when they are not. It can help a lot for you to show them what it means to actually zoom in on the specific words that they have cited, discussing why one word was chosen instead of another, and realizing those choices matter.

Again, students often find it difficult to make the transition from quoting a passage in a text to discussing it, and providing them with transitional phrases can help. These are all phrases to use after one quotes from a text, as above:

- This shows that . . .

- This illustrates that . . .

- This demonstrates that . . .

- Readers realize that . . .

- This changes everything. Whereas before . . . , now . . .

- Readers begin to wonder/question/understand . . .

- The important thing to notice about this is that . . .

- While (such and such) could have (been said/happened/been included), instead this (was said/happened/included).

- It is important to notice that (the author) could have . . . but didn't . . . Perhaps this was because . . .

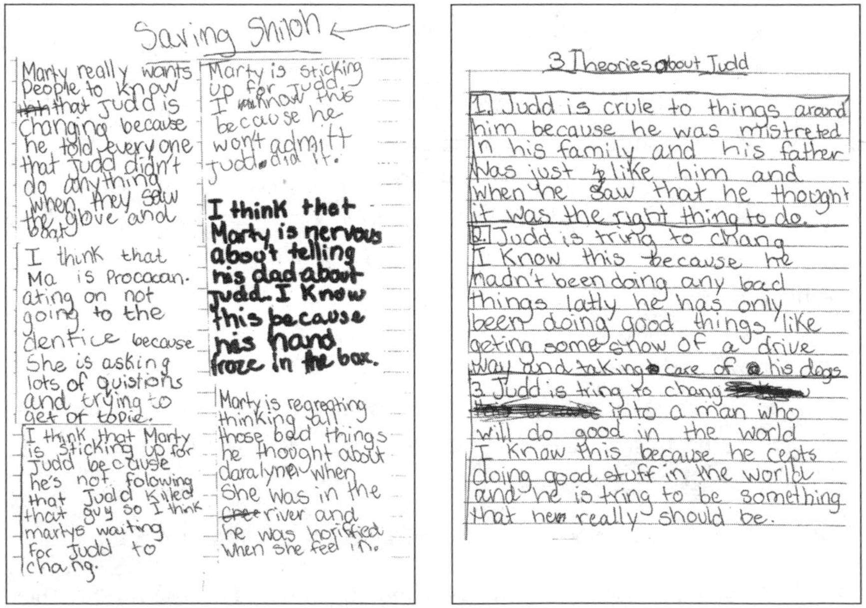

FIG. 10–1 Maddie explores multiple ideas as she reads *(left)* and uses her Post-it-sized ideas to develop larger theories *(right)*.

TEACHERS AND STUDENTS NEED A SHARED IMAGE OF THE GOAL OF WRITING ABOUT READING

Finally, it is critical that there is clarification about the goal for the writing that students do during reading time. I should think that the goal is to lift the level of students' reading—of their insights, connections, and analysis of the text. I should think the goal would be for students to do better work, thinking about the theme of the text, noticing the way that parts of the text support that theme, or thinking about the central ideas of the text, seeing the way the text advances those ideas. I should think the goal would be for students

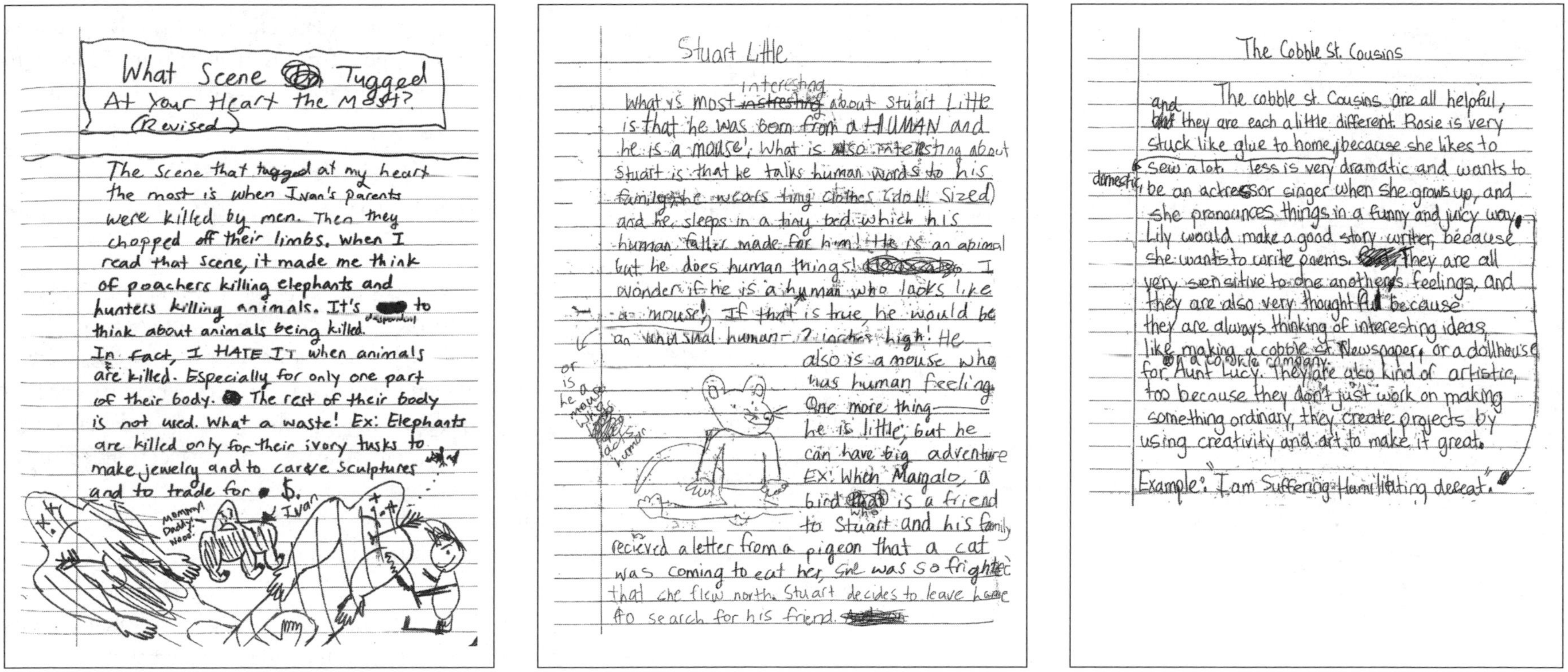

to question, rethink, surmise, hypothesize, remember, connect, deconstruct, doubt, challenge, explore, surmise—in short, to think.

Some of the students' writing about reading will perhaps resemble a literary essay, because there will be times when a student or a group of students develops a hunch about a text and they read on, looking for evidence that supports and disputes that claim. But there will be lots of other times when students' entries and Post-its do not in any way resemble literary essays.

Let me end the chapter by sharing some entries from reader's notebooks that to me, constitute good writing about reading:

FIG. 10–2   Examples of good writing about reading

Chapter 11

Practical Help with Book Clubs

ASK ANY CHILD about his favorite part of the reading workshop, and I can promise you, the answer will be book clubs. Yet all too often, I find that teachers are uneasy about this structure and, instead of launching clubs, rely simply on partnerships for the duration of the year. The purpose for this chapter is to talk back to that decision and to equip you with a collection of accessible, easy ways to launch and to teach into book clubs.

HOW ARE BOOK CLUBS SIMILAR TO AND DIFFERENT FROM LITERATURE CIRCLES?

In the literature on teaching reading, you will see that some people mention literature circles, others book clubs, and you are wise to ask whether there is a difference. In the big ways, these terms refer to the same thing. In both book clubs and literature circles, readers get together to talk about a book they have read in common. Readers generate as well as sometimes respond to questions, and they talk at some length with some independence.

We began using the term *book club* about twenty years ago and have continued since. We deliberately chose the term to highlight a few key choices we advocated that depart from traditional literature circles. Above all, while literature circles often form around a particular book (and disperse once that book has been read and discussed), book clubs are long lasting, with club members choosing the sequence of books they will read.

In this way, book clubs in classrooms resemble the book clubs to which many adults belong. If you have ever been in a book club, you know that one of the great pleasures of such a club is that over time, you and the other readers in the club develop a history of shared books and shared conversations. As you read any one new book, then, your conversations often hearken back to previous books. "Isn't this like . . . ?" you say, layering your thoughts about the current book with references to an earlier text. Of course, the other thing that you do as you and your club mates read together is you bring the conversations and, indeed, the perspectives of your club mates to the current book. That is, because book

Kathy said to the class, "I wonder if in this classroom, you might want to form book clubs?"

She explained to the class, "You'll need to make a few decisions. You'll have to decide what to name your club, what your logo will be, where you'll meet and how often, and what you'll talk about."

Think in your own life about times when you and a group of friends formed a club, a team, a project together. Think of the energy with which you figured out your constitution, your resolutions, and your traditions.

For me, building a book club gives kids a second chance to commit themselves to authoring a rich reading life. It is not unlike the invitation I give kids at the start of the school year when I ask them to think about times that reading has worked in their lives and to think of ways we can make sure that reading works in this classroom, this year. I want as many chances as possible

clubs stay together across time, reading a lot of books together, members of the club find themselves reading and anticipating the ways their colleagues will talk about a book. "Amy is going to love this passage," a reader thinks and reads it extra carefully because of that expectation.

In this series, we first introduce book clubs to third-graders in *Character Studies*, the second fiction unit of the year, after they have already done the work of the first fiction unit. In fourth grade, we follow the same pattern—first a regular fiction unit (*Interpreting Characters*), followed by a fiction unit incorporating book clubs (*Historical Fiction Clubs*). In fifth grade, however, both fiction units—*Interpretation Book Clubs* and *Fantasy Book Clubs*—involve book clubs. The expectation is that if your students have had two years of experience with clubs in third and fourth grade, they will be ready to plunge into club work at the beginning of fifth grade.

THE NUTS AND BOLTS OF BOOK CLUBS

When Kathy Doyle first launched clubs in her fifth-grade classroom, this was an entirely new thing for her students, who hadn't grown up within reading workshop classrooms. She pointed out to the class that many of them belonged to clubs—chess clubs, karate clubs, a Hebrew club. One student, Brian, had just gotten a Holland Lop rabbit and had joined a rabbit club.

What should we think about as we create our book club rules and identity?

→ Determine a club name `CLUB NAME`

→ Designate a meeting spot and a place to post club assignments `To Do:`

→ Make a list of materials that all members should bring to meetings `Materials 1. 2. 3. 4.`

→ Select the number of pages we will read each night `p. 60-78`

→ Come up with a protocol to prepare for conversations `• Reread • Post-it • Write • Talk`

→ Decide on the kind of writing we will do

FIG. 11–1

to allow readers to draw a line in the sand and to resolve, "From this day forward, I'm going to be the kind of reader who . . ." Forming a new book club gives kids a chance to remake themselves as readers. Imagine that this is a club devoted to fantasy reading, and the kids resolve to watch some fantasy movies together—most likely at home, not together, but to all do this and to talk about those movies together. Imagine the kids resolve to make a map of the place for each fantasy movie they watch and each fantasy book they read and to ground their conversation about the unfolding story by planning it on the map. Imagine one of the club members is a great artist and takes it upon himself to make fabulous maps that are front and center in each of the club's text talks. That sort of work makes a difference to a child's self-concept and to that child's concept of what it means to be a reader.

I've always loved survival literature, and I think that the way children create their own clubs within a classroom reminds me of stories throughout literature in which characters do the same. I think about children building a book club together, and I am reminded of the old Disney movie, *Swiss Family Robinson*. After the main characters were shipwrecked on a deserted island, they salvaged what they could from their sinking ship and built a tree house for themselves, as well as a civilization. Book clubs remind me also of Gary Paulsen's character, Brian, whose plane crashed into the Alaskan wilderness and who, with little more than a hatchet, caught fish, started a fire, and built a world. I think I was first drawn to teaching because, in a sense, that is the work that teachers do. We salvage what we can—a spool table from roadside garbage, an old bookcase from our parents' home—and we build a world in the classroom. And surely, that is what readers do when you invite them to form their very own book club.

"What will we call ourselves?" children ask. They create names. They decide on a small bear or a baseball cap that will become their club mascot. They choose a meeting spot. Many clubs make a constitution, and you can help them to do so by suggesting predictable problems that the club will need to tackle. But more on this later.

My first point is that you will tap a huge energy source in your kids if you give them some decision-making ability and allow them to feel as if these are kid-led clubs rather than teacher-sponsored small groups. It won't be any skin off your back for the kids to have a mascot. That little troll with pink hair standing in the midst of their small-group discussion won't take anything away from your ability to work with these readers. And meanwhile, the troll represents something big to the kids.

While children are making choices, you'll want to weigh in and even sometimes to take control. So let me give you a score of small tips, gleaned from decades of work with clubs. Know from the start that if you turn these tips into mandates and essentially take control of clubs away from kids, the clubs will feel like balloons that run out of air. So find ways to finesse some of these points and forego others.

Membership

Generally, clubs are comprised of two sets of reading partners who read close to the same level of text complexity. You may ask kids to write you a note letting you know readers who like to read similar books as they do and at the same pace (that's a code word for kids who are at roughly the same level of text complexity) with whom they think they can work well (emphasis on the word *work*), and then you presumably will put together the clubs, taking kids' wishes into account as best you can. Book clubs do provide support for readers, so this is a great time to move one partnership up a notch to slightly higher books, especially if that partnership will then be in a club with readers who are more experienced at the new level of text complexity. It is helpful if a club can break down into partnerships, because some days instead of a full club discussion, you can suggest partners keep tabs on each other.

Think about a book club as a social structure that will last the duration of a unit and will often be brought into a second unit.

Routines

In most classrooms, a book club meets two or three times a week and agrees not to talk together about the shared book during intervals between the club meetings, so as not to dissipate the energy outside of the club meetings. It is best not to meet too often or kids won't bring that head of steam that provides energy to a club discussion. Most teachers decide to channel all their clubs to meet at the same time, so that perhaps on Tuesday and Thursday of one week, Monday and Thursday of another, the reading workshop ends with fifteen minutes for club conversations. Other days there may be partner conversation, or share time can be devoted to writing about reading or to more reading.

If you find that kids cannot productively sustain a conversation about a text for fifteen minutes, you might plan for the club meetings to be shorter, or you can make it clear to kids that when their club conversations run out of energy, readers return to reading. Keep in mind, however, that you will want to teach kids to sustain conversations for longer, so if a particular club regularly talks only briefly, you'll want to help that club learn ways to talk at greater length. When youngsters can sustain a conversation, this bodes well for them being able to write essays advancing an idea about a text.

There are predictable problems that pop up in book clubs, so club members will need to talk about how they will handle those problems. How do they decide on how much to read between meetings, for example? You may leave that decision up to the clubs and just intervene if their decisions aren't supporting the volume of reading that you expect, or you may find it helpful to fill them in on what other classrooms have tended to do and then let them either go with those decisions or suggest alternative ones. In general, you wouldn't imagine that it would take more than a week for kids to read most books—and that leaves few opportunities for deep conversations about a book. Often the decision is made that readers read other books on the side while also reading the club book, which allows them to read just two or three chapters between club conversations and to sustain work on a club book for a week and a half or two weeks, while maintaining their overall volume of reading. This also allows for a reader who is not as experienced as her club mates to keep up with the club, because that reader can simply do less reading on the side.

It is helpful if club members discuss in advance what the consequence will be when some members haven't done their reading—or their writing about reading. In most classrooms, the expectation is that a club member needs to tell his colleagues that he hasn't done the work, and then instead of joining the club, that student works alone to catch up on the requisite work. The club members also talk about how to make sure that doesn't happen again, often by vowing to text or call the reader the night before to check in. Sometimes a club member will say, "And I'm on the bus with you, so I will check then, and if you are still behind, you can read it on the bus." Sometimes club members have been known to say, "Then if you still need more reminders, we'll call your mother and get her to help." The larger point is that club members act in solidarity with their classmate to make it as likely as possible that the reading is done and the club can continue. This helps keep kids accountable to each other, not just to you.

Decisions also need to be made around writing about reading. In general, the expectation usually is that kids come to clubs having not only read but also written about the assigned chapters. Usually you need to set some expectations about the amount of writing about reading that readers will do in, say, a week. Perhaps the expectation is that each reader will write three pages a week (or two) about her club book, and perhaps it is up to individual readers to decide on any given day whether to write a long entry or simply to make a graphic organizer. Either way, the reader can't come to a club empty-handed.

This is the important part of writing about reading. The club, itself, often decides on what the club members will write about to prepare for the next day's conversation, and every club member writes on the same topic in preparation for a discussion on that topic. But more about this later.

There are also routines around the nature of the conversation. In some clubs, the expectation is that the club discussion will always begin with each club member putting forward one insight or idea that he wants to discuss, round-robin style, setting the group up to look quickly between those ideas and see if there is any overlap before deciding on a direction for that day's conversation. Other clubs begin by asking each other, "Who has a thought or an entry that can get us started in a conversation?" Yet others rotate the job of launching the conversation. No matter how they begin, club members need to know that after a small interval of time—say, three minutes—a club needs to have finished the management and the preliminary hemming and hawing and actually become committed to a line of discussion. Sometimes it becomes necessary to give the club an hourglass or an egg timer so they limit their haggling over what to do.

LIFTING THE LEVEL OF WRITING AND TALKING ABOUT READING IN BOOK CLUBS

Chapter 10 focused on lifting the level of writing about reading in general, but there are particular considerations about the writing about reading that occurs within the context of book clubs. The important thing to realize is that without any input from you, what most clubs will do as they talk and what most readers will do as they write and think about texts is strip mine the book for little surface-level topics, discussing each for just a few minutes, saying the obvious clichés before moving on. And the single most important way to channel readers to think, talk, and write with more depth and substance and new insight is to be sure they stay with a thought longer. So if one reader of *Number the Stars* says, "I don't know why they keep mentioning the dead sister," you already know that the easiest thing for kids to do will be to just chime in, "Yeah, weird," and then quickly move along to another topic. Your hope instead is that if that thought is raised in a club conversation, the club will then stay on that line of thinking for the next five or ten minutes. Ideally, the question is then extended, with kids continuing to think about it as they read in preparation for the next days' conversation. To elaborate in those ways, children might reread passages where the sister is mentioned and think about the role she plays in those passages; they might entertain options for what she could come to mean later in the book, saying things such as "Could it be that . . . ?" They might recall another book where there were frequent references to a now-gone character. They might talk about how different members of the family seem to reference the dead sister in different ways, at different times.

Lingering with one topic in such a manner is not something that is in kids' DNA. Left on their own, they'll skip over the book like a stone skipping across a lake. When left on their own, your students' writing about reading will be similarly superficial, with a sentence or two about the lead of the story, another few sentences about the author's style, some quick thoughts about a character, a bit of prediction, a mention of theme, and so forth.

To change this, I suggest you start not with the club conversations, but with whole-class conversations around a read-aloud text. Imagine you have read a portion of the book that is threading through the unit. You come to a part that you know gets everyone thinking a mile a minute, and you lay the book down, saying, "My mind is on fire, isn't yours? Turn and tell your partner what you are thinking." Then you race among the kids, checking in on their conversations, listening for a thread of talk that you believe the whole class could get onto and sustain for a while. You hear it. Say this is a book talk on *The Great Gilly Hopkins*, and you have heard Geoffrey say, "I think Gilly is like an apple—hard on the outside but soft on the inside." So now you say to your class, "Let's get a whole-class conversation going. Geoffrey, will you get us started?" Then, scanning the room, you say, "All eyes on Geoffrey. Get ready to talk back to his ideas."

Geoffrey states his idea, and if you think your class will need help staying with that idea (which means not playing the card of their own idea, which is burning in the pockets of many readers), then you might repeat Geoffrey's idea as if you are seriously mulling over that fascinating thought. Then you say, "What do the rest of you think? Do you agree? Disagree? Want to add on? See an example? Turn and talk."

If you want to support your children even more, as the children talk, you could call out a voiceover or two. "Find a part of the book that illustrates what you are saying. Open up the book, both of you, and go to that part. Talk about exactly which words get you thinking this."

In any case, after a few minutes, you say, "Who can talk back to Geoffrey's idea?" and perhaps you repeat the idea. If a child talks back but looks at you, aiming his remarks to you, gesture to Geoffrey. Once one person has spoken back to Geoffrey, ask for others to chime in on the same thought. You might

at this point name the goal: "Class, do you see I am wanting you to stay with the line of thinking *Geoffrey* has started. The goal is to keep this ball in play." Then you could, if you wish, distribute a sheet full of conversation connectors, channeling children to use thought prompts such as these to extend the conversation:

- I want to add on.
- Can you say more about . . .
- I think the important thing about this is . . .
- I notice that . . .
- It is surprising that . . .
- I have an example that goes with the idea that . . . On page ___, the text says . . .
- I have another example.
- When I look at those examples, I see something partly different. I notice . . .
- This idea gets me thinking that . . .
- I keep wondering . . .
- So far we have said . . .
- Is there another way to look at this? Could it be that . . .

You can support that whole-class conversation in lots of ways. For starters, stay entirely out of the conversation, so the talk pattern goes child, child, child, child, not child, teacher, child, teacher. Then record the talk, writing a transcript, or record it on your smart phone or iPad if you can't write that quickly. After a bit you can stop the class and suggest they replay the conversation for a particular reason. For example, you might say, "You are not listening to each other and building on what each other says. There are gold nuggets being brought out, and none of you seem to notice. Let's replay the conversation, and this time, listen for when one of your classmates says something that deserves to be followed up on." Then you can display a transcript of the talk you just heard—perhaps enlarging this on the document camera or the Smart Board—and you could recruit the class to talk about how it could have gone differently and then to rewind and try the conversation again, this time making it match their hopes.

That sort of work could be done to help students to linger with and develop the good ideas that are said, to help them not jump away from a topic, and also to help them to reference the text in productive ways.

Once students have learned to stay with a thought in whole-class conversations, you will want to remind them to do this in their club conversations. Lists of thought prompts can help. You can also suggest students literally put a Post-it (or two related ones) at the center of their table (some stick them onto their mascot) and then talk about those two Post-its for as long as seems productive.

One important way to lift the level of these conversations is for children to read and write preparing to talk about the topic they have chosen to discuss. That's why we recommend that club members not only decide on the chapters they'll be reading and thinking about through their writing about that reading, but that also, when possible, the members of a club decide on the topic that they'll address. If the last few minutes of Monday's conversation revolved around the role of the dead sister in *Number the Stars*, your hope would be that in preparation for Wednesday's conversation, readers inquire about the question, using the conversation they already had about the topic as a lens through which they read upcoming text (and reread previously read text). Then they will approach Wednesday's conversation ready to dig deeper.

Note that although children may be reading, say, Chapters 6 or 7 of a book, they aren't writing "all about Chapters 6 and 7." That sort of writing assignment inevitably leads them to skim the surface of the chapters they have read. Instead, they may be reading Chapters 6 and 7, but they are writing about Chapters 1–7 and drawing in any books they have read previously that relate to the topic at hand. This is especially important, because to use almost any skill well, readers need to synthesize. You do not want readers reading with blinders on, thinking only about the text that is before their eyes. Instead, you want them to regularly think between part and whole.

There are other ways to lift the level of club conversations, and one is to consider the issue of who talks and who doesn't talk. I want to caution you against focusing on this to the exclusion of everything else. The work I've described earlier in this chapter will lift the level of conversations more dramatically than will your work with this topic. I also want to caution you against jumping in to quiet your most dominant voices. Presumably, there will be a child or two in each club that carries a lot of the conversational ball for that club, and there will probably be another reader or two who is quiet. Your instinct may be to stop the club and talk to the dominant member about how that child needs to talk less, give others a turn, and so forth. But don't have that discussion in front of the other club members, because if you do, whenever that dominant child speaks, the other club members are likely to roll their eyes, feeling righteously indignant about the one child's dominance. The problem is that this child is not only the dominant speaker, but she is probably also the strongest club member. The club needs her ideas and energy and enthusiasm, because that can lift the level of the entire club. The last thing you want is for that child to essentially have her legs cut out from underneath her by you teaching her club mates to discount what she says.

I suggest that you work with that dominant club member away from the others. Find a way to signal to her that she is again talking too much, taking up too much air space. Perhaps you'll put a finger alongside your nose as a special code that says, "Back down a bit." But also, you can channel that child's enthusiasm to help bring out the quiet voices in the club—and that is work that the whole club can talk about together. Usually we find that one of the problems for quieter children is that the talk gets going fast and furious, and they find it hard to follow the conversation and to fashion an idea worth sharing while the conversation is unfolding at a breakneck speed. So suggest that the conversation usually begin with an idea that one of the quiet voices brings forward. This guarantees that the talk involves that reader, because the idea that is in play was originally his. Yet the quiet voice is able to talk about a thought that he had time to fashion.

Your club can also resolve to take special care of the quiet voices. If one of those readers does speak, it is especially important that no one jump in too quickly, stepping on the heels of what that reader has to say. Instead, let there be a little pool of silence after that reader says something, and perhaps, even, another reader can help the child say more. "Can you explain what you mean? Can you show us a place in the book that made you think that?" Very often we have found that after one of the quieter students in a club or a class speaks, other quiet students follow suit. Club members can let that happen.

WAYS TO TEACH INTO CLUB CONVERSATIONS

While clubs are underway, there are three main ways to teach into them. You can temporarily join a club, functioning as a proficient partner. You can whisper lean prompts into the club, hoping to lift the level of what club members do. Or you can pause the club, do a bit of research on some of your conjectures, and then intervene to give a compliment and a teaching point.

Let's imagine, for example, that a particular club is talking about a biography of Benjamin Franklin, and it seems like the club members don't have the timeline of his life straight. You wonder if one reason may be that the club uses vague references, talking about "this guy who . . ." and "that guy who . . . ," not being specific about names, places, or dates. You also note that club members don't seem to register confusion, so they let people get away with saying things that make little sense.

If you are functioning as a proficient partner, you essentially want to join the club and do the work that a really good club member/reader would do. You aren't going to ask questions, trying to lead other kids to do as you hope they do, but instead, you yourself will carry the ball, for at least a bit of the conversation. So, for example, you might say, "Can I join as a member of the group?" and then you listen for a little bit. Then you say, "You know, I'm not sure about the rest of you, but I'm thinking that I don't have Ben Franklin's life story straight. I am confused about when he did what, and when other people came into his life. Could we make a timeline of his life?" Then drawing a large timeline, you say, "Let me look back for a sec' and see when he was born." You do that, adding it to the timeline. "And remember that school he went to? We should add that here, and the date."

At this point, of course, you could shift so that you take a more backseat role. You could literally leave this group now, saying, "Geez, this is so interesting. I wish I could stay and figure out the rest of that timeline, but I gotta check on the other groups." Or you could simply pass the pen to someone else.

Alternatively, you could listen until someone said something especially vague. The speaker says, "That guy, he, he, he's always doing stuff, like how he invented all kinds of things." At that point, you could whisper in to someone else in the group, saying, "Did you understand what Gerald just said? Do you even know who 'that guy' is?" The youngster will probably shrug and shake his head. So then you could say, "Ask him. Say, 'Can you slow down and explain what you mean? Who is 'that guy'?"

Then again, you can intervene in a manner that resembles research. After listening for a bit, you could say, "Readers, can I stop you?" Once all the children are with you, you'll want to interview them to learn more. "I'm trying to understand a bit about how your club usually works. What would you say is the big goal that you're trying to accomplish right now in your talk?" You'd want to know if the club members were aiming to get the actual content of the whole biography in mind; their talk was mostly literal. "How is it going for you?" you could ask, and see if they had any unease that you could build from.

In any case, at some point you might want to provide some support and some next steps. "I want to applaud you for talking about the whole timeline of the biography, about the basics of Benjamin Franklin's life. Lots of kids just jump to little intriguing parts, but you recognize that first you really need to wrap your mental arms around the who, where, when, and why of this. Good decision." Then you could shift to the tip. As always, it helps to ask permission to give a tip. "Do you mind if I give you two tips about how you could do this work better? Is now a good time to do that?"

Your tips might be that when the basic timeline of a book feels complicated, it can help to almost build a concrete model of the text. You could suggest that the club, in those instances, might work to construct a timeline—in which case you'd be back where you would have been had you entered as a proficient partner. You could also point out that as kids work together to construct a timeline, it helps for them to be more vigilant and to ask, "What do you mean?" or to say, "Can you explain?" when people say things that don't make sense.

Four Easy Ways to Get Clubs Started in Your Classroom

If you worry that clubs won't go well in your classroom and you want to give yourself and your students some scaffolded ways to get them up and going, know that many other teachers have felt the same thing and invented ways to do that work. It helps to think about all the things that make clubs challenging and to think about how you can reduce some of those challenges early on.

Clubs Can Be Challenging Because . . .

- You expect kids to read and write at home; if they don't, the club falls apart.
- You expect kids to read and recall the text enough to talk about it.
- You expect kids to figure out the topic they want to discuss (choosing good ones).
- You expect kids to sustain conversation with each other.
- You expect kids to generate ideas worth discussing.
- You expect clubs to be able to carry on with independence.

You can easily reduce any or all of those challenges as a prelude to your first full-fledged club unit. For example, you might have in mind that you'll soon begin historical fiction clubs, and you even know who you anticipate will work in which club. You could start children off by asking them to sit in those configurations during the whole-class read-aloud—but for now, say nothing about your ultimate plan. Just refer to these as read-aloud clubs. Then read aloud, and when you pause at choice spots, instead of saying "Turn and talk" and channeling kids to talk in pairs, you can channel children to talk with their read-aloud club members. Whereas this might have been a two- or three-minute interval prior to now, you can suggest that the conversations become a bit longer.

Think about how many of the challenges this reduces. There is no longer a worry that some readers won't have worked at home enough that they are prepared for the conversation—everyone will have just heard the text. You can also select talking points in the text that you know will pay off. You could even get the groups started on those conversations, perhaps posing a big alternative for them to think about and discuss.

FIG. 11–2

Then, too, you can listen and watch for how club members get along and alter the social groupings if you need to do so, doing this prior to kids getting going in their own clubs.

If you want to give your read-aloud clubs more independence, you could pause midway through the novel to brainstorm some major topics that are worth thinking and talking about more extensively, and then each club could take on one of those topics as a lens. When a class of fifth-graders did this midway through *Out of the Dust*, for example, one group decided to track and think deeply about Billie Jo's relationship with her father, while another decided to think about the role that music plays throughout the story. The teacher, reading aloud, could signal "listen up," to different groups as she read different parts of the text, but each club sustained its own conversation. Of course, there were times when one club would carry on their conversation while others listened, and then the teacher would say to the other clubs, "Will you and your club now talk about how the things you just overheard relate to the topic you are following."

There are completely different ways to scaffold book clubs. For example, you might decide that the first few days of book clubs might involve discussing short texts only, and those texts are read in school. Then again,

you might launch your entire class in independent reading, and start one book club for students who seemed especially ready for that social structure. You could then help that club get off to a good start, and when you are ready to launch the second club, you could send those youngsters to study the first to anticipate how their club would work. Because you start only one club at a time, you will be able to provide training wheels for those clubs until they gather their own momentum.

Book clubs are not easy work. It takes time and practice for students to engage in thought-provoking and meaningful conversations about a shared text. Taking the time to help readers before clubs even begin will have huge payoffs in the end. Once clubs do start meeting, it is important that teachers take the time to engage in deep and honest inquiry, asking, "What exactly is happening with these book clubs?" Of course, you'll use the data you gather to decide how you'll support and coach that group of readers. Taking the time to assess, rebuild, and rebalance the teaching of reading through book clubs will ensure that your students are learning how to talk about ideas, to change minds, to hold fast opinions, to listen, and to learn.

Chapter 12

Reading Aloud
The Heart of the Reading Workshop

READING ALOUD is the best way we have to immerse children in the glories of reading, showing them both how and why one reads. "Great literature, if we read it well," Donald Hall has said, "opens us to the world and makes us more sensitive to it, as if we acquired eyes that could see through things and ears that could hear smaller sounds." Together with our children, we gulp down stories—stories that allow us to thunder across the finish line at the Kentucky Derby, to live in a thatched hut, and work at the mill. We construct knowledge about weather forecasting and assemble a mental model of a weather station. Together with our children we experience what it means to lose —and to find—ourselves in a story, in history. Word by word, chapter by chapter, we are led into another time and another place and another field of study.

Paradoxically, we are at the same time led deeper into our own lives. We read *Charlotte's Web* and weep as Wilbur the pig comes to realize that "friendship is one of the most satisfying things in the world." We talk and talk and through the talk come to understand that Charlotte's generosity has been as good for her as it has been for Wilbur. "By helping you perhaps I was trying to lift my life a little. Anyone's life can stand a little of that."

"Read to them," Cynthia Rylant says. "Take their breath away. Read with the same feeling in your throat as when you first see the ocean after driving hours and hours to get there. Close the final page of the book with the same reverence you feel when you kiss your sleeping child at night. Be quiet. Don't talk the experience to death. Shut up and let those kids think and feel. Teach your children to be moved."

We read not only because it is good for our children as readers, but also because it is good for all of us as people. I think, for example, of a teacher in Queens whose classroom was one of those rooms where everything seemed to be done perfectly well, but there just was no chemistry. The teacher had a lovely author's chair at the front of her meeting area, lovely charts around her room, a daily reading workshop and writing workshop, but it often seemed like her children were going through the motions when they were reading and writing.

Then one day, when the Teachers College Reading and Writing Project staff developer arrived in this teacher's room, everything was utterly different. The room was charged with energy and intensity. During writing workshop, kids were pouring their hearts out onto the paper, and during reading the room felt brim full of care and investment. "What happened?" my colleague asked.

The teacher nodded, knowingly. "Can you believe it?" she said, scanning the room.

"What'd you do?" my colleague asked, big-eyed with amazement.

"We read together," the teacher said. "That's all. We read sad, sad stories, like *A Taste of Blackberries* and *Bridge to Terabithia*." Then she said, "I think I'd been pretending that stories have happy endings. Reading those sad books, it tapped into the pain in children's lives and in mine. I started telling the children about how my parents are moving and it's killing me. I told them about all my years of plastic surgery on my face and how I always thought I was ugly, and they started telling me their stories, too, and writing them."

A young boy had written about seeing his father go into diabetic shock, and a little girl had written about seeing her father released from jail and how she hugged him and he hugged her and "it is like the greatest love of all."

How powerful it is to read aloud, right smack in the midst of the hopes and heartaches of a classroom, amid friendships that form and dissolve, invitations that come and do not come, clothes that are in or out of fashion, and parents who attend or do not attend the school play. Here, children work out their life and death issues. Doing so with books at their side is a way to help them make sense of it all. Ralph Peterson, author of *Life in a Crowded Place* (1992) suggests that we respond to the challenges of elbow-to-elbow classroom living by using ceremony, ritual, and celebration to create a sense of community in the classroom, and he further suggests that one way to create that sense of community is to read aloud poems and stories as a way to cross the threshold, to mark the classroom as a world apart. It may be that every day the class joins into a shared reading, perhaps of a poem such as Shel Silverstein's "Invitation," which invites dreamers into the circle. As the poet Julius Lester says, literature can "link our souls like pearls on a string, bringing us together in a shared and luminous humanity."

And so we read aloud. We read aloud several times a day; we read to greet the day, to bring a social studies inquiry to life, to learn about molecules or gravity, and to fall through the rabbit hole of story.

CHOOSING TEXTS TO READ ALOUD

So how does one choose the texts to read aloud? My advice is this: choose carefully. Spend your summer reading one book, another, and another and mulling over your decisions. Think about texts that will open up new topics for your class, turning your students into scientists, historians, anthropologists. Think about the texts that will bring your class together—to laugh together, to be outraged together, to cry together. Think about books that are more complex than those readers can read on their own, books that can take your children toward more complex understanding of characters or settings or issues.

But think, too, about books that match those that your kids who struggle with reading are reading. By reading a book such as George and Martha aloud, you use reading aloud and grand conversations to elevate the books and the authors that are fundamental in the reading lives of some of your students who struggle with reading. When you read one of these "simpler" books, emphasize the way the books make you think and think and think, perhaps saying something such as "I want to read to you one of my all-time favorite books. It's a story that can really make you think, so turn your brains on to high and get ready." If you follow that with a reading of Poppleton or a Pinky and Rex book or Katherine Paterson's *The Smallest Cow in the World*, you will have made an important statement.

As you mull over your choice of books, you'll want to consider the length of books. Chances are good that you might want to read aloud powerful, complicated books such as *The Great Gilly Hopkins*, *Bud, not Buddy*, or one of the Narnia books, and if you make reading aloud a mainstay in your classroom, by all means turn to books such as these. But if you tend to have a bit of trouble actually finding twenty to thirty minutes a day for reading aloud, then you'll want to opt for shorter books such as *The Hundred Dresses* or *My Name Is Maria Isabel* because you won't want your read-aloud to drag on over too many days.

It's helpful to think about the band of text difficulty within which most of your children tend to be reading (or will soon be reading) and to make sure that for a fair proportion of the year you are reading aloud from within that band. I describe these bands of text difficulty in more detail in *Reading Pathways*, but for now let me simply say that the challenges readers will tend to encounter when reading level K, L, and M books will be different than those they'll encounter when reading level N–Q books, and those are different than those readers will tend to encounter when reading level R–T books, and those are different than readers will encounter when reading level U–V books. For example, if your read-alouds tend to be books from within the level U+ bands of text difficulty, as you read aloud, you and your children will need to spend a fair amount of time wrestling with subplots, with gaps in time, and with shifts in perspective. Readers will often know more than the characters themselves. If your children are meanwhile reading mostly in the level N–Q band of text difficulty, the challenges they'll need mentoring with will be more like those involved in understanding that the main character is not just one way and learning to notice ways the character changes from the beginning to end, often by resolving some of her ambivalence. Granted, you will often want reading aloud to invite children into heady intellectual work, and more complex books are especially supportive of that work, so you won't want to limit yourself to only reading aloud books that are similar to those your children can read, but there will be advantages to some alignment.

Then, too, you'll need to think about the relationship between your read-aloud books, your reading units of study, and your content area units as well. Think about the relationship between the read-aloud and your units not only in topic, but also in place. If you weave a chapter book and a shorter text or two into a reading unit, building many of your minilessons around that text, as we tend to do, your read-aloud of that chapter book will probably be held in check by the fact that particular parts of the book will be aligned to lessons you want to teach—and those lessons sometimes require prior work. And so, for example, in the historical fiction unit, it takes a week between the day we read aloud the first page of *Number the Stars* and the day we start Chapter 4 because of the amount of teaching opportunities (minilesson opportunities) that are too good to miss in those first chapters. In an instance such as this, you will presumably want to maintain a second read-aloud.

When you choose books for nonfiction read-aloud, choose these with equal care. Often, it's helpful to assemble a text set, so that your read-aloud work will lead and mirror the work that you want children to do in their own texts. For example, if your children are going to be reading texts to construct an argument, you'll want to have a collection of texts on a topic that the whole class will engage with during your minilessons, as a way to anchor the unit. You'll want to launch the unit with one or two texts that support both sides of

an argument. These should be texts you can return to across the unit, so they need to be engaging enough that students can glean information from them quickly, yet well written enough that you can return to them later to study their language and structure.

When you read nonfiction aloud, remember to attend to your tone of voice and body language, just as you do when you read fiction. Watch some great nonfiction videos, such as the "Planet Earth" series, and listen to that "newscaster" or "nature specialist" tone of voice, which imbues great drama into even a flight of geese. Just as you use your voice to help children follow a story, you can use your voice to help them follow meaning in nonfiction. You can also exaggerate your own response to the content of what you are reading, giving a kind of "Wow, can you believe that?" expression, or a "Hmm, what does *that* mean?" look, to show your children what engaged readers look like as well as sound like. Children need us to make nonfiction as engaging as fiction, and read-aloud is your chance to really bring that sense of avid curiosity to life.

When I'm considering texts, I try to choose texts that are well written as well as informative, both so kids will fall in love with nonfiction, and so that if I decide to study perspective, or interesting craft or structure, the text is rich enough to reward these lenses. I also think about how I will layer texts in my read-aloud so that we build toward complexity. Children sometimes read nonfiction a level below the level at which they read fiction, so I try to begin with fascinating and accessible texts and gradually lead into more challenging ones. Most importantly, I look at my read-aloud texts and compare them to the texts children will be reading, and I double-check that the texts pose similar challenges. This mirroring of text complexity accomplishes two things. It means that I can return to these texts during my minilessons, and my read-aloud text will allow me to teach into these challenges. It also means that the work we do during read-aloud will either foreshadow or give children extra practice with work they need to do in their own texts.

For both fiction and nonfiction texts, we make clear suggestions for texts to anchor these units. Of course, you can choose other texts. Just remember that these text selections were strategic, and the order of the minilessons often mirrors the way these texts unfold. If your texts unfold differently, you may need to reconsider this order, which introduces other issues as the lessons build on each other. All completely solvable, especially if you enjoy unit planning, but it's just something to keep in mind.

USING THE READ-ALOUD TO TEACH THE SKILLS OF PROFICIENT READING

In the classrooms I know best, although texts are read aloud throughout the day for multiple purposes, there is one time, several days a week, that children refer to as read-aloud time, and this is an instructional, interactive read-aloud. This is often at an entirely different time than the reading workshop—perhaps after lunch or at the end of the day—and it generally lasts at least twenty minutes and usually more like half an hour.

The book that is weaving its way in and out of a unit of study is sometimes read aloud during this time, with the teacher pacing that read-aloud so as not to read past the portion of the book needed for an upcoming minilesson. Other times, other texts are read aloud—a second chapter book that may be woven through the unit and other texts of all lengths and all sorts.

Spy on Yourself while Reading

To plan your read-aloud, you need first to read the book (or the portion of the book) that you will be reading aloud to your children and spy on the work that you do as you read the text. Ideally, you'll do this in the company of some colleagues, and you'll note the work that each one of you does. In this way, you'll cumulate ideas for the reading work that portion of the text supports, and you'll form a consensus about some of the especially essential work.

Let's imagine, then, that you were going to read aloud the first chapter of E. B. White's classic, *Charlotte's Web*. You may have read the book before, but you'd try to resurrect a "first" reading. You begin reading:

> "Where's Papa going with that ax?" said Fern to her mother as they were setting the table for breakfast.
>
> "Out to the hoghouse," replied Mrs. Arable. "Some pigs were born last night."
>
> "I don't see why he needs an ax," continued Fern, who was only eight.
>
> "Well," said her mother, "one of the pigs is a runt. It's very small and weak, and it will never amount to anything. So your father has decided to do away with it."
>
> "Do *away* with it?" shrieked Fern. "You mean *kill* it? Just because it's smaller than the others?"
>
> Mrs. Arable put a pitcher of cream on the table. "Don't yell, Fern!" she said. "Your father is right. The pig would probably die anyway."

You and your colleagues might pause for a moment to come up with a list of ideas for the reading work, such as this:

- **Envisioning.** The story begins in action and dialogue. We might cue children in that when stories start this way, readers are expected to envision who is talking and what is happening. We might elaborate by pointing that right from the start of a book, readers are alert to the fact that characters have different voices, different speaking styles. Part of envisioning is constructing the soundtrack of a story, and this involves hearing characters' distinct voices.

- **Character.** The story presents a problem at its very outset: a runty pig is going to be killed, and a little eight-year-old girl is upset—even outraged. She confronts her mother. We might decide to let children know that because we know how stories tend to go, we approach a story

FIG. 12–1

looking for what the main characters want and for what gets into their way. This sets kids up to think that the tension in this scene may well underlie the story. We pay attention to problems that could be central to a story, and in this instance we are wondering about whether this pig will die or be saved. We can also point out that we look for clues to help us answer a question such as that, and in this instance, the picture of a beaming pig on the cover of the story hints that this pig will not only live, but will probably be featured as a main character.

You and your colleagues continue reading a bit further into the chapter, thinking about the essential work that children will do.

"Please don't kill it!" she sobbed. "It's unfair."

Mr. Arable stopped walking.

"Fern," he said gently, "you will have to learn to control yourself."

"Control myself?" yelled Fern. "This is a matter of life and death, and you talk about *controlling* myself." Tears ran down her cheeks and she took hold of the ax and tried to pull it out of her father's hand.

"Fern," said Mr. Arable, "I know more about raising a litter of pigs than you do. A weakling makes trouble. Now run along!"

"But it's unfair," cried Fern. "The pig couldn't help being born small, could it? If I had been very small at birth, would you have killed *me*?"

You and your colleagues might pause once again to add to your list of ideas for the reading work students will do in this section:

- **Setting.** We might teach children that readers pick up clues to figure out the setting. There's mention of a hog house and a pitcher of cream being set on the table, so readers might guess that this opening scene is set in the kitchen of a farmhouse. We could point out that readers often need to construct their own sense of the setting, because a book might not come right out and name it. You might note that there are places in the chapter that give readers a rich sensory image of the setting—passages such as "Fern pushed a chair out of the way and ran outdoors. The grass was wet and the earth smelled of springtime. Fern's sneakers were sopping by the time she caught up with her father."

- **Interpretation.** We might use this read-aloud as an opportunity to teach kids that we don't wait until the end of a book to interpret. We

approach a book, thinking, "Might this teach readers about . . . ?" At the outset, we get an inkling that this story might advocate a humane treatment of animals or that it might deal with issues of justice. We could set readers up to view upcoming text with this lens to see if this will be a recurring theme. Could this book be about standing up for what one thinks is right? Could it be about bringing about a change by taking action?

You and your colleagues continue reading, building your consensus of the essential work that the text asks readers to do.

Mr. Arable smiled. "Certainly not," he said, looking down at his daughter with love. "But this is different. A little girl is one thing, a little runty pig is another."

"I see no difference," replied Fern, still hanging on to the ax. "This is the most terrible case of injustice I ever heard of."

A queer look came over John Arable's face. He seemed almost ready to cry himself.

"All right," he said. "You go back to the house and I will bring the runt when I come in. I'll let you start it on a bottle, like a baby. Then you'll see what trouble a pig can be."

Choose the Skills to Teach

After (or before) spying on yourself to see the work that you tend to do as you read the passage, you need to decide on the purpose of this read-aloud. While reading those five or six pages, you will have envisioned, predicted, monitored for sense, made personal responses, asked questions, inferred, developed theories about the characters, and interpreted. So you'll need to decide which sequence of work the read-aloud will bring readers along, so that you can demonstrate those skills and channel readers to use those skills themselves, first with more and then with less scaffolding. In many ways, this process is similar to riding a bicycle, which also requires the seamless integration of many different actions. A biker pedals, steers, balances, distributes his weight on a slope, monitors speed and momentum, and occasionally brakes. Yet while teaching someone to ride a bike, you would support a few of these actions yourself so that the learner need only focus on a handful of skills at any given time.

With training wheels, you take balance and weight distribution *off* the instructional radar completely so learners can focus on pedaling and steering—and ringing the bell. Teaching reading, in many ways, is no different than teaching swimming or dance or tennis or painting. When any of these activities are done proficiently, the effect is that of effortless synchronization, but to the practicing novice, it is easier to focus on a small cluster of related skills, learning to achieve the fluidity or fluency with those skills before adding on other new skills.

When you do teach three or four reading skills at a time, you might attempt passing the read-aloud text through the sieve of just these skills. That is, even though reading a text as rich as *Charlotte's Web* will often lure you into focusing on envisioning, interpretation, critical thinking, and empathy—often all on the same page—if your instructional aim at a given time is to support envisioning, synthesis, and growing theories about characters, then you'll presumably prepare for teaching by again spying on yourself as you read the text, this time highlighting those skills.

Spy on Yourself as a Reader Again, with Particular Skills in Mind

Let's imagine how this might go. Suppose you decide that on this particular day during the read-aloud, you want to teach synthesizing and developing theories about characters. You'd spy on your own reading, noting the thoughts you have when you read to develop a theory about a character and also how you *synthesize* this theory across the book.

To begin, you might point out to students as you read aloud that when you are hoping to grow theories about characters, readers note their reactions to each new character as she is introduced. When Charlotte the spider enters the story, calling out a friendly "Salutations!" from her web in the barn door to Wilbur, the pig in the manure pile below, Wilbur has no idea who Charlotte is at this point and neither do we.

Wilbur jumped to his feet. "Salu-*what*?" he cried.

You might set the book down for just a second and mention, "When a new character enters the scene, there's always the question on my radar: 'Is this a goodie or a baddie? Is this character a hero or a villain?'" You read on with a kind of bated breath, checking your intuitions, noting little clues that the text provides.

"Salutations are greetings," said the voice, ". . . it's just my fancy way of saying hello . . ."
At last Wilbur saw the creature that had spoken to him in such a kindly way.

You pluck out the word *kindly* and use it to begin creating the picture of Charlotte in your mind: kind, quirky, has a peculiar way to greet people.

"My name," said the spider, "is Charlotte."
"Charlotte what?" asked Wilbur eagerly.
"Charlotte A. Cavatica. But just call me Charlotte."

The more Charlotte talks, the more this canvas fills up, because she has such voice, such presence. "I think I like her," you say to yourself. Then you hear Charlotte describing herself:

"Well I *am* pretty," replied Charlotte. "There's no denying that. Almost all spiders are rather nice-looking. I'm not as flashy as some. But I'll do."

"Quite a personality," you think as you read. "She's not entirely immodest, because she admits that there are spiders flashier than she is, but she *is* confident and assertive. Knows how to take a compliment, too!" Though you're having this thought silently as you read quietly, you might say it out loud, as an aside, during your read-aloud. Then you slip back into reading in Charlotte's voice:

"I wish I could see you, Wilbur, as clearly as you can see me."
"Why can't you?" asked the pig. "I'm right here."
"Yes but I'm near-sighted. I've always been dreadfully near-sighted."

Now you're developing a theory about Charlotte, about a character. Because you're using this specific sieve as you read, filtering out only the skill that you want to highlight—that is, developing a theory about a character—you're allowing other "teachable points" to fall away. Note that you're making no effort to offer any *predictions*, though you may have a few predictions up your sleeve. Nor will you alert yourself to how you're *monitoring* for comprehension here. And by no means will you pick up on how E. B. White, in making this spider spunky and beautiful, defies familiar spider stereotypes where they fall out of dusty cobwebs in dark haunted houses, inspiring shrill, terrified shrieks from hysterical arachnophobes. You might reserve that observation for when you use this text to teach *critical reading*. For the moment, stick solely to highlighting the specific skills you want to teach—developing theories about a character and synthesis.

At this point, you haven't accumulated enough information about Charlotte yet to *synthesize*, but that work is about to follow. Though first impressions often endure, you know that developing a theory about a character across the story arc will usually require readers to *revise* their first impressions as the character reveals greater nuance, depth, and complexity. As new information about the character piles up, you'll want readers to retain and revise the old. And so it is with deliberateness that you read this following new thing about the likeable Charlotte:

> "Watch me wrap up this fly."
> A fly that had been crawling along Wilbur's trough had flown up and blundered into the lower parts of Charlotte's web and was tangled in the sticky threads. The fly was beating its wings furiously, trying to break loose and free itself.
> "First," said Charlotte, "I dive at him . . . Next I wrap him up. . . ." Wilbur watched in horror. He could hardly believe what he was seeing . . . although he detested flies, he felt sorry for this one. . . .
> "You mean you *eat* flies?" gasped Wilbur.
> "Certainly . . . Of course I don't really eat them. I drink them—drink their blood. I love blood," said Charlotte, and her pleasant, thin voice grew even thinner and more pleasant.

If you, like me, are mesmerized by how the spunky, likeable spider is now shown to be a darker, more sinister queen of the web, you will flag this part. If there had been background music to this reading, it would have switched at the point where Charlotte says, "I love blood."

> "Don't say that," groaned Wilbur. "Please don't say things like that!" . . . He was sad because his new friend was so bloodthirsty.

This is the perfect chance to teach that readers *synthesize* their theory of a character based on the changing, occasionally conflicting information they receive about a character. You'll want to bring this up in your think-aloud when you're reading to the children. Then again, you may decide that you have set students up well enough that they can, with your support, do this thinking on their own.

In this way, continue to go through the read-aloud text armed with tiny Post-its or flags, and perhaps a pencil, to enter small instructional think-alouds in the margins. You can sift through the upcoming text with the same sieve, picking up and marking off the parts that will further synthesize this developing theory of who Charlotte is. Along the way, you'll have important teaching points to insert. You might tell kids, "Even though she's good and noble, she's complicated. Characters aren't just one way." "Readers constantly revise their first impression of a character to reach a more complete picture."

You'll know that you've picked the text well if the upcoming story supports the work you're trying to do. A page or two later:

> Wilbur lay down and closed his eyes . . . "Charlotte is fierce, brutal, scheming, bloodthirsty—everything I don't like. How can I learn to like her, even though she is pretty and of course, clever?"
> Wilbur was merely suffering the doubts and fears that often go with finding a new friend. In good time he was to discover that he was mistaken about Charlotte. Underneath her rather bold and cruel exterior, she had a kind heart, and she was to prove loyal and true to the very end.

You might use a special new sticky flag to mark this part. "Characters are complicated!" You'll remember to nod, when reading this. In this way, as Charlotte goes through her short life, weaving miracles of literacy with her spinnerets, you'll follow her alertly with a pencil so that when you read aloud her story to children, they'll have synthesized a theory about who she is and use her as a reference point to understand the scores of *other* characters they'll read about on their own.

Read-alouds are an enormously powerful tool in teaching reading because they dramatize—and therefore make visible—the internal work of proficient reading. Step into classrooms where read-alouds occur, and you'll see that the most rapt audience belongs to the teacher who can muster up the greatest drama. This teacher will often alternate between voices and even accents, so you know which character is talking, turning squeaky one second, adopting a baritone in the next. Goose will have her own fast-talking, phrase-repeating speaking style, and Templeton the rat will be decidedly nasal. When Charlotte tiredly announces that she won't be returning to Zuckerman's farm, this reading teacher's voice will turn quiet and her shoulders will droop. When Thing One and Thing Two run around with a kite that goes bump thump, thump bump, her voice too will race with all the adrenaline that Seuss unleashes in that tale. Much like Oscar-deserving actors, therefore, teachers who read aloud most effectively adopt the characteristics of their character—*become* their character and enter the story.

READING ALOUD ACROSS THE CURRICULUM

What a powerful tool this is to bring to science! To social studies. To history. Narrative reading can be exhilaratingly close to actually experiencing, and this is true for narrative nonfiction as well as for fiction. Children learn that they can climb into the character or subject, whether that is a caterpillar as it eats its way out of its cocoon to become a butterfly, experiencing the thrill of metamorphosis, or George Washington, gathering his weary troops on a wintry Christmas morning, trying to inspire the men to stay with him. You can expect that the child who can stand with other soldiers on that snowy battlefield, who can climb aboard a red blood cell to ride the roller coaster of arteries and veins, will be an avid reader.

You'll certainly want to bring this magic to expository nonfiction as well as to narrative nonfiction. There are few ways more effective in demonstrating that expository and narrative texts sound, feel, and are structured differently than reading these different kinds of texts out loud. In fact, you can actually read expository texts aloud in ways that highlight specific text structures, where you might state the *boxes* in a stronger tone and proceed to count out *bullets* on your fingers. Or, while reading, you might motion one way and another with a hand, wherever similarities and differences are being enumerated. You might read aloud a part and then stop to restate its main idea to the side.

Then again, if your instructional focus is on synthesis and retelling, you might say, as you read aloud, "Let's listen to this next part and see if it adds onto what we just learned or if it is a whole new thing." After reading a bit, you could pause, externalizing the reasons for pausing: "Let's pause. I do that when I'm reading expository nonfiction and my mind is full, don't you? Let's see if we can collect what we have learned so far."

MAKING READ-ALOUD MORE INTERACTIVE

Reading aloud in a way that is spellbinding is an acquired talent, one that requires practice and planning. The teachers who are best at the art don't need to rehearse the thump-bump scary parts, the balloon-floating happy parts, and the slow, sad, knot-in-the-throat parts. Their reading aloud is an extension of their reading itself. These teachers use their hands, their eyes, their posture, their voices, and their hearts. But no matter how thrilling the dramatic impersonation is, to optimize instructional potential, it is important to provide children with the chance and space to actually respond to the texts you read aloud to them.

Imagine for a minute that someone was teaching you to drive. There is something to be said for getting into a moving car with a proficient driver, hearing a steady commentary on why he's choosing to brake, why he's accelerating just so during an overtake, and what he'd do at a busy roundabout. The next step, however, is for you to actually take your *own* spot behind that wheel, for you to actually have your proficient driver egging you on with advice and encouragement when you enter the traffic flow on our first busy roundabout. A read-aloud accompanied by your out-loud thinking might serve as a great demonstration, but instruction requires the learner's active involvement.

To pass the baton to children, you'll go from pausing to think aloud yourself to becoming adept at saying, "Stop and think" and then leaving a pool of silence, or saying "What are you thinking? Turn and talk," sending children into partnership conversations. Sometimes, instead of saying "Turn and talk," you'll say "Stop and jot," and duck your head to do this while others do as well. Of course, there are many variations on these prompts. Instead of saying "Stop and think," you can say, for example, "Oh my gosh, what's going to happen next? Predict, will you? Make a movie in your mind of what will happen next." Then, after the pool of silence, "Let's read and find out." That is, any of the prompts can be made more specific. "Stop and jot" could be "Stop and jot. What's this *really* about?" or "Stop and summarize. What's happened so far?" Still, the three main invitations you'll give will be to think, to talk, and to write.

Each of these three prompts invites children to develop and articulate their own independent response to the text, and each does this in a different way. Silent thinking is the most introspective of the three methods and is perfectly suited for especially moving or poignant parts. The turn-and-talk incorporates a social element, allowing peers to model, imitate, or reinforce each other's ways of responding to text. The stop-and-jot differs from a written response by allowing children just a moment in which to scribble a few words, quickly catching the images or thoughts that bubble to the surface of their minds before they're dragged back into the flow of the continuing read-aloud.

When you plan, then, you'll think about not just the specific skills that you'll teach during a read-aloud and not just the *points* at which you'll nudge children into responding, but also about the various ways to scaffold their response—through silence, through talk, or through pencil and paper.

Of course, there will be days when you pause more or less or not at all. Indeed there will be days—and books—that remind you of Cynthia Rylant's advice to end with quiet reverence, to "be quiet" and not "talk the experience to death." There will be other days and books that will invite, almost beg, questions, discussions, and hot debate. You and your children will decide which those days and books are for your community. The best thing about a read-aloud is that it can be tailored to fit time, need, and instructional agenda; when done often and done well, it can be the binding cement that holds your community of readers together.

SUPPORTING A WHOLE-CLASS GRAND CONVERSATION

When you finish reading for the day (and sometimes in the midst of a day's reading), you'll want to support your children in talking together as a class about the text. You'll use those whole-class conversations as opportunities to teach children to grow ideas about texts, to hold themselves accountable to what the text actually says, to mine passages of the text for meanings that may not at first be apparent, to think across texts, and to use their higher-level comprehension skills to comprehend with depth, harvesting all the insights and feelings, understandings, and knowledge that the texts can yield. These conversations are enormously important. If I had more time, I'd write one more book for the series —one that supported reading aloud and whole-class conversations.

For now, let me tell you how I tend to launch whole-class conversations early in the year. I read aloud a chapter, pausing half a dozen times to think aloud for a few sentences. Perhaps once or twice I pause to support children in thinking to themselves about something I got them started thinking about. Then I suggest they talk to a partner ("Turn and talk.") before I resume reading.

I come to the end of the chapter. At this point, I'll need to decide whether I want to channel the conversation in a particular direction or let the children develop an idea. Let's imagine that I choose the latter alternative, as I'm prone to do. I'll probably close the final page of the chapter and say, "Oh my gosh, my mind is on fire. Isn't yours? So many thoughts right now. Whoa! Turn and tell your partner what *you're* thinking. Go!"

The room will erupt into conversation, and as the children talk, I crouch among them, listening in. Frankly, I'm hoping to overhear a child who is full of an idea that I believe will pay off easily in a whole-class conversation, but I don't let on. Just to let you in on all my secrets, I confess that there have been times when I enter into a peer conversation and get a couple of kids going on a question or an idea that I'm all excited about. If the children have two or three minutes to talk about that idea, I know I can call on them to share their thinking, and the origins of the thinking will have slipped from their minds.

In any case, after children talk for a few minutes, I convene their attention and start the whole-class conversation with an invitation that will become part of the fabric of the classroom. "Who can get us started in a conversation? Who's got an idea to put on the table?" (There is not really a table—we're just sitting in a bunch.)

Later, I may take the time to put a magnifying lens up to this particular juncture, showing children how to sift through their various thoughts to find a thought that is (as my colleague Donna Santman likes to say) provocative, compelling, and central to the text. It is, after all, worthwhile to teach readers to pause a bit and think, "Will this thought that I have pay off? Will it be an important one to develop?" If readers become skilled at this, their conversations about books will head toward interesting terrain—as will their writing and thinking about books. But if they have trouble getting started in lines of thought that will pay off, I might step in to teach them some universal questions that almost always work when we're thinking about a text.

Questions Readers Ask of Fiction

- **Is this a journey?** So many books are, so it is interesting to think if this book qualifies as a journey. If so, who is traveling, and where? Is it an external journey, or is it also an internal journey? Will the protagonist end up where she started or somewhere new?

- **Why did the author decide to write it this particular way?** Why is it titled this? Why might it start this way? Why might it contain whatever characteristic bits of craftsmanship it contains—such as the italics in *Baby*, the quotes from Pushkin in *Letters from Rifka*, the free verse format in *Love that Dog* and in *Home of the Brave*? How might these decisions go with what the book is really, really about?

- **What takes on special importance in this book?** An object? A place? A name? A saying? How does that object (place, name, saying) connect with what the whole book is really about?

- **What lessons does the protagonist learn?** What do I learn alongside her?

- **Think about one of the minor characters.** What role does he play in the book? Why is that character here? How would the story have been different had that character not been here?

I would rather children not reach for one of these ever-ready invitations to think, but that they listen, question, conjecture, notice, and hypothesize and that they are willing to cup their hands around a fleeting thought and to put that fleeting thought at the center of a conversation.

In any case, once I have nodded to a child who signaled with a thumbs-up that he could get a conversation started, I'll probably make sure that members of the class look at that child, giving him their attention. "All eyes on Tyrell," I might say, and signal for Tyrell to wait until he has his classmates' attention. I might also coach Tyrell to say his idea to them (not to me, not to his collar, not to a hand held over his mouth).

He puts his idea out there. Now I want the others to ponder it, and I want the idea to spark thoughts in them. I'm apt to model the way I listen deeply, taking in the idea that someone else has put onto the table. "Hmm," I say, as if the idea is a new one, dawning on me as I reflect on it. I repeat it to myself aloud, making sure that my mind is going ninety miles an hour as I think about my response to that idea. I know that children can see and feel the wheels of my brain spinning, and I know that I'll help them think in response to this idea if I actually do so as well.

If I think the children don't have much to say in response to this idea yet, I'll give them a few minutes to develop some thinking. I might say, "Let's take a second and jot our thoughts about this, okay?"

If I want to support children as they do that thinking, I might say, "Can I have a few of you jotting on white boards?" And then I can distribute small white boards to three or four children, dispersed throughout the group. That essentially makes eavesdropping inevitable. Additionally, I might say, "Can I have a few readers thinking on our easel and our big white board?" And then a couple of children can jot their thoughts on some large space at the front of the circle. Then again, I could do that myself. Or I could start jotting, and after children have started jotting, I could reread a few relevant sections of the original read-aloud passage, helping them ground their thinking in the text.

Then again, if I want to support children's thinking, I could suggest that instead of writing, they talk with each other. That means that in the end, if one of the two partners has a thought, that person can carry the other partner.

If I want to be sure their ideas are text based, I might distribute copies of a relevant passage and channel students to annotate, then to talk in pairs, linking that passage to the ongoing conversation.

In any case, I'll soon say, "Who can talk back to the idea?" and I'll reiterate the idea. The next speaker may address her comments to me, in which case I'll signal that she needs to speak to the group and to the original speaker. Now a second related idea will be on the floor. I'll probably raise my eyebrows and scan the group, asking without words for someone to add on, and when one child catches her breath like she can hardly contain the idea that has come to her, I'll try to refrain from calling on her with words, using a gesture instead. I'm hoping that before long one child will speak and another and another, without me needing to emcee the entire conversation.

This portion of the conversation, again, merits more instruction. Another time—or even this time—I'll want to help children talk back to each other. There are lots of ways I can help them with this.

Ways to Help Children Talk Back to Each Other's Ideas in a Book Talk

- I might repeat the ideas on the floor and then say, "One way to develop an idea is to say to yourself, 'I agree (or I disagree) because, for example (and then we retell a part of the story that goes with—or doesn't go with—the idea).'" Then I could say, "So pick up your pen, and let's talk on the page right now. Try writing, 'I agree/disagree because . . .' Then retell a part of the story that builds your case."

- I might say, "Readers, one way to grow an idea is to repeat it in our own words and then use a thought prompt to get ourselves to say more about it, to think more about it. Right now, I'm going to repeat the idea that is on the table right now, and then Partner 2, turn to Partner 1 and, one, repeat the idea in your own words and then, two, grab one of these thought prompts, any one, and say it next, seeing if an idea comes to you as you say that thought prompt. It might, and it might not—but try." The thought prompts could be, "This is important because . . ." or "As I say this, I realize . . ." or "The surprising thing about this is that . . ." or "This connects with . . ."

- I might say, "Get with a partner. I'm going to help you say more about this idea. Partner 1, repeat the idea, and then, after a minute, I'm

going to say something. Whatever I say—repeat it, and then keeping talking and thinking about the idea." Partner 1s could then have two minutes or so to say the idea before I call out, "In other words . . . ," and wait for Partner 1 to reiterate the idea in different words. "The interesting thing about this is . . ." "What I wonder is . . ." "One answer might be . . ."

- I might transcribe a conversation among children that jumps from topic to topic without developing any of those topics and display this to the class, suggesting we "rewind" and try again, this time using thought prompts to develop an idea before jumping to a new idea.

As the conversation unfolds, there will be other ways that I support the conversation, and all of these are "conversational moves" I might later teach children to do for themselves. So, for example, after children have talked for a bit, I might say, "We've been talking for a bit. You know how, when we read nonfiction, we read until our minds are full and then we stop and think, 'So far, what the text has said is . . . ,' and then we say it back? Well, I find that it helps to do that in a conversation, too. Let's see, so far, what we've said is . . . ," and then I say back the conversation. Of course, another time I might, at that point, suggest, "Turn to your partner, and Partner 2, say back the conversation, and Partner 1, you add in bits you remember as well." Alternatively, I might say, "We've been talking for a bit. Let's take a second to crystallize what we've said so far. Use writing to capture what the main ideas are that we've said so far." Again, I could, if I wanted to provide some scaffolds, do this myself on the easel, working alongside the others in ways that I know the kids will learn from and emulate, or I could, alternatively, say, "Partners, help each other to do this."

There are other conversational moves I'll make that I'll in the same way teach the children to make on their own:

- For example, if someone has put a theory into the air, I'm apt to say, "What do you base this on?" or "Can you show us what part of the text made you think this?"

- Later, if an idea has been stated, and no one but me seems to feel the need to ground it in a text, I might make a tiny gesture to one child, surreptitiously hinting to him that it would be great to ask his classmate,

"Where in the book did you see evidence of that?" If the child needs me to be less subtle, I'm happy to whisper to a child, "Ask for evidence," and then, when the child does as told, I'll give a thumbs up.

- Then, too, if a child takes the conversation to left field, saying something totally unrelated, I'll try to make it clear to the class that it is okay to say, "I'm not sure how that goes with this idea," and if, in fact, it doesn't go with the current line of thinking, to say, "Can we talk about that later, 'cause right now we're talking about . . ."

All of these conversational moves are turns of thought. Teaching students to *talk* well about a book teaches them to *think* well about a book. What could matter more?

Chapter 13

The Special Importance of Nonfiction Reading

OST OF THE READING that any of us do is nonfiction reading. In the last two days, I've read the Metro North train schedule, reviews of restaurants, persuasive letters to New York State's governor about changes in state policy around teacher evaluation, newspaper articles about people elected to the board of regents, a number of articles on websites, a draft of chapters of this book, a research chapter, the *New York Times*, letters to the editor in our local town, a pamphlet about a bird walk, a review of doctoral programs to which my nephew has applied . . . and probably a score of other nonfiction texts as well.

Nonfiction is the primary reading fare of almost every teacher and every literate adult. We read nonfiction continuously. We read it as we inhale, and we do this for an enormous range of purposes. We read nonfiction to catch up, to locate, to rank, to be surprised, to overview a topic, to answer questions, to become knowledgeable—above all, to learn. As Nell Duke (2000) asserts, "informational literacy is central to success, and even survival, in advanced schooling, the workplace, and the community" (202). But beyond academic and life success, reading informational texts has many other benefits for our children. Nonfiction can open doors for students, offering them opportunities to pursue their interests and passions and to develop new areas of expertise (Caswell and Duke 1998; Duke 2000; Moss et al. 1997).

Yet, despite the clear, rich benefits of nonfiction texts, there is very little of this going on in schools.

Almost twenty-five years ago, Christine Pappas (1991) wrote about "narrative as primary ideology" in classrooms. By this, she meant that there was a predominance of stories, of fiction texts, in classrooms and a lack of informational texts. Her article "Fostering Full Access to Literacy by Including Information Books" cautioned educators that using only stories in class could end up "being a barrier to full access to literacy" (461). In 2000, Duke studied twenty first-grade classrooms and found that in addition to there being a scarcity of informational texts displayed in the classroom or in classrooms' libraries, children in these classrooms spent on average only 3.6 minutes a day with informational texts. Children in low-SES classrooms, in many cases, spent even less time with informational texts.

I've written this chapter because nonfiction is especially important and especially ignored. Also, of course, the Common Core standards and other iterations of global standards place a new premium on information texts (as the standards call nonfiction). Chances are good that your school has decided it is a priority to bring nonfiction texts front and central. This chapter, then, should help you take some steps toward doing so.

No one chapter can possibly do justice to a topic this large, but I thought it might help for me to highlight some key points and suggestions.

FIRST THINGS FIRST

As the leader of the Teachers College Reading and Writing Project, one of the most important jobs that I do is support the learning life of my organization and of the adults who work within it. One of the quotes that I have tacked to my bulletin board is this one, from Seymour Sarason, author of *The Culture of Schools and the Problem of Change*:

> The notion that teachers can create conditions that are vital and stimulating for students when those same conditions do not exist for teachers has no warrant in the history of mankind.

That quote from Sarason reminds me of the time when Roland Barth, founder of Harvard's famed Principal Center, visited my organization and said to us, "The health and well being of a school has everything to do with the learning lives of the people who teach in that school. A school needs to be a place where everyone's learning curve is as steep as it can be."

The wonderful thing about the new spotlight on information reading (and writing) is that this is a goal worth living toward. It can vitalize a school. Doug Reeves encourages schools to think about power standards—those that can pay off across the curriculum and across years—and surely this is one of them.

If your school decides to support more nonfiction reading, my first suggestion is to bring teachers together to think about predictable problems and be willing to talk honestly and openly about how best to handle them.

CREATING CLASSROOMS IN WHICH NONFICTION READING THRIVES

If your first goal is to turn students into avid readers of nonfiction—as I hope it is—remember that motivation is everything. Although you will want to comb nonfiction across the curriculum, and that will be important, reading assigned texts on the state-approved curriculum sequence probably should not be the sum total of your emphasis on nonfiction texts. Consider also ways to support reading nonfiction that allow students to see nonfiction reading as a magical way to pursue their own quirky personal interests, hobbies, and passions.

Fifth-grade teacher Kathy Doyle launched her work with nonfiction without mentioning texts at all. She simply asked her fifth-graders to teach each other their hobbies and interests. You can imagine: soon the classroom was filled with talk of rockets, skateboards, basketball, art projects, trail guides for ski mountains, raising guide dogs, combing the beach, and taking care of a new baby brother. Annie Dillard describes her view of the universe by saying, "There must be bands of enthusiasts for everything on earth . . . there is no one here but us fanatics; bird watchers, infielders, detectives, poets, rock collectors" (1989, 159).

After a few days in which students "came out" as fans and enthusiasts, Kathy said, "I've been thinking about all the hobbies and interests we've been talking about, and here is my question: in what way could reading help us enjoy these things even more? Talk to your partner. Have you—or could you—weave reading into the interest you shared with us, or into another interest that you could have shared?"

Soon Kathy called the class back together again. "I've been talking with Emily. Her interest is sleepovers, and she isn't sure if reading could make a better sleepover. But Nicole, her partner, told her there are articles in magazines about how to make a better sleepover, and I'm wondering if any of you have other ideas for ways reading could help even this interest in sleepovers?" Soon the class had listed an abundance of ideas. She could read joke books and get good jokes or scary horror stories to tell at the sleepover. She could find a recipe for taffy and make that as part of the party. She could learn to tell her friends' fortunes.

Meanwhile, Jeremy told about how he plays chess, and he had just done exactly what his teacher suggested. He'd read a book on strategy—specifically about a play called "annihilation of defense"—and tried it on his dad. "I won in three moves!" he said.

As you can imagine, students were soon pursuing reading that related to their interests—and bringing that reading to school. Kids shared a website about outer space, brought the sports page to school, and swapped texts on ferrets. The students brainstormed ways to get more reading material related to their interests, and soon a request letter was sent to the parent association for financial support subscribing to magazines. Parents, too, were asked to support magazines related to their child's interest, if they could. The class began subscribing to a few newspapers. First, a task force of students interviewed adults to learn how they go about reading the paper and shared their results with the class. One thing they learned is that most adults have a few topics they follow—the economy, schools, sports. Based on that, children decided they would each approach the newspapers with their interests leading the way. Different children took up topics to follow and read everything they could find related to their theme: sports, the environment, music, and so on.

While attaching reading to students' hobbies and passions, you will also want to bring irresistible nonfiction texts into your classroom. You have probably already found that when you get terrific stories into your school, it's easy to turn kids into avid readers. The books are just so good, and there are so many of them now: Magic Tree House, Time Warp Trio, American Girl, the Narnia series, Gregor the Overlander, Fudge-a-Mania. The list goes on and on, and each character is more amusing, provoking, or endearing than the next. Many of your children will have already been lured toward reading simply by having easy, constant access to fascinating fiction. You will want to rely on great nonfiction texts in just this same way. Richard Allington reports that access to high-interest texts is one of the single most important factors accounting for students' success in reading.

There was a time when finding irresistible nonfiction was challenging, but that has changed. Now there are lots of nonfiction books that are spellbinding to your readers. If you provision your class with high-interest nonfiction, children will devour those books as eagerly as they devour fiction. I can't say enough about the importance of filling your shelves with the DK Readers and with books by authors such as Gail Gibbons, Seymour Simon, Bobbie Kalman, Jean Fritz, Melissa Stewart, Steve Jenkins, and Nic Bishop. Look for well-written texts on high-interest topics: planets, poisonous snakes, spies, ballet, weather disasters, far away places. Check out some of the new, interesting collections: Split Histories, which teach about a historical time period from two different perspectives; Who Was . . . ? books, which each describe the life story of a famous figure in music, government, science, and

so on; National Geographic Readers/Kids, which teach about a variety of fascinating topics from sloths to forensic science at a variety of levels; the You Wouldn't Want To . . . series, which take a critical (and often humorous view) of famous events/time periods. Add in great nonfiction journals—*Odyssey, Ask, Cobblestone, Junior Scholastic, Ranger Rick, Scope*—and your kids will soon be carrying nonfiction in their backpacks, reading nonfiction on the bus and at home, perhaps even perusing it in the bathroom, as so many adults do! You'll also add in websites and digital texts such as nature, history, and science videos; all of these are easy to find now. Consider creating a basket called "New Hot Reads" and fill it with nonfiction. My colleagues and I have seen students grabbing for nonfiction books when they look inviting. After all, what kid wouldn't want to read books that sound as intriguing as *Alien Deep* or *Survival! Ocean*?

So your first lens is to look at the nonfiction in your classroom and ask, Will these books and magazines turn my students into avid nonfiction readers? Have I done my best, when possible, to assemble nonfiction in topics and baskets, so kids can read more than one book or article on a subject? Have I gone to my public library, asked parents and friends, done everything I could to get better nonfiction into my classroom? Reach out if you need help. Trade book distributors such as Booksource will assemble leveled nonfiction sets for you, on topics of your choice, or there are digital nonfiction libraries, such as StarWalk kids, which holds hundreds of titles that you can sort using a variety of categories, including age range and reading level. You can visit the TCRWP website (readingandwritingproject.org), and the online resources that accompany these units, for text lists. The main thing is—your kids are likely to turn into nonfiction readers if they have access to great nonfiction, and unlikely to if they don't.

In their article, "Teaching about and with Informational Texts: What Does Research Tell Us?" Beth Maloch and Randy Bomer (2013) argue that one of the most important things we can do is to fill our classroom libraries with engaging nonfiction. As they assert, "It is clear that one important (perhaps the most important) step in growing young children's knowledge, understanding, and use of informational texts is making these texts available and accessible to them" (442).

You will also want to be sure that your own nonfiction reading life is a resource that you bring to your teaching. Think of some topics that you enjoy reading about, and make sure you are public about those topics in your classroom. If you're obsessed with the fate of sea turtles, your children should know that. They should be alert to anything they come across about turtles, bringing those texts to you. Be prepared for your collection of turtle texts to expand dramatically as children add to your turtle corner! I'll never forget seeing a fifth-grade teacher at PS 6 gather his children for morning meeting to say that he just had to read them a snippet from a news article about a fisherman pulling up a live coelacanth! He was fascinated by this prehistoric fish, and his children had become equally fascinated. In fact, the class had become somewhat obsessed with all prehistoric marine life, and children could debate knowledgeably about whether or not megalodon (a giant prehistoric shark) might still dwell in the depths of the ocean. This teacher, Steve, said to his children, "Part of this article is too hard for us, I think—it's for scientists—but I think we can make sense of the beginning, and if you want, we'll try to figure out the rest as well." What authenticity.

In summary, we all know there are conditions that make it likely that students will love nonfiction (and conditions that make it unlikely). If students can choose the texts they read most of time—even within some constraints—they'll like nonfiction more. If kids can proceed at their own pace through texts, they'll like nonfiction more. You can see students' enjoyment (or lack thereof) by doing a quick scan of the classroom. Are students' eyes on the text, or are their eyes darting to the clock, to their book, back to the clock, to the classroom door? Are they reading, sitting on the edge of their seats or sitting slumped in their chairs? When students discuss their books with their partners, do they talk excitedly, pointing to pages and lines in the texts, or do they struggle to talk about what they've read? Be on the lookout for these "red flags" of disengagement, and begin by stoking the fire and enjoyment of nonfiction.

Nonfiction reading is sociable. When kids have chances to teach each other what they have learned, to talk about confusing parts, and to share notes or questions, they will like nonfiction more.

UNDERSTANDING HOW NONFICTION BECOMES MORE AND MORE COMPLEX, AND MATCHING READERS WITH TEXT

If you begin your nonfiction units by helping students link nonfiction to all that they love most, you go public as a reader of nonfiction, and you create a culture in your classroom where people share their interests and texts with each other, you will be well on your way to cultivating new skills in nonfiction reading.

I also recommend you study text complexity in nonfiction texts. Just as your knowledge about levels of fiction texts and of the bands of text difficulty allows you to put the right book into each child's hands and to make a pretty good guess about the skills that reader will need to tackle particular books, a knowledge of text complexity can allow you to do similar work with nonfiction texts.

We recommend you collect a ladder of texts representing increasing difficulties and study for yourself what makes one text more challenging than another. As I describe in Chapter 5 of *Reading Pathways*, my colleagues and I found it challenging to ascribe specific levels to nonfiction texts with confidence—there seem to be so many ways for a nonfiction text to be hard—but we did find what we refer to as strands of text complexity. That is, we found ways nonfiction texts become increasingly complex. For example, texts written to support third-grade readers often contain topic sentences that are prominently located at the start of a paragraph or a section of text, and by fifth grade, the main idea is more implicit. I've written about half a dozen ways in which nonfiction texts become more complex in that chapter.

In *Tackling Complexity: Moving Up Levels of Nonfiction*, we explicitly teach fifth-graders ways that nonfiction texts become more challenging, and we teach them strategies for tackling those increasing challenges. We've created a set of text complexity cards that match the ways that texts become challenging, with strategies readers can use to tackle those challenges. These cards give young people a lighthearted, concrete, practical way to spring into action when the nonfiction text they are reading is too hard for them. Simply helping readers name the difficulties they confront and reminding them that they have a toolkit of concrete strategies has been enormously helpful.

In *Reading Pathways*, you will also see a text that we have written up the ladder of levels. That is, the same text has been written at increasing levels to illustrate the increasing challenges nonfiction readers will face. You can find other texts such as that one if you read places where a text has been rewritten at easier levels to accommodate all students. Newsela (www.newsela.com) provides daily articles on current events, which are written at different levels. National Geographic and Scholastic do similar work.

Understanding ways nonfiction texts become more complex can help you to spot the challenges in texts that your students hold. All too often, kids actually do no reading at all during nonfiction reading workshops because they are holding books that are inaccessible to them. Perhaps the pictures make the book look deceptively easy. In any case, ask a child to read aloud to you, and listen for fluency (you can hear that in a minute) and accuracy. Allington suggests simply asking every child in the school to lay out all the books from his desk that he is expected to be reading: the history textbook, the math book, the works. Then ask the child to open those texts to a random page and read aloud, testing using the five-finger rule (if there are five words you can't read on a page, the text is too hard.) Allington suggests that the day that a child can spend 100% of her day reading books she can actually read will be the day we make major headway toward supporting nonfiction reading. Allington's article is aptly called, "You Can't Learn Much from Books You Can't Read."

Reading Up a Ladder of Books to Develop Background Knowledge and Access Harder Texts

But here is the good news. When you go to read a text and it is hard—you can't read it with 96% accuracy or even 90% accuracy—there *is* a fast-track detour that can often allow you to access that book. Don't wait until your general reading level advances so that book is within your grasp. Instead, make the book more accessible by building your background knowledge, simply by reading easier books on the topic. That is, any reader can always ratchet up his ability to read more complex texts on a particular topic by reading a lot of easy texts on that topic. Those easy texts teach you the vocabulary and the concepts that will make the challenging texts vastly easier for you.

Whether students are trying to learning about photosynthesis, the English colonists, or gravity, they can learn to build knowledge quickly by reading texts that are fast and easy. Therefore, organize your classroom libraries and digital collections in ways that help students read up and down a topic. For example, you might pull together a bin of books on "animals that live in the ocean" or "texts about the Boston Tea Party" with a variety of texts at easy and increasingly harder levels. At the start of any unit of study or nonfiction

study, therefore, kids need access to some fast and easy texts. Eventually, kids also need to develop agency in anticipating upcoming studies and/or evaluating when topics and texts are hard, quickly seeking some easier texts on their own and building up background knowledge fast to tackle a topic or a text more successfully.

It is problematic when students are either left to flounder with inaccessible texts (after all, kids are taught to monitor for sense and not to persist when texts make no sense to them), and it is equally problematic if students are too dependent on the teacher to provide all background knowledge. If teachers dole out that background knowledge in a slow trickle, parsing out bits and pieces of information, kids learn that knowledge comes only from one source— the teacher. That means a student's access to that source controls how much knowledge can be accessed, and that learning requires the teacher's presence. When the teacher is the only way that complex texts become accessible, the result is that kids all read the same text at the same rate, rather than each child reading as much as she can.

When there are no accessible texts for kids to deeply immerse themselves in and no way for kids to make inaccessible texts accessible, when the library is not organized to reflect topics/levels of text complexity/structures or genres, kids are left passive and dependent. It is crucial to design text collections that facilitate an ease of compiling background knowledge, where every reader in the room can find an entry point into the topic of study.

INDICATORS OF A THRIVING NONFICTION WORKSHOP AND RED FLAGS

In the best nonfiction reading workshops, there are some clear patterns. That is, there are indicators that show that the work going on in these rooms is creating a thriving nonfiction reading workshop. These indicators of what occurs in these exemplary classrooms can become guidelines for how to create a thriving nonfiction workshop. Conversely, there are also red flags associated with these indicators that can mean that a nonfiction reading workshop needs to be brought back on track—and fast.

Students Need to Read for Stretches of Time/Text before Pausing to Take Notes

Students benefit from reading a large chunk of text and only after reading that entire chunk, stopping to think, "What was that mostly about? How was it structured? What was the main idea or most important ideas? The most important supportive details?" The work of note-taking should provide kids with daily practice determining importance, synthesizing, taking into account text structure, and citing details that support main or central ideas. This is only possible if students take brief, organized notes after big intervals of reading. The size of those intervals should vary based on a reader's skill, with children reading at levels L/M perhaps pausing every ten minutes, and students who are reading more complex texts pausing around every twenty minutes. What you don't want to see is kids who read for two minutes and then record facts for a minute.

If students are reading with pen in hand, recording a series of facts as they read, note-taking swamps their reading time and doesn't provide them with opportunities to practice reading skills other than, at best, paraphrasing. At that pace, not only are students getting little reading done, but they are also not using note-taking as an invitation to do important higher-level work. It is especially problematic if the notes that students do take reflect no evidence that they are organizing information, or slotting information from one text into the right place in notes taken during work with another text. If your nonfiction readers are spending more time writing than reading, coach them to take in more pages of text before pausing to record all that they are learning and thinking.

Students Need to Talk about What They're Reading

Students benefit from talking often about what they're learning from nonfiction texts. Nonfiction texts are packed with information, and if students don't pause often to talk about that information, they will have difficulty digesting it. There are many options for students to talk about what they are reading and learning:

- They might teach each other what they learn.
- They might explain some of the important visual graphics or charts to a partner.
- They might decide what's worth taking notes on.
- They might compare and contrast the information they have learned from multiple sources.
- They might debate positions on an issue or topic.

Just remember that talk is essential to increasing comprehension and building higher-level interpretations about a topic or text.

Notice if kids are reading silently and taking notes that are rarely shared or discussed with others. It's a red flag if kids who, when asked to explain what

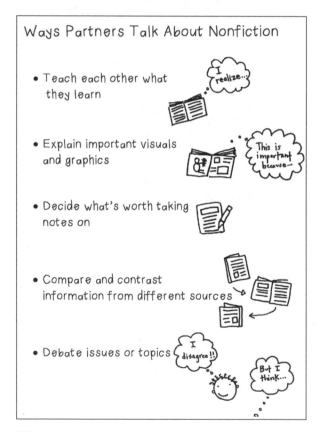

Ways Partners Talk About Nonfiction

- Teach each other what they learn
- Explain important visuals and graphics
- Decide what's worth taking notes on
- Compare and contrast information from different sources
- Debate issues or topics

FIG. 13–1

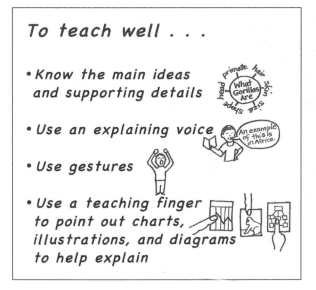

To teach well . . .

• **Know the main ideas and supporting details**

• **Use an explaining voice**

• **Use gestures**

• **Use a teaching finger to point out charts, illustrations, and diagrams to help explain**

FIG. 13–2 A chart to help partners talk about their nonfiction texts

they just read, have a hard time talking about the text or topic. If you notice problems with this, coach students to begin sharing, perhaps by providing a few thought prompts, such as "This is making me think . . . ," "Something important I just learned . . . ," "One thing I find surprising is . . . ," "Something that doesn't fit what I'm learning is . . . ," or "The author is trying to . . ."

Students Need to Preview a Text to Figure Out the Kind of Text It Is and Vary Their Expectations for Reading Accordingly

It is critically important for students to look over a text prior to reading it (and again midway into it as they approach new chunks of the text), thinking, "What kind of text is this? How does it seem to be organized?" And they need to vary their expectations for what they'll learn and for how that learning will be organized based on the genre/structure of the text. If the text is a nonfiction narrative, for example, students should draw on their knowledge of story structure, anticipating that the text will tell about a subject who has traits and needs/motivations, who encounters trouble, and who eventually responds to that trouble. On the other hand, if the text is expository, students will probably

read looking for main ideas and supportive details. These texts may be structured into a problem-solution structure, a cause-and-effect structure, or a compare-and-contrast structure, although usually it will work for students to read, culling main ideas and supports. And nonfiction texts are often hybrids of narrative and expository structures, with elements of each, so students will need to draw on their knowledge of how both genres are structured. If students are reading texts that are level T and above, it is important for them to know in advance that the text will probably teach several main ideas.

It is a problem if you see students begin reading nonfiction texts without taking any time to preview those texts. It is also problematic if they preview texts to anticipate only the content that will be taught, without any awareness that anticipating the structure of the text can affect how they read. Be on the lookout for students' notes that are just a laundry list of information that does not mirror the structure of the text or reflect the reader's purpose. If you notice these things, model how to preview a text, especially highlighting the text structure and typical parts of the genre. Lead in with angled research questions during your conferences, asking students, "What are your expectations as you begin reading this text? How does the way the text is organized or the way the author previews the information help you form your expectations as a reader?"

Students Need to Read Texts They Can Comprehend with at Least 96% Accuracy, Fluency, and Comprehension

Scaffolding, when it is provided, should be a temporary support and needs to be withdrawn within a few days. If the scaffolding is appropriate, the student will soon be able to do the work with independence. Nonfiction texts can be deceptive. The presence of large colorful pictures, diagrams, and charts can sometimes make a text look more accessible than it really is. If students are reading texts that they cannot understand and cannot read with fluency (and this will be the case if they are reading below 96% accuracy), then they are not able to use and develop the reading strategies that are all important to their continued growth as nonfiction readers.

Instruction should march ahead of development, thereby making development possible. For this to happen, you need to see what your students can almost—but not quite—do with independence and to provide the limited and light scaffolds that will make the difference, allowing them to do that work because of the presence of those training wheels. The scaffolds—the training wheels—need to be withdrawn or decreased after a few days of work. For example, a fifth-grade student reading level M texts might profit from support when reading level N texts. For a day or two, the teacher might provide this reader with an introduction and a shared-text partner. After a few days, the teacher simply puts Post-its in parts of the text that she hopes the reader and the same-book partner will talk about before they begin to read, allowing them to give themselves a text introduction.

It can become a problem if you interpret the term "scaffolding" to mean that the teacher or other students do most of the work, leaving just bits of work for the student in need to do on his own. You want to make sure the student isn't carried along by the scaffold, pretending to do work that is actually many levels beyond what is within his actual reach. If the assistance given by the teacher or by peers supports a learner doing work that is well beyond what he will soon be able to do with independence, that is not a scaffold. Students who are well below grade level need massive amounts of time practicing the reading skills that are imperative for them to learn. It is important that they are making progress, but the level of work the students can do with independence should be a big part of what is assessed, with progress noted and expected.

text, may offer additional ideas and information. As students read across a text, and then across more than one text on a topic, they need to name the big or central ideas that seem most important and gather up details that also seem important to these points—looking across all the parts of the text and expecting that all the parts matter and may offer something new.

Be on the lookout for kids who read a text that clearly makes a few big points, yet the students summarize what they are reading with one main idea. Another red flag is when kids talk about a complicated topic, yet they make statements that are too general as they try to fit it into one main idea. If you notice this, coach students to embrace the layers of the text, by asking, "What other ideas might the author be teaching?" or "What else could this text be about?" or "That's a big idea of the text, but what might be a smaller idea that the text is teaching?"

Students Need a Repertoire of Ways to Read Closely and Reasons to Read Nonfiction Closely

For close reading to be purposeful, students need to be doing some bigger work that requires them to look closely at texts. TCRWP schools use three main methods to increase kids' engagement with close reading of nonfiction: gathering evidence for debate, synthesizing information on a topic from a variety of sources (which are sometimes conflicting and sometimes involve compare-and-contrast work), and reading like a writer. In the first of these—gathering information for a debate—children either participate in flash debates or prepare for argument writing, and they read closely to gather evidence for a particular side of an issue. In the second—synthesizing information on a topic from a variety of sources—they work with a variety of texts that offer information that can be synthesized together, with some of it containing conflicting perspectives or information. As they read a new text on the same subtopic, they think, "How does this fit with what I already

Students Need to Embrace the Complexities of a Text as They Read

As kids encounter texts that make more than one point, it's important that they don't oversimplify these texts to just one idea. Sometimes the author makes several points that are threaded through the text, and other times the author makes major related points in various sections of a text. Once kids are reading texts that are level S and beyond, they should expect that many of those texts will teach more than one thing. They should also expect that some of the text features, rather than explaining points made in the read? Is this adding to what I already read? Conflicting with it?" In the third way that students become engaged in close reading of nonfiction, they study the craft and structure of nonfiction from the perspective of a writer, either because they are writing nonfiction in writing workshop or because they are thinking about the craft decisions an author made to make readers think or feel a certain way.

It becomes a problem when the act of close reading is done solely for test preparation purposes or because it has been assigned. Close reading shouldn't keep students working on a short leash, controlled by a teacher or assignments. That is, students should be taking up their own important purposes to read a text closely and do so with independence. Be on the lookout for students who tend to read straight through one entire book on a subject and then move quickly onto a second text on the same topic. Notice if they don't pause to think about the intersections of their learning. What is this text teaching? How does it fit with what I've already read? What is different about how this text is teaching about the topic?

LEARNING FROM TEXTS: VOCABULARY ACQUISITION

Vocabulary acquisition has a special place in reading nonfiction. Although it is important to boost students' vocabulary knowledge across the curriculum, in nonfiction reading workshop and in the content areas, students are reading primarily to learn, and key to learning about a new topic is learning the vocabulary of that topic. So, as students are reading about wildlife conservation, for example, they are coming across terms such as *endangered*, *habitat*, *critical*, *conserve*, *threatened*, and so on. Now imagine that if students are reading a small text set on a topic, they are likely coming across these sorts of key terms repeatedly and seeing more about how these terms are used as well as the meanings they carry. If students are talking to partners about their reading and writing about their reading, better yet, now they are being given opportunities to use this vocabulary in oral and written contexts, thus supporting their understanding of these terms and increasing the chance that these terms will become part of their vocabulary base.

And, of course, students should be learning not only domain-specific vocabulary terms (terms that are directly linked to the content, e.g., *force*, *motion*, *gravity*, *accelerate*, *friction*) but also academic vocabulary (terms that go across content and that are necessary to know to truly understand what one is reading, because these terms help link and explain concepts, e.g., *confirm*, *conclude*, *distinct*, *external*, *imply*). This academic vocabulary is also tricky, because these terms are often used in multiple forms (e.g., *imply*, *implications*, *implicated*, *implying*). Isabel Beck and her colleagues (2002) refer to this second type of words as tier II words and suggest that these are the terms on which vocabulary instruction should focus.

There is some evidence that suggests that the act of reading itself can foster vocabulary growth. Nagy and Anderson (1983) investigated incidental learning of word meanings through normal reading and concluded that the act of reading did lead to vocabulary growth. As they concluded, "the results of this and our earlier studies indicate that wide, regular reading will itself provide the necessary exposures to words in a variety of meaningful contexts" (266).

Nagy and Anderson (1983) caution that, of course, multiple encounters with a word in a variety of meaningful contexts is necessary for a student to gain a depth of understanding of that term. They also caution that especially in expository or nonfiction reading, exposure to a word is important, but students also need to understand the relationships among concepts, so they need repeated exposure to the new term but also to the "system of ideas in the new domain" (266) to deeply grasp the term. Beck, McKeown, and Kucan (2002) echo this caution, arguing that for students to learn words from reading, they must read widely enough to encounter a "substantial number of unfamiliar words," and they must have the skills to "infer word meaning information from the contexts they read" (4). They also argue that there does need to be direct vocabulary instruction in some words, because not all words require equal instruction. They claim that direct teaching into words that are found across a variety of domains—the academic vocabulary I mentioned earlier—will be most productive.

So, clearly, we need to teach students how to figure out the meanings of words, and there does need to be some direct instruction targeted to words that will pay off the most in helping students become "mature language users" (Beck et al. 2002, 8). Still, direct instruction in vocabulary cannot account for all the new terms students learn during their elementary years in school (Nagy et al. 1987). Duke and Moses (2003) cite Nagy et al., asserting that "researchers estimate that 5–15% of all the words we learn we learn from reading." In addition, students who do not read widely are unlikely to have strong vocabularies. Stanovich and Cunningham (1996) concluded, "Inadequate exposure to print prevents children from building important knowledge structures, such as vocabulary, metalinguistic knowledge, and general world knowledge. These knowledge sources are necessary for efficient reading comprehension at the more advanced levels" (29). After citing Stanovich, Allington (2012) concludes, "So expanding volume of reading, as suggested in the previous chapters, is a good first step to increasing knowledge of word meanings" (141).

Therefore, in addition to vocabulary instruction, students must be reading nonfiction regularly to build world knowledge and vocabulary.

One of the important things we can do for students then is not only to provide some direct instruction around terms, but also to teach students how to better figure out the meaning of the unfamiliar words and phrases in their texts. To do this, some understanding of how texts teach and employ domain-specific and academic vocabulary is necessary. In Chapter 5 of *Reading Pathways*, I explain ways that nonfiction texts tend to get more complex, and I encourage you to read that chapter for more detailed information on the strands of nonfiction text complexity that my colleagues and I have researched. One of those strands is a strand that relates to vocabulary. So here I will briefly describe the way that texts tend to get more challenging in terms of language and vocabulary.

A Strand of Difficulty: Language and Vocabulary

As texts become more difficult, they contain longer, more uncommon and discipline-specific words that may be difficult to decode. Tricky words are less apt to be defined.

As a reader progresses toward more challenging nonfiction texts, she can expect to encounter an increasing number of challenging words. For example, in a hundred-word passage in a level N nonfiction book about wild animals, there were nineteen two-syllable words (e.g., *blooded*), nine three-syllable words (e.g., *family*), one four-syllable word (i.e., *scientific*), and one compound word. On the other hand, think about the words I just listed as exemplars, and you'll see that many of these words could be sight words for students reading level N books (e.g., *family, blood*).

In contrast, in a hundred-word passage in a level U book about Albert Einstein, there were nineteen two-syllable words (this time, they tended to be words such as *captured* and *announced*), sixteen three-syllable words (such as *universe*), four four-syllable words (such as *expeditions*), and three compound words. As a reader progresses to even harder texts, the number of complex words will increase. The words themselves get harder, both because they are

unfamiliar or technical (such as *parallelogram* or *monarchy*), and because the meaning of a term is the secondary meaning (such as *grave* meaning serious or *cabinet* as a governing body).

Most of the two- to four-syllable words that students have difficulty reading in books at higher levels are unlikely to be sight words for most readers. Also, often the challenging words in these higher-level texts contain unusual spelling features that make the words difficult to decode, and they often contain affixes (*con-*, *-tion*) and inflectional endings (*-ed, -er, -est*), which means that it is helpful for students to understand how these parts of a word affect the word's meaning. In these complex nonfiction texts, the challenging academic vocabulary is often essential to the passage's meaning, and miscues often completely change the meaning of the passage. In a level N article about endangered animals, a student read this sentence, "By 1986, this ferret species was nearly extinct, or totally wiped out," as follows: "By 1986, this ferret species was nearly *extended*, or totally wiped out." Hopefully, the reader is reading the passage with enough accuracy that he can notice the miscue, self-correct, and correct close to the point of error.

More Challenging Words, Less Support for Figuring Them Out

Of course, the challenge here is not only to pronounce the word, but also to figure out its meaning. In the easier texts, the hard words are followed by a synonym, and there may also be a text feature or an example as support for the word. Readers can be taught to "read around" the word in question, and when they do this, they often find, right nearby, other words they can use instead of the hard word. The reader may also encounter a word more than once while still being given support. For example, in the level N book, *The Life Cycle of an Emperor Penguin*, by Bobbie Kalman and Robin Johnson, the text says,

> On the ice, a colony travels from 31 to 75 miles (50–121 km) to reach its **breeding ground**. A breeding ground is the area where a colony of penguins mates and lays eggs. The penguins travel for days by walking or **tobogganing**. Penguins toboggan by sliding on their bellies, using their wings and feet to push themselves along.

Notice that the tricky words are bolded and then explicitly defined in sentences that exist for the purpose of that job only. Granted, although definitions are provided for those words, this text contains a density of academic

FIG. 13–3 Students can accumulate new vocabulary in a topic-specific word bank.

vocabulary that is greater than that which one would usually find in easier books. But on the whole, in the harder texts, the tricky words are left for the reader to figure out, and the reader needs to rely on a broad understanding of the text, not just the surrounding words, to ascertain what the word probably means. Plus, at this level, that word might be referred to through different synonyms. Readers read about the penguins' down, then about their feathers, then their under layer—and are expected to understand that these are all restatements of the same word or concept.

Let's look, in contrast, at the level T text, *Earthquakes*, by Seymour Simon. Scanning the book, there are certainly lots of technical words introduced, and Simon does not go so far as to write a whole-sentence definition for each new word. But Simon does tuck definitions into some parts of his writing, while in other instances he leaves technical vocabulary to the reader.

Cracks in the rocks, called faults, run through the crust. The rocks on one side of a fault push against the rocks on the other side, causing energy to build up. For years, friction will hold the rocks in place. But finally like a stretched rubber band, the rocks suddenly snap against each other. The place where this happen is called the focus on the earthquake.

In the above passage, *friction* is never explicitly defined, although the passage absolutely describes what the term means in this context. The "focus on the earthquake" is defined, as are the faults. Still harder texts expect that readers come to a text with a knowledge of expert vocabulary on a topic or are willing to seek out and learn that vocabulary from external sources. In these texts, context clues are rarely present for readers to draw on, so using morphology will pay off in bigger ways.

More and More Various Connective Words

It's interesting (and not surprising) to notice that as texts become more elaborate, they include more linking words, or conjunctions. In more complex texts, one is much more apt to encounter additives such as *furthermore*, *thus*, and *in the same way*. We're also more likely to encounter adversative connectives such as *yet*, *but*, *however*, *on the other hand*, and *in any case*. Then, too, in more complex texts, one is more apt to encounter causal connectives, such as *so*, *because*, *it follows*, and *as a result*. We're also likely to find temporal connectives such as *finally*, *meanwhile*, and *to sum up*.

When readers have a sense for the way words such as these tie a text together, this can help them build relationships between one part of a text and another. As soon as a reader sees the word *but*, that reader needs to begin thinking, "Get ready, this author is going to say something that is an exception to the first part of the sentence."

More Complex Pronoun Referents

In addition to understanding the words and phrases writers use to tuck in subordinate points and elaborate on their ideas, readers of more complex texts will also need to have finesse with understanding pronoun referents. To make the ways nonfiction gets more complex more clear, my colleagues and I have written a text on the topic of the octopus at different levels of complexity (you can read more about this work in Chapter 5 of *Reading Pathways*). In the level six version of the octopus text, called "Lessons of the Deep," notice the mental gymnastics a student must go through to keep the information about the octopus's methods of defense.

> An octopus can also protect itself by squirting ink at a predator, obscuring its view and causing it to lose its sense of smell temporarily. This makes the fleeing octopus difficult to track. And if a predator manages to grab an octopus by the arm, the octopus has one more trick up its sleeve. This escape artist can break off its arm, swim away, and then grow a new one later with no permanent damage.

In the first sentence, notice that the pronoun *it* has different forms and different meanings—the octopus and the predator. The next sentence also contains the demonstrative *this*—meaning the predator's temporary impairment of smell and sight.

Try reading a piece of text without using any of the forms of reference given above. For example, you would read the above text,

> An octopus can also protect *the octopus (itself)* by squirting ink at a predator, obscuring *the predator's (its)* view and causing *the predator (it)* to lose *the predator's (its)* sense of smell temporarily. *The temporary impairment of sight and smell (this)* makes the fleeing octopus difficult to track. And if a predator manages to grab an octopus by the arm, the octopus has one more trick up *the octopus's (its)* sleeve. *The octopus (This)* escape artist can break off *the octopus's (its)* arm, swim away, and then grow a new one later with no permanent damage.

Continue reading the remainder of the article with this lens. When you try to read a text this way, you experience the kind of thinking students must do to truly comprehend text.

Teaching into Vocabulary Acquisition

Having an understanding of how texts tend to get harder in terms of language and vocabulary (in addition to understanding other ways that texts can get harder) can help you to be better prepared to support students in addressing the challenges that texts pose. For example, if you wanted to teach directly into determining the meaning of vocabulary, you might gather a group of students reading the same article and craft a text introduction around the vocabulary in their text. This might sound something like "There's one other way the texts you're reading now are getting hard. Authors are using more

sophisticated vocabulary. This author uses a lot of fancy vocabulary words, especially words to describe the octopus's body. Some will be names of body parts we don't even have! I've highlighted some of those words in your copy of the text. When you get to them, see if you can work to figure out what they mean. The text will give you the answers." With your text introduction complete, you can launch students into their reading, moving from student to student to coach in. You might pull from the list of prompts shown on page 137 and give these to students to help you specifically address language and vocabulary work.

Supporting Students in Taking Risks to Use New Vocabulary

In addition to supporting students in figuring out these terms, you also want to support students in *using* these terms. In "10 Research Tested Ways to Build Children's Vocabulary," Duke and Moses (2003) outline ten research-based practices that will support vocabulary development, drawing on the work of multiple researchers to support each of the strategies outlined. One of these practices is supporting rich conversations in which students have the chance to use the vocabulary they are learning. As Duke and Moses (2003) assert, "In school we need to involve children in rich, meaningful conversations whenever we can" (5). Our students need to engage in high-level conversations and to be encouraged to take risks in using new vocabulary. That means that you'll want to suggest to students that as they read, they keep notes on new terms they are learning (or for some students you may want to preteach a small set of a terms related to a topic they are studying and suggest that they keep track of their learning of these terms). It also means that giving students time to talk about their reading is essential, and so is pushing them to take risks when using new vocabulary. Encourage them to point to illustrations or diagrams to help them offer concrete examples of the terms they use, and especially encourage them to use the more abstract, conceptual academic vocabulary that helps to explain relationships.

If you see a student talking with her partner about her ideas about why the Revolutionary War might have been fought, you might coach in and offer some high-level academic vocabulary. "Ah, you are letting your partner know some conclusions you have come to after reading about the causes of the Revolutionary War. *Conclusions* means the big theories or ideas you are taking away from your reading. So what have you concluded about the causes?"

Prompts for Language and Vocabulary ✺

Easier Texts

- I found the tricky word _____. The explanation the author gave for this word is _____.

- I found the definition for the tricky word _____ in the _____.

- When I looked around the word _____, I found the synonym _____.

More Complex

- I found the tricky word _____. The clues the author gave to help me understand it were _____ and _____.

- A tricky word in the text is _____. An example of it is _____.

- Is there another meaning for the word _____ that might fit here?

- This word might mean _____, but it also might mean _____. The meaning that fits best is _____.

Most Complex

- Some of the vocabulary I already know about this topic is: _____, _____, and _____.

- A word part or root I recognize within this word is _____. That part means _____. So, I think this word might mean _____.

- I know other terms that relate to this word such as _____. This is how those other terms relate to this word: _____.

- This term has other meanings that I also know, such as _____. But that doesn't seem to be how it is used here. Here it seems to be used to mean _____.

- A resource that I could use to learn what the word _____ means would be _____.

And push the students to try out using the word *conclude* or another form of it. Welcome their attempts. If they say, "I conclusioned that . . ." don't jump in and say, "No, that's not it! That's not how you say it!" If that's how their attempts are met, they'll likely never take another risk again. Think of how you'd react to a young child (even younger than your students—say, three years old) trying out a new term. If that three-year-old said something like, "I brang it home," you would not jump all over the incorrect grammar. Instead you'd probably say something like, "Oh, you *brought* your drawing home?" (emphasizing the word *brought*). And you'd be patient and realize that the child might make that same mistake again in the future. One time using a word does not mean the word is known. The same attitude applies here. So if a student says, "I conclusioned that . . . ," you might say, "Oh, you *concluded* that . . ." and raise your eyebrows, eagerly waiting for her to continue.

Or you might tell yourself that you are so thrilled that this student has taken this risk that you are not going to say anything this minute, but instead let her finish voicing her ideas, and at the end of the conversation, you might provide the student and her partner with an index card or Post-it with some prompts based off what you heard, such as:

- After reading, I concluded that . . .

- After reading, one conclusion I drew was . . .

- After reading, some of the conclusions I drew were . . .

You'll want to see students also using new terms in their writing about reading. If your students are using their new domain-specific vocabulary but no new academic vocabulary, you might decide to do a mid-workshop or share on a few new academic vocabulary words for your students, ones you think could run across multiple texts. Push students to think of examples of these (as well as nonexamples) and try sketching them out.

For some students, and in particular, your English language learners, you'll want to preteach a small set of words every few weeks, ones that you think they are likely to see repeatedly and to which they will be able to have multiple exposures. Try to make your preteaching of these words as visual and concrete as possible. Again, examples, nonexamples, and sketching are all great ways to help students get to know words better. You might even have students write some of the new terms on index cards and then jot examples of a term around the term, so when they are in conversation or writing about reading, they can turn to their set of words and see examples of those terms in front of them. (For more detailed information about supporting English language learners, please read Chapter 14 of this guide).

The nonfiction reading workshop, content areas, and related read-alouds are rich spaces for vocabulary growth. Of course, your students will also be learning new vocabulary in writing workshop and reading workshop around literature, but reading to learn offers special opportunities to build world knowledge, an understanding of historical and scientific concepts, and a rich vocabulary base.

PLANNING AUTHENTIC READ-ALOUDS THAT FOSTER A LOVE FOR NONFICTION AND MODEL HIGH-LEVEL READING WORK

We know that reading aloud is the best way to create glorious reading experiences for students, so naturally, we can use read-aloud as way to teach into these pillars of a hearty nonfiction reading workshop. To support students in being avid readers and lovers of nonfiction, we need to model deep engagement with nonfiction, as well as support students in practicing that deep engagement. Read-aloud is the best time we have to do that. In reviewing research on informational texts, Bomer and Maloch note the value that is seen in conducting interactive read-alouds around informational texts with students, asserting, "A third theme in the research on informational texts is the value of engaging young children in interactive read-alouds and discussions of these texts" (444). In addition to being a way for students to practice and see in action the skills needed for deep nonfiction reading, interactive read-alouds can also support their genre knowledge, as well as help build content knowledge. For all of these reasons, you will want to ensure that you are offering your students nonfiction read-alouds that are as powerful as your fiction read-alouds.

First, decide on the nonfiction text you want to use. Keep in mind all that was discussed above; when picking an excellent nonfiction text, run down a list of qualities to be on the lookout for. Quality nonfiction advances more than one idea, uses multiple kinds of evidence, leans on a variety of text structures, offers multiple perspectives, uses words in interesting ways, and is written well with descriptions, comparisons, and analogies. Of course, one piece of excellent nonfiction won't meet every set of criteria. But read-aloud is a special time to lift up quality examples of nonfiction for your class

to experience. Don't waste time on texts that don't reach your standards of excellence!

Once you decided on a text, such as *No Monkeys, No Chocolate*, by Melissa Stewart and Allen Young, for example, you could let yourself react to the text as a reader, marking your own ideas and questions and then turning these into think-alouds or prompts for turn-and-talks or stop-and-jots. On the other hand, you could decide that you want to do a read-aloud focused on some of the particular work in which your students need to strengthen their skills. In this case, you would study your data, decide on what work feels most important, and then prepare a read-aloud that pops out and highlights this work.

Let's imagine how this might go. Suppose you decide that on this day during read-aloud, you want to help your students preview the text and vary their expectations, talk with their partners about what they are reading, and read with a standpoint of embracing text complexities. To begin, you might point out to students that when you begin reading a nonfiction text, it is helpful to do a quick preview of the text, noting how the text is organized and making a plan for yourself as a reader.

After reading the title, *No Monkeys, No Chocolate*, you might set the book down for a moment and say, "Hmm, . . . *No Monkeys, No Chocolate*. That's kind of a funny title. Normally, I wouldn't pair together chocolate and monkeys. Could that be a mistake? But Melissa Stewart has written more than 150 science books for kids. I bet she has a reason for this title. Why might the author have written the title in this way?" You might pause and then turn a few pages and say, "The book starts by listing chocolaty desserts, and then it says":

But you can't make chocolate without . . .

"Hmm, . . . that 'dot dot dot' (writers call that *ellipses*) makes me pause while I read. Watch me." You might reread that line with a dramatic pause while you turn the page and finish the line:

. . . cocoa beans.

"Ah, do you see how Melissa Stewart finishes her thought on the second page? We just went from chocolate to cocoa beans. Let's see what's on the next page.

Cocoa beans can't develop without cocoa pods.

"Hmm, . . . do you notice what Stewart is doing here as a writer? How is she structuring the text?" Only a few hands might raise, so perhaps you'll continue by turning the next few pages and reading:

Cocoa pods can't form without cocoa flowers . . .
. . . and midges.
Cocoa flowers can't bloom without cocoa leaves.

"Aha! Thumbs up if you see how Stewart is organizing this text." After many thumbs are raised, you might say, "It looks like the author is going back in time, right? She's organizing the text in a sort of cause-and-effect structure. You can't have chocolate without cocoa beans. And you can't have cocoa beans without cocoa pods. And so on." After a moment's pause, you might slowly make the connection to what a reader might learn from this text. You'll continue by saying, "So, readers, if this is how Stewart organized this text, what might you expect to learn? What expectation do you have for yourself as a nonfiction reader and learner?" Have students share in partnerships and then pick a few student goals to share.

As you jot some of these expectations on a chart (either physical or digital), you might continue, "Readers, do you see how you formed your own expectations by quickly previewing the text and asking yourself how the text was organized? Now we have some learning to do! Make sure you hold these expectations in your mind as we read. I bet Melissa Stewart will teach you information to help you become smarter about this topic, and you'll want to talk with your partner about all that you are learning. Quickly, looking at this list of expectations, share your expectations that you have for yourself as a reader and learner with your partner. When you share a goal or expectation aloud with a partner, you're more like to have success with that goal!"

After a moment of setting intentions, you might begin to move to class toward your other two goals: talking about what they are reading and embracing the complexities of a text. You might say, "So readers, as we read, you'll want to check in often with your partner to share your journey of learning. One way to share your learning journey is by thinking about the information you are learning and the ideas you are having. Remember that as texts get more complex, they have more than one main idea. So as I read this, let's be thinking, "What ideas am I starting to see in this text?" As I read these next few pages, keep those questions in mind. You'll have an opportunity to chat about them with your partner in a moment."

You might read the first few pages, ending with:

Cocoa beans can't develop without cocoa pods.
Cocoa pods are the fruits of the cocoa tree. They look like small, lumpy footballs growing on the tree's trunk and main branches. Inside each pod, white, gooey pulp surrounds thirty to forty cocoa beans—just enough for one candy bar.

You might then have students turn and talk, sharing the information they are learning and the ideas they are having. It's predictable that students will be captivated by the content they are learning, so be on the lookout for talk that centers more around facts than ideas, and coach in to help them notice more complexity than they might have noticed at first. You might capture students' conversations visually, writing the information down in one color and ideas in other, drawing arrows illustrating the connections kids are making through their talk. You might continue this process across a few pages, also layering other ways nonfiction is complex. Voice over some tips to help raise the level of what the entire class is doing. Here are you some tips that you can turn into coaching or voiceovers to support students in seeing more complexity in texts.

- **Tell students to expect relationships as they read.** These are not relationships between characters, but relationships between different bits of content. You might say, "Readers, one way of seeing more ideas in the text is to consider relationships. Earlier, we discovered that Melissa Stewart uses a cause-and-effect text structure to tie her chapters together. That means, as we read, we might wonder, 'How does one thing lead to another? How does one thing affect another in this process?' Or even 'If this part was left out, how would the entire process be affected?' What new ideas does that give you? Keep talking to your partner."

- **Teach how authors layer their writing with multiple ideas.** Some of these will be super clear and obvious, some less clear and subtle. As students talk in partnerships, coach them, asking, "What are some ideas that are easy to spot in this section? What ideas stood out to you during your first read of this text? What ideas are harder to find in this section? What ideas slowly came through as you read this part of the text again or talk about it again with your partner?"

- **Explain that an author's job when writing nonfiction is to teach a lot of information about a topic.** Students' jobs as readers are, at times, to prioritize the information, ranking it in importance as it relates to the overall topic or idea or in a matter of relevance. Readers can ask themselves, "Which detail relates most closely to the idea the author is teaching? Which detail most strongly shows the main idea of this part? Which detail is most important to teach others about this topic? Least important? What does that let you know about which idea might be most significant in this text?"

- **Teach students how authors of nonfiction often give a call to action toward the end of their books or articles.** Coach students to use their partnerships to find possible calls to action and discuss ways to become involved with the topic in their own communities. You might pose the questions, "What bigger issues is Melissa Stewart tackling in this text? What things can you and your partner do to get involved with this topic? What would you teach others to do about this topic?"

Nonfiction read-alouds are a time to shine a light in all the different corners of work students can engage in when reading independently. It's a special time to gather kids together, calling them to the different layers of work that await them when reading to learn about their world. Teaching students to think complexly as they read nonfiction shows them all the different ways they might think and talk about a book, boosts them toward a higher complexity of comprehension, and most importantly, fosters a love for nonfiction reading.

As you prepare for your nonfiction read-alouds, you also can consider other possibilities for how to engage children in informational texts. Some teachers have found "video-alouds"—times during read-aloud where students watch clips of videos—to be very powerful. They prepare for these times the same way they might prepare for a traditional read-aloud—choosing where to pause the clip to think aloud, where to push students to turn and talk to discuss why an author might have included a particular part or what different ideas this text seems to convey so far or the author's point of view on this topic so far. A visual text can help to pop out some of the work in ways that are more overt to children. Of course, you will not want video-alouds to be your main read-aloud, by any means. However, now and again, you may find that varying your media can rally children to work that might be otherwise difficult and less than engaging.

Then too, other teachers have found that giving students some materials during read-aloud can support their engagement in the text, as well as cross-text work. They offer students maps to hold as they listen to read-alouds about a particular American Indian tribe, letting students discuss what that land is called today and how it is different from what existed then. Or they provide students with a word bank with a few key terms, both academic and vocabulary, that will be most important and powerful to use across the read-aloud. Or they offer students images, photos, diagrams, or a timeline that can better support their learning. My organization has videos of nonfiction read-alouds in action on our Vimeo website (www.vimeo.com/tcrwp), and I especially encourage you to watch the videos that Kathleen Tolan ("Bringing Close Reading and Accountable Talk into an Interactive Read Aloud of Gorillas, Grades 3–5") and Amanda Hartman ("Bringing Close Reading and Text-Based Questions into an Interactive Read Aloud of Bugs! Bugs! Bugs!, Grades K–2") have made around nonfiction read-alouds. These will likely offer you additional ideas and methods for conducting your own nonfiction read-aloud.

Chapter 14

Helping All Learners Access the Curriculum/Differentiation

THE STRUCTURE of the reading workshop and its sister, the writing workshop, are both deliberately kept simple and predictable, because the work of helping individual readers and writers requires teachers to be able to do the complex work of listening, adapting, and teaching responsively. The simplicity and clarity of workshop structures have allowed both reading and writing workshops to be built around what is almost a reverence for listening and for responsive teaching. Open any page of the texts written by Don Graves and Marie Clay, two of the most influential people upon whose shoulders reading and writing workshops have been built, and you will hear them rhapsodizing about the need for teachers to take cues from learners. Visit any school that leads effective reading and writing workshops and you will come away describing those classrooms as responsive and intimate.

In this chapter, I'll try to address the challenges and promises of responsive teaching. Clearly this is one of those topics that deserves a book unto itself, and this may in fact be the topic I take up next. Surely, there are few topics that matter more.

I'll write about ways of giving all kids access—and also about ways that I don't think make sense. I do this based on the assumption that saying *yes* involves saying *no*. Warren Buffett, one of the world's top investors, recently said, "People ask me for the secret of my success. It's my ability to say *no*. Day in and day out, I look at investment proposals and I say, 'No, no, no, no.' Then one comes along that looks exactly right and I say, 'Yes.' One *yes* can get you very far."

You and I are, in a sense, investors. We look over proposals for what will help our students, and we, like Warren Buffett, need to say "No, no, no, no." Then when one comes along that looks exactly right, we can say *yes*.

READING WORKSHOP AND RESPONSE TO INTERVENTION (RTI)

Meeting the needs of the diverse learners who enter our classrooms each day is a shared concern for school districts across the country. As outlined in the Individuals with Disabilities Education Improvement Act (IDEIA), reauthorized in 2004, it is critical for schools to meaningfully and proactively address the needs of all students, including struggling readers, within the regular education classroom, thus reducing the need for special education services. IDEIA mandates that before school districts can identify a child as having a specific learning disability, they must first determine if a child responds to "scientific, research-based intervention" (IDEIA 2004).

Many districts have turned to response to intervention (RTI) as a way to best meet students' needs. RTI requires teachers, schools, and districts to administer research-based universal screening assessments to all students at the start of the school year and then to design classroom-based and out-of-classroom interventions based on that data. Those interventions are to be implemented with fidelity, so they are closely aligned to the curriculum taught in the classroom.

Running records are an approved universal screening tool for RTI, and these assessments will provide useful data about which students are not making progress at the expected rates (rate, accuracy, comprehension), which teachers can use to provide appropriate data-based instruction to meet students' needs within the classroom setting. For additional information about administering running records and analyzing assessment data, see Chapter 3 in *Reading Pathways*. It will be important to create a protocol within your school that details how staff will administer running records so the validity of the data is boosted.

RTI relies heavily on high-quality instruction within the general education classroom, referred to as Tier I instruction, with the goal of meeting 80–90% of student needs within this setting. This is done through the use of scientific, research-based approaches that include explicit and systematic instruction in phonics and phonemic awareness, vocabulary, fluency, and reading comprehension. These are precisely the principles on which the reading workshop is based. Schools and districts that adopt reading workshop and RTI find that they are well equipped to meet the needs of their students through increasing tiers of support.

Reading workshop classrooms are designed to support all learners in the classroom, whether or not they are reading on grade level, through differentiated small-group work and one-on-one conferences as well as through minilessons which are broadly supportive and sometimes include differentiated scaffolds. Reading workshop classrooms are proactive, rather than reactive, with teachers modifying instruction based on the specific needs of their learners. Suggested modifications that can be made to units of study based on data are detailed across this chapter. Then, too, teachers pull flexible, planned small groups based on a host of data collected from progress-monitoring tools, including running records and performance assessments, as well as analysis of students' writing about reading.

In one classroom, during a third-grade reading unit on nonfiction reading skills, after teaching a minilesson on identifying the structure of a text and using that structure to guide note-taking, the teacher sent students off to read independently from their within-reach books. From her analysis of students' running records, the teacher identified a small group of readers who needed additional support with fluency, so she designed a series of small groups to support students with their intonation. On this day, she gathered these students together for small-group instruction designed to help them read texts fluently. After providing a quick demonstration to highlight how she used her voice to pop out the structure of the text, she got to work coaching readers while they tried the same work in different accessible texts. Then, the teacher conferred one-on-one with a different student whose initial performance assessment revealed that she needed more foundational support with identifying details that supported the main idea of a text, before moving on to confer with another reader. Across these small groups and conferences, the teacher kept careful records that she could study later to design her ongoing work with students around these skills.

Within an RTI model, children spend their bulk of their time in Tier I instruction, which means that high-quality classroom instruction in reading is critical. The very best reading intervention, administered in a thirty-minute chunk of time, cannot make up for the five hours of time children spend in the classroom. Because of this, school districts are wise to invest a significant amount of time and energy into strengthening teaching and learning within the classroom.

While the classroom-based interventions are underway, teachers are expected to regularly monitor student progress toward goals and benchmarks and make adjustments to instruction, providing necessary levels of support until all students are able to achieve success. At times, progress monitoring of student achievement may reveal that students are not making sufficient progress toward benchmarks, and students may be moved into Tier II support. At Tier II, support becomes increasingly intensive, with teachers gathering together smaller groups of students several times a week for extended periods of time. This support is provided in addition to, not in place of, Tier I reading instruction, and students cannot be removed from reading, writing, or math instruction for this intervention.

This Tier II support can be provided within and outside of the reading workshop classroom. Teachers identify a target need, design a series of small-group or guided reading sessions to support students with that need, and use assessments for progress monitoring before, during, and after the intervention to evaluate whether or not an intervention is working and to make adjustments to better support students. If an initial screening reveals that a small group of students are having difficulty summarizing narrative texts, the teacher might design a series of small groups across a six- to nine-week span that will support students with strengthening this skill. We recommend that this instruction draw on the wealth of resources available in this series.

Of course, it's likely that a small number of students will not make adequate progress with the Tier I and II supports you provided, and you'll want to transition those students to Tier III support. This support, which occurs outside of the classroom, is in addition to the Tier I interventions provided in the general education classroom. This level of support is typically reserved for 1–5% of students. During this phase, you may choose to draw on supplemental programs designed to target students' specific needs, or you may choose to provide school-designed interventions.

You will find it useful to keep your school's RTI framework in mind as you read through the remainder of this chapter, considering ways your school's RTI program already meets the needs of your diverse learners. As you read on, be on the lookout for additional ideas you can say yes to, ideas that data shows your students need.

ADJUST TEACHING BASED ON YOUR DATA

The start of the school year is a critical time for assessment. In *Reading Pathways*, we give detailed suggestions for how you can assess your readers

to determine their precise needs before making adjustments to your instruction. As detailed above, running records are a universal screening tool for RTI. The previous year's teacher will have passed along data about levels of text complexity that each of your children can and cannot tackle, and your own running records will confirm or alter that information. Be sure that if you have many readers below level L, you look to the battery of foundational assessments that are discussed in the K–2 series and are available in the digital resources. For instance, you might decide it is important to assess some of your students on their ability to read high-frequency words with automaticity.

It's likely that you'll also give a performance preassessment prior to the launch of each unit, and you'll want to look across these assessments as well. At the start of the year, you'll note cross-class trends that can shape your whole-class instruction. Perhaps fourth-grade teachers will notice that many students summarize texts by trying to give a blow-by-blow recap with no effort to prioritize and be selective. If this is the case, teachers at that grade level may want to talk with each other about ways to adjust unit plans based on these assessments.

As you get to know your students, you'll construct a portrait of who each reader in your class is. This will be based on your running records and performance assessments, and it will also draw on your studies of behaviors during reading workshop. For example, it will be important for you to sometimes scan the room to see whose eyes are focused on text and whose are roaming the room. It will be important for you to analyze students' Post-it entries and their talk about texts. You will want to draw on these broad understandings of data as you design your instruction.

Although you will tweak and revise your units, you can rest assured from the start that these units were piloted, taught, and written so that they support a wide range of readers. After all, this entire curriculum has been piloted in the most high-need areas of New York City, the most affluent suburbs around NYC, and in countries as diverse as Singapore, Jordan, Austria, and Chile. Teachers in a wide range of schools have all taught these units using whole-class and small-group instruction, conferring, and techniques of differentiated instruction to bring all kids to high levels of success.

This doesn't mean, however, that there won't be ways you need to adjust the tempo and flow of these units of study based on your data. If you have analyzed your initial assessments prior to launching your reading instruction—that is, if the sequence of units you will teach is still an open question—and if your students' skills are extremely low or extremely high, I recommend that you and your colleagues turn to the introduction of the *If . . . Then . . . Curriculum* book for your grade level. That introduction will suggest how you might alter the sequence of units in ways that are responsive to your students' needs. For example, perhaps fifth-grade teachers should provide students with a preliminary nonfiction unit before Unit 2 to shore up their foundational skills. *If . . . Then . . . Curriculum* summarizes the way a number of auxiliary units could go.

One caveat. If you and your students are new to reading workshop, I recommend you start with the first Units of Study book for your grade level. If you decide to teach your first unit of study by relying only on the summary of a unit (such as those provided in the *If . . . Then . . . Curriculum* book), you will be foregoing the tremendously supportive scaffold of a Units of Study book—the day-to-day guidance that details how your instruction might unfold and provides you with the coaching, support, and materials you need to teach that unit well. My advice, then, is for you to self-assess, and if this teaching is new to you, no matter what your students' skill levels might be, stay with the first Unit of Study book, adjusting it somewhat based on your assessment of your students. The only exception I'd make to this is that if you are teaching in a school that has Units of Study books at every grade level and if the first book in the grade before yours is not already being used by that teacher, borrow that book and teach at least the first bend from it as a precursor to the first bend of your own book (or teach the entire unit from the earlier grade).

Of course, if you are already well into the first unit, it won't be an option to alter the sequence of units for at least the start of the year anyhow. Know that the series as a whole provides you with many resources that should help you add sessions designed especially for your students, should your assessments reveal additional needs. For example, if you are teaching fourth-grade character work in reading, and some of your children are having trouble figuring out how characters are feeling in the stories, if you look through the first- or second-grade fiction reading units focused on character or through the *If . . . Then . . . Curriculum* book for second grade, you will find lots of lower-level tools, mentor texts, teaching points, and minilessons. You can also invent minilessons yourself that address the skills students need to learn. To develop those minilessons, you can draw on your students' reading, the strands of the learning progression that describe what you hope students will learn to do, and on relevant conferring and small-group work suggestions found as part of every session.

Although it is entirely reasonable to plan a detour in your unit of study, I want to advise you against stretching out a unit to longer than six weeks. That is, if you do bring some supportive instruction into a unit, you might need to lop off the last bend. Always, the most sophisticated work in a unit is what comes in the final stretch. Youngsters need to be finished with a chunk of work and to have the chance to get a fresh start on some new work. Rest assured that there will be opportunities to cycle back to skills your readers need particular support with in future units of study.

NO MATTER WHAT, YOU NEED TO CONSIDER WHERE LEARNERS ARE AND SUPPORT THEM IN MAKING PROGRESS FROM THERE

My colleagues and I find the principles of Universal Design for Learning (UDL) to be a helpful tool in guiding educators to consider how to support all learners. As defined by the National Center for the Universal Design for Learning, UDL is "is a set of principles for curriculum development that give all individuals equal opportunities to learn" (www.udlcenter.org/aboutudl/whatisudl). At the core of UDL are three principles: provide multiple means of representation (the *what* of learning), provide multiple means of action and expression (the *how* of learning), and provide multiple means of engagement (the *why* of learning). These principles help educators design instruction that, from its creation, is accessible to all. These principles relate directly to workshop teaching.

Workshop teaching is a curriculum designed to offer access to all students. The very structure of the workshop allows for and expects that teachers will provide intimate instruction that addresses each learner's needs. The structures of workshop teaching call for teachers to adapt a responsive stance to instruction, taking their cues from children and planning instruction that articulates next steps or goals that address their needs. The minilessons are already multilevel. For example, think about a minilesson that teaches students that readers read a nonfiction text, raising questions and carrying those questions with them to grow new thinking. I, myself, raise questions and carry them with me when I read the latest reading research, and that is also a teaching point that first-graders would benefit from hearing. Students in your classroom might be asking different questions that align with the reading goals specific to their needs. For instance, some students might carry questions pertaining to author's craft and structure, while others carry questions that help them figure out the sequence of events. The units brim with examples of instruction such as that—instruction that can at one and the same time support readers who are working at very different places on the learning progressions.

All of this means, then, that workshop teaching is the absolute opposite of one-size-fits-all instruction. The principles of UDL, such as utilizing different methods to teach students, giving them access to different digital tools or supports to express their learning, and engaging students through providing opportunities for choice and self-assessment, are just a few examples of where workshop teaching and principles of UDL intersect.

There are some in education who suggest that some children should not attend minilessons if they are reading at what is considered far below grade level. They suggest to teachers that a few students, for whom the whole-class minilesson does not seem exactly suited, should instead work on word work activities or something of that nature while the rest of the class gathers for the minilesson. On the whole, the idea that a few students would be segmented from the rest and perhaps thus be made to feel that they are not capable enough to attend the whole-class lesson is troubling to me. I see the minilesson as not just the teaching for that day, but also as a community-building experience. Just like we believe you might read an Emily Dickinson poem aloud to students who are not sophisticated enough to grasp its full meaning but who will benefit from hearing the poem, there are important reasons to give students access to ways of talking in the intellectual community of the class. Minilessons help develop the language, the ways of being, that characterize the intellectual community in your classroom.

Of course, if you teach in an integrated coteaching classroom, you might use the coteaching method of parallel teaching to meet the needs of your students performing far below benchmark. On occasion, one teacher teaches a minilesson from the unit, and across the room, the other teacher adapts that minilesson in ways that especially support the less proficient readers at the same time. When you teach in a self-contained special education classroom, sometimes it may be difficult to find one minilesson that meets the needs of a majority of your class. In that case, you might take advantage of station teaching, where you teach three different minilessons to three different small groups. While one minilesson is happening, the rest of the class reads independently. Of course, these aren't methods that would happen every day. These methods of teaching would be layered into your unit plans as needed.

PLAN ON MAKING YOUR MINILESSONS DIFFERENTIATED

There are a number of very accessible ways you can make any minilesson more differentiated. These methods support the principles of UDL by providing multiple entry points to the learning, meeting the students where they are so that you can support them in making progress from there.

Assigning Roles within Partnerships

Let's think, for example, about the partnership work that occurs in the midst of minilessons. You will quickly find that if partnerships are left on their own, what tends to happen is that the same student—usually the more proficient or dominant student—will take the lead. So if you say, "Turn and tell your partner how you think this part of the text connects to what we read before. How does it fit?" and you give just a minute or two for students to talk about this, the dominant partner is apt to talk first, while the less dominant partner listens, nods, and follows along. There often isn't time for both youngsters to talk, so typically the stronger student does the work, and the less proficient student becomes his sounding board.

Because this is predictable, you can add a layer of support to your minilessons by assigning roles to students within their partnerships. I recommend that one student be named Partner 1 and the other, Partner 2, and you can make a point of asking for one or the other to talk first, alternating this over the course of days. This means that when you say, "Turn and tell your partner how you think this part of the text connects to what we read before. How does it fit?", you can add, "Partner 1, go first."

If you decide (quietly) which member of each partnership is Partner 1 and which is Partner 2, making the more proficient one Partner 2, you can make deliberate decisions about whether you want the more or the less proficient reader to do the talking at any one time. For example, if you are asking about what we already know about a character, the first person to be able to offer a thought is probably in the easier position, able to choose the low-hanging fruit, so in that instance, you may say, "Partner 1s go first," or "Partner 1s, you say something you already know about the character, and Partner 2, you think of an idea that gives you about the character." Sometimes, of course, if the more proficient partner goes first, this provides the less proficient partner with a second demonstration text, making it more supportive to be the second partner to speak. Similarly, sometimes the work will be particularly difficult. You might ask for the more proficient reader to have a go, and then at the end of the minilesson, you might say, "Will Partner 1s, who didn't have a chance to try this during the minilesson, stay with me while Partner 2s, you get started on your reading?"

Embedding Assessments and Coaching Responsively

Another way you can differentiate your minilesson is by embedding quick assessments across your minilessons and coaching responsively based on your observations. In the midst of a minilesson, you will often channel students to turn and talk to practice what you have just taught, and while they do so, you will want to listen carefully to ascertain whether or not they are grasping what you are trying to teach. Carry (or think about) relevant strands of the Informational Reading or Narrative Reading Learning Progressions with you as you listen into conversations, and listen for roughly where students' work falls. Or you might choose to handle this differently and ask students to write on white boards instead of talking to a partner and then hold the white boards high afterward so you can quickly keep tabs on their work. Alternatively, if you want to take account of what your more struggling readers are thinking, you might call, "Will Partner 1s say aloud what you are thinking, and Partner 2s, will you record your partner's words exactly, writing his or her name as well, so I can look at those later?"

Be prepared to coach your students in response to what you overhear. You might say something like, "Many of you are talking about tiny lessons the character learned, lessons learned in just one paragraph. Try to name the lessons characters learned across the text." A minute or two later, you might intervene again and provide a bit more support, saying aloud, "I'm hearing . . ." and then repeat what you've just heard a student or two saying that can function as another example or as a template.

Varying Your Coaching to Meet the Range of Needs in Your Class

Of course, you may also choose to ask a student or two to report to the class in a way that functions as a model for others. If you want this to provide the rest of the class with a mentor text, you'll want to call on a student you overheard earlier whose response is what you are after.

Just a word of caution, the trick is to do this without extending the minilesson beyond ten to twelve minutes in length. You may need to crop part of the written minilesson to stay within that time frame, and you certainly will need to leave many issues left to be tackled in small groups.

Providing Visual Texts as a Scaffold

Another way to adapt your minilessons so they support all your students is to offer visual examples as scaffolding across the parts of the lesson. If you feel that the work might be particularly difficult, or if a strategy taught includes several steps, you might post a chart listing the steps of the strategy. During the teaching portion of the minilesson, touch each step on the chart as you demonstrate that step, helping students connect your demonstration with the step of the strategy. Then, during the active engagement, you might say something like "Remember, I have a chart up here with steps you can follow to do this work. Use it if you need it." Adding illustrations to your charts whenever possible will offer additional support. Illustrations often function to make an abstract concept more concrete and accessible for diverse learners. Study the suggested anchor charts in the Online Resources for examples of ways illustrations can capture complex activities and concepts. Whenever possible, keep your illustrations consistent across charts, so that whenever you're asking students to stop and think, you use the same thought bubble. Your charts could also provide access for more of your students if you included exemplars for students working below and above the level at which the minilesson was taught. For example, if you taught a minilesson on jotting about characters in fourth grade and your exemplar jot was a fourth-grade, R/S/T level, you might also provide an example of what a jot would look like for students reading levels N/O/P/Q and U/V/W so that all students understand what their work should look like.

You might even provide a small group of students with a mini-version of the day's chart and ask that they hold the chart as you demonstrate, touching each of the steps as you model how a proficient reader does the work. Then, as students work with their partners, the chart could function in a similar way, guiding them through each step in the active engagement.

Using videos or digital texts in reading instruction can hit multiple points for UDL. This increases engagement for all children, and it's particularly helpful in making sure that high-level thinking work is accessible to all children. Two kinds of videos particularly spring to mind as useful for classroom teachers: short narratives (ones that tell a story) and short informational texts (ones that teach).

When considering how you might use videos in your teaching, especially for children who might read at lower levels, there are many options. When teaching an especially challenging concept, you may decide to ground this work in a video, allowing students to grasp an advanced concept through an especially accessible text. For example, if you were teaching your readers to investigate symbolism as a way to think about theme, you might gather children around a music video or an advertisement that incorporates symbolism in striking and obvious ways. Then when you introduce the work with print texts, your children will already be familiar with the thinking work.

You can also use videos to beef up students' background knowledge on a topic. Their social studies texts will seem easier when they know a little bit about the topic—say, the colonial period in American history. Students' science experiments will make more sense if they know something about how plants grow. Science, nature, and history videos can really add to children's knowledge base. You might, therefore, bookmark some good sites for parents and students. You might make sure that you have some videos in most of your text sets, so that children can learn from digital sources as well as print. You can use movie scenes (available on YouTube), for instance, as great texts for comparing character traits or for thinking about the way the setting affects the characters. Many music videos tell stories, and these make for great short texts for studying themes or symbolism.

A word of caution: you can't rely on having fast or open Internet service while you're teaching. You don't want to depend on an online video for your lesson, only to find that the server is down that day and the video is unavailable. To avoid that, download the videos you want to use ahead of time, placing them in a folder on your desktop and/or a flash drive. There are a variety of tools that will let you download YouTube videos. Look them up online, talk to colleagues or to a fifth-grader, and get your folders set up in advance to save you time.

You'll also want to turn to the archives of museums and other educational sites such as National Geographic, the History Channel, and the Discovery Channel. Look on these sites and create some lists of helpful videos. If you can download them, do so, because they may disappear later!

Guiding Students toward Appropriate Texts

You can also decide to make your minilessons differentiated by channeling groups of students toward texts your assessments reveal to be especially appropriate for them. Say, for example, you are teaching a lesson about identifying shifts in text structure in informational texts. Some of your students will be ready to make sense of rapidly shifting text structures, so you might provide them with a text that provides opportunities for that work. Meanwhile, you might give another set of students a text with sections that have explicit text structures, marked off by headings. This type of differentiation occurs naturally anytime you ask students to pull out one of their texts to use during the active engagement, because students will then be working with texts at their independent reading level.

You could choose, instead, to ask all students to read the same text, and then channel the more proficient partner (Partner 2) to read aloud, asking Partner 1 to do other intellectual work.

Seating Students Strategically

Of course, strategically seating students will also help boost success during minilessons. You might want to assign students to spots on the rug, next to their reading partner, and make careful choices about which students will be seated in the most easily accessible spots on the rug. If you have a paraprofessional or another colleague in the room during your minilesson, you might suggest that she sit near particular students. That is, there are lots of ways to adjust the minilesson to make it differentiated for different students.

Supporting Students Who Need Additional Help Getting Started

If you are concerned that despite your best efforts to differentiate during a minilesson, some students may still not have gotten access to the content, you can end the minilesson by asking students to get started doing their work, and then you can use that time as an opportunity to notice students who aren't able to get started. The students who need further scaffolding will become apparent to you, and you can ask them to linger in the meeting area for some follow-up instruction that you'll make more accessible. This approach is especially useful if the strategy you are teaching is particularly new or essential.

USE CONFERRING AND SMALL-GROUP INSTRUCTION TO RESPOND TO STUDENTS

Ideally, when you confer and lead small groups, you are inventing instruction that addresses problems you may not even have known existed until you gathered with that small group or that individual. The ways that you teach responsively can end up being broadcasted more widely through mid-workshop teaching points, instructive share sessions, and newly invented minilessons.

Perhaps, in a nonfiction reading unit, a handful of your fifth-grade students are reading texts far below grade level and having trouble naming the topic of the text even when the topic is conveyed through explicit topic sentences and headings. Meanwhile, imagine you had planned to teach a minilesson emphasizing the fact that main ideas in a text are sometimes merely implicit. Readers may need to infer the main idea. While that teaching point addresses grade-level standards, you know that readers who can't determine main ideas even in texts that highlight them explicitly probably won't have success inferring *implicit* main ideas.

When you pull a chair alongside such a reader, you'll want to determine where this student's skills fall on the learning progression for reading for main ideas. If you find that this reader's work with main idea falls on the second-grade level of the "Main Idea(s)/Supporting Details/Summary" strand of the learning progression, it will help to look to the third-grade level to determine a next step.

It can help to envision your small groups and conferences not as stand-alone conversations with a child, but as sessions that make up a larger course of study on a topic. If you identify that a major need for one reader is word solving, you might plan several conferences and small groups around the topic, accelerating the student in this particular area. Your performance preassessment might reveal that another reader is meeting grade-level expectations for analyzing author's craft, so you might design a series of conferences that continue to push the reader's skills in this area. Working with students over time to accelerate their progress around a target need is a central tenet of RTI. It is important to set clear short- and long-term goals with students. Frequently, students performing below grade level feel overwhelmed by the amount of growth they need to make to be reading the same levels as their peers. By setting short-term goals that you share with students, you allow them to work toward something attainable and to see their progress. Always,

your small-group work and your conferring will show children how to do something they can do first with scaffolds and supports and then, soon afterward, with independence. Chapter 8 explains in detail ways you might remove scaffolds with your small-group instruction. Rest assured that even if you maintain a focus on one skill for a chunk of time in your conferences, helping students to become more proficient with that work, your students will have opportunities to practice a repertoire of skills during your minilessons and read-alouds.

You might also choose to use some of your conferring and small-group work time as a way to orient readers to upcoming work you anticipate will be difficult. Let's say you are planning to teach a lesson on growing ideas about characters. In a small group the day before the lesson, you might preview some of this work by showing students a video of a commercial featuring characters with distinct actions. You might also show them a comic strip and ask them to name what the characters are doing, then say what those actions make them think. In this way, you would be providing multiple means of representation of the content you are teaching, while also helping students practice the work first on a more accessible text. The next day, when you gather students in the meeting area for a minilesson on growing ideas about characters, this time using the class read-aloud as your demonstration text, these students will be better able to access that content.

Support Readers with a Variety of Methods

In addition to your minilessons, conferences, and small groups, you may provide differentiated instruction in a number of other ways. These methods can be used flexibly as part of small-group work and conferences for specific readers, and some can be brought into share sessions, mid-workshop teaching, and connections.

Shared reading is a particularly effective method for helping students who need extra support with particular skills. Gathering students around a shared text and reading the text together is especially useful for teaching word-solving strategies and for helping students orchestrate information, as well as for supporting fluency. In primary classrooms, teachers may do shared reading with the whole class every day, but you might instead decide to use this structure to support small groups. These brief (typically ten-minute) sessions often begin with a warm-up in which you and the students read a familiar text in unison, almost singing along together. Then you'll want to draw students' attention to a new text that you'll leave with them to work on after the shared reading is over. You may read that text several times in shared reading sessions before leaving it with students to reread on their own. Note that its not shared reading alone that helps—it's this and also the decision to revisit texts many times.

Guided reading sessions are very useful to support students in accessing texts a notch above those they would be able to read independently, and you can read more in-depth information about these sessions in Chapter 8. When planning a guided reading session, you'll want to design brief text introductions that focus on the tricky aspects of the text, keeping these to just a minute or two in length so you move students quickly toward reading the text. Students sit alongside each other reading the text silently until you come close and ask for them to read a bit aloud. Coach the first reader quickly, with lean prompts, and then move on to offer brief support to the next reader. You can tailor these groups to meet individual student's needs by layering in scaffolds, such as coaching students to carry a bookmark with questions to remind them to monitor themselves as they read. These extra supports can be the entry point students need to progress to more challenging texts.

Reader's Theater, which connects oral reading to genre and drama, allows students to work on fluency while being part of the story. This allows students to work on fluency and character theories simultaneously. Students who have difficulty inferring traits when reading can benefit from Reader's Theater as well. There are Reader's Theater sets from Benchmark Education that are leveled. Within one text, the character lines are leveled as well. For instance, one text might have character lines that go from level F to M (they are available in Spanish as well).

While many of your students will be ready to engage in partnerships and book clubs as we've described them throughout in this guide, you may have a few students in your room who would benefit from the kindergarten and first-grade model of partnerships. In those early grades, students transition from independent reading to partner reading midway through the workshop. The transition to partner time gives those readers a second wind, allowing for more time dedicated to eyes on print, this time reading with the company of a peer. Partner time can also give students time to practice fluency or can serve as an alternative to jotting, where students read side by side and turn and talk when they have ideas. Over time, you'll want to move students toward progressively longer and longer periods of uninterrupted reading time so that eventually the bulk of their time can be spent on independent reading.

You may find that some of your students, in particular those who have difficulty with fluency or word work, may benefit from having kindergarten buddies and visiting the kindergarten classroom around three times a week (outside of reading workshop time) to help the kindergarteners with their reading and to read to these younger buddies. This arrangement provides powerful support to these younger buddies—but it also can reinforce important foundational skills for your students and dignify the time they spend reading very accessible texts. After all, they are teachers and need to choose books for their tutees.

Above all, keep in mind that students who are having difficulty in reading need even *more* time to read—not less. So they should be getting every minute of reading workshop, possibly in addition to more time to read outside of reading workshop time. Buddy reading time can be valuable for these readers if it offers them authentic powerful reasons to practice their reading, but this needs to happen outside of your reading workshop time.

Be extremely cautious before letting these readers be pulled from your reading workshop for any reason. Richard Allington has cautioned that this pulling of readers who need the most support leads to less reading time for them, confusion in terms of not knowing the content the rest of the class has learned, and disjointed instruction. It does not lead to reading growth. So be protective of your reading workshop (as you are of your writing workshop) and think carefully about how to maximize each minute.

Use Materials to Differentiate

You may wonder how it is possible to support all your children, working at their just-right levels, while still teaching a compelling unit. The easiest way to do this is to differentiate expectations by differentiating the materials you provide to students.

If a child is a novice reader, it doesn't do any good to put *Bridge to Terabithia* in her hands. She needs to read books that are at the high end of what she can handle, and she needs to be supported and taught in ways that help her progress quickly up the ladder of text complexity. A good teacher needs to ascertain what a child's just-right level is and teach at that point and then progress expeditiously from there.

Reading workshop classrooms include a range of readers, and it's likely that your first running records revealed that your students are reading on a wide range of levels. Be sure your classroom library features books on the reading levels of all students in your class. As UDL has taught us, students need choice and engagement in content. Your library showcases your beliefs about literacy and lets students know what books are valued in your classroom. So if you are teaching a fourth-grader who is reading at a first-grade reading level, you need to have books in your classroom library at levels G, H, and I, perhaps borrowed from a first-grade teacher who isn't currently using them, so the reader can fill her baggie with books from those bins. Finding books at levels G, H, and I that a fourth-grader finds engaging takes some doing. The time that you spend finding engaging materials for this child will be worth its weight in gold because this can help you support a love of reading. You might rotate lower-level high-interest book bins with other teachers in your grade, trading book bins with another teacher every few weeks to give students access to a broader variety of books at their reading levels. Your school may decide to keep some level E–J books out of primary classrooms, using them only with older, below-benchmark readers, so those books don't become identified as "baby" books. Many schools have done this with James Howes' Pinky and Rex series.

To increase engagement for your below-benchmark readers, you might decide to dedicate part of your read-aloud time to books that they will know well. Imagine that you are an I-level reader in fourth grade. Your peers are gobbling up engaging titles such as *Bridge to Terabithia*, similar to the read-aloud texts that you experience in the classroom. One day, your teacher reads aloud *There's a Nightmare in My Closet*, by Mercer Mayer, or Caldecott Medal winner *The Stray Dog*, by Marc Simont (both level I texts). Your classmates talk in deep thoughtful ways about the book—and suddenly you see yourself as a reader, an integral part of your classroom.

If you have students reading at the second-grade level or below, you'll want to talk with your primary colleagues or look at *A Guide to the Reading Workshop: Primary Grades* to get a sense of volume expectations for these readers. While it's reasonable that a fifth-grader holding a copy of *The Lightning Thief* by Rick Riordan might read one book over the course of a week, you'd want to sound the alarms if you saw a student who is reading at a first-grade level doing the same. That is, I'd expect that a student reading at level G would need a baggie of perhaps ten books, reading these again and again over the course of the week. You will want to provide these students with materials to support the rereading of texts such as book logs that ask them to tally the number of books read rather that writing out the title of each text, or you

might teach students to plan out the order of the texts that they will read and then reread.

Students who are preemergent and emergent readers in upper grades will need additional supports. These students will need time reading with a partner, listening to books, and working on high-frequency words, as well as reading independently. You will want the book baggies for these students to be filled to the brim with books at their level, and you might also include shared reading and shared writing texts with which students are familiar. Some teachers find it helpful to type up (and correct) student's writing and put it in their book baggies to read during reading workshop. Students often write a level or two above their reading level. They can use their knowledge about their stories to read more complex sentences.

You might even create a schedule for students to follow during reading workshop that breaks their independent time into reading tasks such as ten minutes for reading and rereading just-right books, five minutes for partner reading, five minutes for going over high-frequency work flashcards, ten minutes for listening to books read to them on the computer. Schedules that break independent reading time into more manageable chunks can also be beneficial for students with low engagement.

If you teach a classroom full of students who are working way below benchmark levels, you may decide that some of the units recommended in this series won't work with your students. Fantasy, for example, may be hard to teach if students are well below benchmark. In this case, some teachers borrow units from previous grades; some put children into more general genre books, such as fiction, and tweak the minilessons in the unit to sound less genre specific. Although the teaching points within those units teach into specific genres, they also hit upon essential reading skills for students of all levels, such as the important role that setting plays in a text. In units such as this, read-aloud becomes the place where students reading below grade level access the genre-specific work of the unit.

You might also choose to differentiate the learning progressions that students use to self-assess. Chapter 6 in *Reading Pathways* particularly supports this work. Imagine that in your classroom, all of your students are self-assessing their work around analyzing author's craft. Some students are using the strands of the progression for grades 2, 3, and 4, while other students are using the strands for grade 3, 4, and 5. A few students even have level 6. All of your students are engaged in goal-setting and making action plans; however, each student is working on this at the level that is right for him. I recommend that you use your students' performance preassessments, as well as your formative assessments of students' work across the unit, to determine which levels of the learning progression you place in students' hands. Keep in mind that your students will likely need different progressions for different skills. That is, although a student might need the second-grade progression for analyzing point of view, he might be ready for the fourth-grade progressions for monitoring for meaning and word solving. Across the Units of Study books that make up this series and the *Reading Pathways* book, you'll find transferable examples of tools teachers have created to support students as they use the learning progressions.

When considering writing about reading in your classroom, you might decide that not all of your students need to write on their Post-its. Perhaps some students can record symbols or sketches on Post-its. Other students may type reading responses on iPads or use an app that allows them to speak their jot rather than using reading notebooks and pencils. Suppose you have a student who jots character traits on Post-its, but she has difficulty looking across these ideas to develop theories about the main and supporting characters. You might teach her to draw a web in her notebook for each character. This way, she can see the changes or consistency of characters' traits on one page, and she can start to do the deeper thinking of theories about characters and their relationships. All of these are ways to support learners to make sure that each student is accessing the content.

SOME GENERAL PRINCIPLES TO KEEP IN MIND ABOUT SUPPORTING ALL LEARNERS

It is difficult to write a chapter on supporting students with IEPs, when the biggest point to make is that these students are not the same. Every child who has an IEP (just like every child) has strengths and needs that are unique. Therefore, the same strategies and accommodations will not work the same way for each student. For example, Gene is a student who has great difficulty organizing his thoughts and articulating what he's thinking. He has no shortage of ideas, but he finds it challenging to express these ideas. In the same classroom, Stephanie is a student who is considered to have autism spectrum disorder. Inferring emotions is challenging for her, which makes it especially difficult for her to infer characters motivations. She also finds it difficult to

be flexible in her thinking and revise her ideas. She loves nonfiction and is always carrying around the latest issue of *Ranger Rick* magazine. Just looking at these two students, one can see that they need totally different types of support to help them to access the curriculum.

As different as every learner is, however, there are some important principles to keep in mind. These apply to working with any learner, but they are especially important when working with your students who need the most support.

Access to Curriculum Is the Overall Goal

Your objective is always to support all learners in accessing the curriculum. That means that when planning, you will want to ask questions such as "What might be difficult for certain students about this lesson (or series of lessons)?" "What will it look like when students do this work?" It also helps to ask, "What content from this unit is essential—and what content is nice, but not crucial?" Thinking about these goals can help you prioritize the accommodations you will make for your learners.

Prioritize Your Accommodations to Offer What Is Most Important for Each Student, and Teach toward Independence

It is true that there are endless things you could do to support learners. You could cover the feet of your chairs in cut-out tennis balls to minimize any undue background noise. You could set up listening centers. You could create bookmarks of every sort for every lesson. You could make graphic organizers. You could illustrate every chart. You could enlarge any text or make individual pocket-size copies of it. The hard truth is that there are a thousand things you could do for any student—but not a thousand hours in the day.

Prioritizing the supports for your learners is important. This means that some days you will offer more support to some groups or individuals than others. I want to caution you against believing that you need to spend endless hours developing materials so each child is always being given a new scaffold. I get a bit concerned when supporting all students sometimes translates into you making graphic organizers and other paraphernalia. In some cases, a particular graphic organizer may be useful, but each new scaffold is not necessarily a blessing. Sometimes it seems, in fact, that we inadvertently clutter up readers and writers with far too many demands. Certainly, if you do introduce a scaffold, you need to be sure to introduce it to students as a temporary scaffold, saying, "I'm giving you this chart now to help you organize your thinking about how these parts fit with the rest of the text. In two weeks, you'll need to do this organizing and thinking on your own, without the support of this tool." Make it clear to students from the outset that the ultimate goal is for them to work with less support.

I would suggest that the best and most important thing to do is to deeply know your students. Sometimes, especially at the start of the year, instead of conferring, I suggest you simply conduct an interview (a conversation really) in which your primary goal is to get to know the student better, so that you can better understand how to help that student learn. I also find it helpful to think about what previous students a current student might resemble. All students are unique, but there are certain strategies that can hold across students. For example, one year a colleague of mine had a child in her class who had great difficulty dealing with anger and would become upset easily and then be difficult to reach. This colleague spent some time educating herself about the rage cycle and what causes anger. Then, for the rest of her teaching career, she told me she felt better able to deal with students who had emotional issues, in particular, anger.

Focus on Students' Individual Goals and How You Are Helping Them Make Progress toward These Goals

When you are deciding what to prioritize, setting goals for a student (which could be the IEP goals) can help you to know what accommodations to make. For example, if a primary goal for a student is to get her to express herself and participate in class conversations more, then before reading workshop starts, I might talk to the student a bit about the content of a certain day's lesson, even perhaps helping her to think ahead about what she might say during the lesson. If that student was working with an adult volunteer during breakfast time twice a week, for example, I might ask that volunteer to read parts of that days' read-aloud and to converse with the reader about the passage, setting her up to feel more confident in class. That is, supporting a student before the class studies something will often be helpful when rehashing a lesson. That way, when the lesson occurs, the student feels more comfortable participating. In that instance, my goal for the student was not

so much to master the content of the lesson as it was for her to express herself and participate. It is important to plan with student goals and IEP goals in mind, making sure that you are supporting students in making progress toward these during the workshop.

Collaborate and Communicate with Other Invested Adults

Too often, the invested adults in a student's life don't always talk together about the instruction they are providing for that student. That is, the reading intervention specialist has one goal and pathway for instruction she is following, the classroom teacher has another, and the speech therapist has a third. The result is that the student ends up feeling scattered. Be sure that all service providers talk together about their goals for the student and how to help the student meet those goals. This matters tremendously. For example, if you give the reading intervention specialist a copy of a few strands of the learning progression that the student is focused on, when the student reads with that specialist, she also can ask the student to reflect on how well he is meeting his goals. Service providers are invaluable to the student, and making sure that the classroom teacher and service providers, in addition to parents/guardians are all a team and on the same page can help the student to feel as though he is getting a cohesive education. When students know exactly what is expected of them and how to help themselves to make progress, they feel empowered.

Know What Resources Are Available to You for Support

It is a Herculean task to support all learners—a monumental task that changes from year to year, class to class, and child to child. My respect for you is enormous. It is my hope that you will find the resources provided in these Units of Study helpful to you as you work to support all of your students in accessing the curriculum. The *If . . . Then . . . Curriculum* book can help you adjust your teaching based on your data and also offer you support in your small-group work and conferring. *Reading Pathways: Grades 3–5* will help you to gather that data and see how to analyze it to know where learners are and how to help them to get to the next step. The Units of Study themselves are filled with examples of small-group instruction and conferring to offer support and enrichment, as well as coaching notes for how to adjust the teaching of certain lessons, if needed. And the fact that the units unfold across the years means that you can easily look to a unit above or below your grade level for more support in tailoring your instruction.

In addition to the Units of Study, there are resources and materials that I would suggest as helpful to you. Two books that I recommend for you to read are Richard Allington's *What Really Matters for Struggling Readers: Designing Research-Based Programs* (2011) and *Understanding by Design*, by Grant Wiggins and Jay McTighe (2011). And, of course, remember that you and your colleagues are each other's greatest resources. When instruction is aligned across grades, whole-school conversations around reading instruction are possible. Your colleagues are treasure troves of information, and I highly encourage schools to make time, not only for grade teams to meet and plan, but also for cross-grade teams to meet, as well.

A SPECIAL NOTE ON SUPPORTING ENGLISH LANGUAGE LEARNERS

Because the Teachers College Reading and Writing Project is deeply involved with schools where classrooms brim with English language learners (ELLs), we spend a lot of time thinking about ways the reading workshop can be adjusted so that it is especially supportive for our ELLs. In many of our schools, teachers, coaches, and administrators have been working for decades on teaching reading and teaching language simultaneously throughout the workshop.

Balancing both—teaching reading and teaching language—is challenging but greatly rewarding for students and teachers, and the English learners in our classrooms are eager for the challenge.

Provide Consistent Teaching Structures

Workshop classrooms are organized in clear, predictable, and consistent ways that allow children to quickly become comfortable participating in the work of each day. Very early in the school year, ELL children come to understand that reading workshops start with the teacher giving a minilesson, and that during the minilesson they learn strategies that they are then expected to apply to their independent work. Children know that after the minilesson they will be expected to read independently and that the teacher will circulate around the room, conferring with individuals and with small groups. Children

also know that they will be expected at some point to share their work with a partner. When the reading time is over, children know that they need to put their materials away and gather with a partner (or in the meeting area) for a share session. When teachers follow these routines day after day, students can focus their energies on trying to figure out how to do their work, rather than on worrying about what they will be expected to do. The predictability of the workshop provides tremendous reassurance to a child who is just learning English, and this is amplified if workshop structures repeat themselves across other subjects.

Use Consistent Teaching Language

In addition, reading workshops are characterized by a consistent instructional language. The consistency of this language scaffolds each child's classroom experience, making it easier for a child who is just learning English to grasp the unique content that is being taught that day. For example, it helps that most minilessons start in a predictable manner, with teachers saying, "Readers," and then reviewing the content of previous minilessons, perhaps referencing a bulleted entry on a class chart. It helps children that every day the teacher encapsulates the day's minilesson in a sentence or two (the teaching point), which is repeated often, using the same language each time it is referenced. It does help that the teaching point usually becomes a bullet on a chart.

Offer Plentiful Opportunities for Reading Practice

Of course, the predictability of the workshop also means that teachers needn't invent a new way each day to support their English language learners. Because the same classroom structures are in place day after day, solutions that help on Tuesday will also help on Wednesday, Thursday, and Friday. In a workshop classroom, a sheet of language structures that you give to students one day can be threaded through partner conversations on many days.

The predictable structures also mean language learners can count on having not only a space for learning language, but also a place to practice. Whether your English language learner is a beginning speaker of English or an advanced one, she will have the opportunity to work on her reading and language skills each day. Repetition and practice are two important scaffolds that English language learners need to grow their literacy skills. They need to expand both their receptive language skills—their listening and reading—as well as their expressive language skills—their speaking and writing. The reading workshop is one more place where both of these skills can be cultivated.

Provide Access to a Broad Variety of Texts

All students benefit from seeing books in the classroom library that match their own experiences and culture. That is, it is extremely important, not just for your English language learners (but especially for them) that you made an effort to have books in your library that they will relate to. This includes having books in other languages, when you can. It is easier to find popular titles and series in different languages than you would think. Mo Willems' Pigeon and Knuffle Bunny series is available in Spanish, as are several Dr. Seuss books, The Magic Tree House series, and The Lightning Thief series, just to name a few.

Carefully considering what books are in your room also applies to your choice of read-aloud. If you have a few students whose home language is Spanish, think how much they would appreciate if your read-aloud was written in both English and Spanish. Think how much more comfortable those students would feel—how they would feel a sense that "This classroom welcomes me and my language." Or think how much these students would love if your choice of read-aloud was about a main character for whom English was not her first language. Teachers love titles such as *How my Parents Learned to Eat*, by Ina R. Friedman, *I Hate English*, by Ellen Levine and Steve Bjorkman, *Everybody Cooks Rice*, by Nora Dooley and *Home at Last*, by Susan Middleton Elya. This is, of course, not always possible, but keeping your classroom library and choice of read-alouds in mind is important for all of your students, but especially for your English language learners. A few titles that include lines in Spanish are *Abuela*, by Arthur Dorros, *I Love Saturdays y domingos*, by Alma Flor Ada, *Too Many Tamales*, by Gary Soto and Ed Martinez, *Hairs/Pelitos*, by Sandra Cisneros, and *Subway Sparrow*, by Leyla Torres (this has Polish lines too).

Use Assessment to Provide Extra Support for ELLs in All Stages of Learning English

Of course, there is no such thing as the "typical" English language learner. Like all learners, ELLs differ one from the next in many ways. Two significant factors contributing to their unique needs are the child's level of competence in his first language and the child's English proficiency.

Knowing where each student is in his English acquisition allows you to plan minilessons, confer with students, and set up supportive partnerships more strategically. Assessing your students' language proficiency, just as you assess their reading skills, allows you to identify goals and expectations that you will help them work toward in reading workshop. Ninety percent of the language we have is acquired over time. So knowing what areas of language your ELLs know—for example, conversational English versus academic English—will help you coach your students during reading time. For language they don't know yet, you can create partnerships in which they will hear those parts of language in context, and you can use those parts of language with kids during conferring and small-group sessions. Identifying language that kids use but confuse can help you identify goals that you can work on with kids, encouraging them to use those words with more effectiveness in their talk (and their writing about reading).

Most school districts have a formal language assessment, but you are able to collect language samples from your English language learners every day in the reading workshop. Every time a student talks during the minilesson, during partnership time, and during small-group work and conferring, you

can consider her language skills and needs. Many days you will also have examples of the student's writing about reading to consider. The more you listen to the language she uses throughout the day, in different contexts, the more you will be able to identify where she needs to move next linguistically and support her in reaching that goal.

Each of the components of a reading workshop can be altered to provide ELLs with the language support they need. Most language learners go through predictable stages of language acquisition as they move to full fluency in English. When you plan the reading workshop, you need to think about how you are going to meet your children's needs as they develop English language skills and how you are going to adjust your expectations while children are moving toward full fluency. Methods such as shared reading and interactive writing can provide immersion and practice in grammar and language, in addition to fluency work, word work, and comprehension. These structures draw on students' ideas, language, and vocabulary, resulting in the creation of more texts students know how to read independently. These texts can be copied and placed in students' book baggies for use during independent reading, and students can also create approximations of these texts during writing workshop. You'll always want to consider vocabulary—both content vocabulary (Which words that students need to know are specific to the content of this lesson?) and academic vocabulary (Which words that run across many disciplines can be taught in this lesson?). All students who are learning English benefit from targeted instruction in a few vocabulary words with extended time to study these words across a period of time—say, a week. They benefit from seeing these words illustrated, generating (or being provided with) examples and nonexamples, and using these words in conversation and in writing.

Let's think now about specific ways each of the components of the reading workshop can be altered just a bit so that the workshop as a whole is especially supportive for ELLs at different stages of English language acquisition.

Support the preproduction and early production stages of learning English.

When students are in the first few stages of language acquisition (the silent period, called the preproduction stage, or the early production stages), they are generally working on learning such things as common nouns, prepositions, pronouns, and present tense. To support these students, make your teaching and the words you use as clear as possible. You will want to help students build language by exposing them to language they can understand. Let's consider some ways you can make your teaching and talk more comprehensible to these learners.

Use visual examples in your teaching.

You might, for example, put up an illustration of one of the characters your student is discussing or an image from a book that captures some of the information about the character. Or you might sketch an abstract concept to make the meaning clearer to students. You might even try using your whole body when teaching a lesson, becoming highly animated. This helps not only because animated teaching can grab and take hold of students' attention, but also because doing so makes your teaching and language more comprehensible. Use gestures, facial expressions, and intonation to dramatize your teaching and talk to help make it more comprehensible. Recruit students to join you in these dramatizations, acting out new vocabulary words or becoming characters and role-playing their feelings.

Modify your minilessons to be as concise as possible.

If you are working with a large ELL population, you will likely want to trim the minilessons in this series. Make a special point of using examples that children can relate to. It's also helpful to repeat the teaching point more often with children who are learning English. Similarly, when asking children to turn and talk, it can help to set them up with cue cards. In a lesson on considering author's choices, for example, you might give them cards that say "The author wrote/drew . . . ," "This makes me think . . . ," and so forth.

Weave a double active engagement into some of your minilessons.

Some teachers find that if they've demonstrated something slightly more complex and want children to learn from their example, children profit from first repeating the teacher's model before they apply these principles to another section of text or their own book. This leads some teachers to set up a double active engagement within many minilessons.

Provide readers with topic-based text sets.

You might find it useful to provide students with text sets of leveled books about a topic. Within a baggie of books on the topic "food," for example, readers might encounter the words *lunch*, *eats*, and *hungry* several times.

Days with Frog and Toad	
Character	Ideas
Toad 	• Toad is grumpy. • Toad cares about what other people think. • Toad is a good friend.
Frog 	• Frog is considerate. • Frog is hard working. • Frog is a good friend.

FIG. 14–1

Repeated exposure to words supports students in the early stages of learning English in building vocabulary. When introducing a new baggie of books to a reader, you might preteach a few words using labeled pictures to help the reader access the texts. To prepare these baggies, lay out the bin of books a reader is reading, and look for similarities. You might create simple text sets on food, families, animals, homes, sports, cities, and more.

Do shared reading to support fluency, comprehension, and word work.

Some educators think of this as a method generally used with primary students, but the truth is that shared reading can be extremely potent for upper-grade students as well. Shared reading can be done with the whole class, but in particular, this can be a method of small-group work that is especially powerful for your English language learners at every level. You might find it helpful to use the same text across, say, five days, each day planning

to support students in studying the text for something new—comprehension on day 1, fluency work on day 2, word work on day 3, vocabulary on day 4, and higher-level comprehension on day 5. With your preproduction students, you will want to choose a text that is very visual and that offers the kind of language they most need to see—common nouns, present tense, and so on. Shared reading can be done with fiction, informational texts, poems, songs, even small snippets of text that the teacher makes up. It is especially powerful if students bring their own books to the shared reading lesson, so that at the end, they can look at their independent reading to try some of the same work, perhaps asking, "Do I see any of those same nouns and verbs in my book?"

Provide opportunities for listening and learning the social language of the reading workshop.

Children who are in the preproduction or early production stages of learning English will have few oral English skills, but they will be listening carefully, trying to interpret what is going on around them. It is okay for children to be quiet at this stage, and it is important to understand that they are taking in a lot of information. The English words, phrases, and sentences that will make sense to them first will probably be the predictable sentences related to concrete classroom activities, such as "Get your books," "Start reading," "You can go to your seat now," and "Let's gather in the meeting area."

Opportunities for listening, really listening, are important, and the expectation that these children will participate in the comings and goings of the class spotlights the importance of them learning the social language that is most within their grasp. It is important that these children are being told, "Get out your book baggie" and "Let's gather in the meeting area" (with accompanying gestures) and that they are expected to do all these things along with the others.

Establish partnerships and triads that support ELLs' burgeoning language development.

Language is learned through interactions with others. The reading workshop is an especially rich context for language development because children are not only reading and listening, but they are also talking—and much of that talk happens in the small, supportive structures of partnerships. Eventually, these partnerships will give children important opportunities to discuss their ideas about texts, but when children are in the preproduction stage of learning English, a partnership with one other child could make the child at the early

FIG. 14–2

production stage feel trapped, like a deer in the headlights, with nowhere to hide. Still, it is crucial that new arrivals are expected to join into the class as best they can right from the start. There is never a time when new arrivals sit on the edge of the community, watching. Instead, the rug spot for the new arrival needs to be right in the center of the meeting area, and from the start, when children turn and talk during the active engagement section of a mini-lesson, these children must know that they belong to a conversational group.

Children in the early stages of learning English benefit from being in triads, not partnerships. Ideally one child in that triad will share the new arrival's native language but be more proficient in English, and the other child will be a native speaker of English (and a language model). Make use of every opportunity possible to pair your students learning English with the strongest English language models in your class. Granted, children who are in the pre-production stage of learning English will mostly listen. You can teach their more English-proficient partners how to use lots of gestures and to ask the child questions that can be answered with a yes or a no, a nod or a head shake.

You will want to coach your kids on how to work together in various configurations in the classroom. Many students benefit from meeting often with a peer to read pages of their books together or talk about them. These conversations not only give them valuable feedback, but they also create opportunities for comprehensible language input from a peer. This is a good use of partner time in both the upper-grade and lower-grade classrooms.

Provide your ELLs opportunities to read in both their home language and in English.

When a child in the first stages of acquiring English arrives in a classroom, the first goal is to make sure that child is immediately active and interactive. If this child is literate in his home language, then by all means it is important for him to read (and to write) in that language in school. If there are people in the classroom or the school who can speak the child's home language, you can rely on this buddy to convey to the child the kind of text that the class is reading in this unit and some of the main aspects of that type of reading. For example, this buddy might convey, "We are reading stories and thinking about the people who are in them. We are trying to say ideas we have about the people in the stories."

Whether or not the new arrival is literate in his home language, you will want that child also to have opportunities to begin doing some reading in English. Some teachers find that it helps for these children to have time slots for home-language reading and for English reading, with the child perhaps starting the reading workshop with fifteen minutes to read in his home language. During this time, the child can read with volume that is comparable to other children and build his identity as a child who reads a lot. Then, the child can transition to reading books in English.

Usually we start by asking the child who is in the early stages of learning English to read texts that are very short and have recognizable patterns when reading in English. These texts are generally filled with pictures that support readers in making sense of what the text says, often before they can even read all the words. This, of course, is reminiscent of what we ask kindergarten and first-grade children to do. There is nothing "elementary" about learning a second language, and yet taking children new to English through the progression of work that younger children in a reading workshop experience has all sorts of advantages. After a child has read at one level for a bit, you can informally or formally assess the child and then move the child to the next level with a transitional book baggie that contains the child's previous level and current level. If possible, providing students with theme-based books can be very supportive. These children need the same kinds of methods that are so powerful with primary readers. You might find it helpful to do interactive writing in small groups with English language learners, specifically creating writing that matches the language goals for a group of students. This interactive writing can take the form of books that can then be added to a child's book baggie, and the student can read these books in addition to others. The advantage to this is that the story or information text can be tailored to student interests or home culture.

Plan instruction with your ESL instructor to maximize learning in the reading workshop.

If you have children who are in the early stages of English acquisition, it is especially important to provide them with extra help understanding the content of a minilesson. If there is an English as a second language teacher who is willing to provide support, this can also be extremely beneficial. Some ESL teachers "push in" to classrooms; some ESL teachers "pull out" children for work in the ESL room. While not always possible, we recommend that ELLs remain in the classroom to maximize interaction and instructional opportunities. But, in either case, working in tandem with your ESL teacher will benefit your ELLs.

If classroom teachers and ESL teachers have opportunities to plan together, the ESL teacher can support the children during reading workshop by preteaching the concepts and developing the vocabulary necessary to understand what will be taught in the minilesson. For example, if the minilesson will teach children how to read looking for main ideas and support ideas, the ESL teacher might use a nonfiction content-area book and lots of gestures to convey that the title of the book is the main idea or the big idea, and then to convey that some of the subtitles are support ideas (or smaller ideas). The teacher could reinforce the concept of ordination and subordination (without using those terms) by showing that if the classroom represents a big topic, the library area could represent a subtopic.

Many ESL teachers also work with groups of students to help target specific parts of language. They may use shared writing or interactive writing as a way to build language structures that relate to the unit of study that students are in. Many teachers also then conduct group conferences with students who are working on the same parts of language.

Support the later stages of learning English.

It is important to celebrate the work that children at this stage of early emergent English are producing, focusing on the content of their speaking and writing about reading, not only on the correctness of the syntax. These children are taking risks, and your job is to help them to feel successful, while also accelerating their forward progress. There are many ways you can tailor your teaching to provide particular support to students at these stages of English language acquisition.

Move students in this stage from triads to partnerships or pair them with an early emergent ELL.

As children begin to acquire more fluency in English, they will be better able to understand written and spoken English when they have concrete contexts (pictures, actions, sounds, and so on). As they develop these proficiencies, you might move them from triads to partnerships, or you might nudge them to become one of the more vocal members of a triad, with a new preproduction ELL joining in as best as she can. These learners will not always use correct syntax, but it is important to know they can and must participate fully in partnership work. Remember that all language learners need the best language models possible. So keep this in mind as you determine your partnerships and triads.

Extend the language ELLs are producing.

As children become more proficient in English, their answers to questions will become more extended, even though their hold on English grammar and vocabulary will still be approximate. Again, partners (and teachers) can be coached to realize that this is not a time for correcting grammar. Instead, it is a time for expanding on what the child says. If the child points to a picture in her book and says, "Shark," then you'll want to expand on this. "That's a shark?" Pause for a nod. "Sharks," pointing, "have sharp teeth?" Point again and wait for another nod. "Yes, you're right. What else do you notice about them?" Gesture to illustrate that the question pertains to sharks' bodies. If the child isn't sure how to answer, you can eventually supply options. "They have tails, right?" pointing, "And fins," pointing. "What else?"

Scaffold children's thinking and writing about reading with conversational prompts.

To help children bring a growing repertoire of language from the minilessons into their independent work, you might scaffold the thinking and writing that children do (and also the conversations that children have during work time with their partners) by providing them with conversational prompts. For example, in a nonfiction research unit, you might teach children to write or say, "This text is about . . . and this text is about . . ." and then to shift and write or say, "One thing that is the same is . . ." The thought can be elaborated on when the child learns transition phrases such as *for example*. Children who are just learning English may rely heavily on these sorts of prompts, and you may even write cue cards for them.

Provide time for in-context grammar instruction.

While it is important to support children's attempts at emerging syntax, children also need instruction. For example, if children are reading biographies, you might teach and then post or create cards with transition words used to show that some time has passed, such as *then, later, after a while, years later*, and *next*. You might remind children that as they talk about a person's life, as they move from one moment in time to the next, they will often use a transition word to show that time has passed. To practice this, you might ask one partner to tell another what he did since walking into the classroom, remembering to insert words that show the passage of time. When partners meet, you can suggest that they talk through the sequence of events in each child's book, using transition words as the student progresses from telling one moment in time to the next. Each child will also benefit from having a list or cards of these transition words during work time.

Support students in acquiring academic English.

Children who are in later stages of language acquisition also need special support during reading workshop. When children reach intermediate fluency, they demonstrate increased levels of accuracy and are able to express their thoughts and feelings in English. They often sound as if their English is stronger than it is. Although these children may have developed conversational skills, often they still do not have academic English language skills. These children have a strong command of social English and can use English to chat with each other, to learn what the teacher expects them to do, and to talk about the events of the day. They may sound "fluent" in social conversation where complex structures can be avoided, but it is often difficult to follow them when they describe events from another time and place.

One way to determine whether a child needs help with academic English is to talk to the child about a story in a novel or about something that happened in another time and place. Invite the child to retell an episode from the book or from the child's experience; listen well. If the child's language is such that you have a hard time piecing together what she is trying to say, chances are good that this child needs support with academic English. The term *academic English* does not refer only to the language that is used in discipline-based studies. It refers to the language that a person must use to communicate about times and places that are distant and unfamiliar and that must be created with words.

The challenge for these children is that they now need to learn academic English; to do this, they need input from people who can provide strong language models and from skilled teachers.

Scaffold students' work on talking and writing about reading with description and specificity.

At this stage, it is very important for teachers to work on elaboration and specificity to help children use more descriptive and extended language. You might teach children adjectives or adverbs that can help make their language more specific (colors, textures, speeds, and so on). It is also important for these children to be partnered with children for whom English is their first language, children who can function as strong language models. Often, when teachers have a handful of children who are in the earliest stages of language acquisition and a handful who are further along, teachers devote most of their special attention to the children who are the newest to English. However, if you set new arrivals up with the proper invitations to work, support structures from other children, and ways of being interactive, they can learn a huge amount from each other. Meanwhile, you can devote additional time to children who have a good command of social English but not of academic English and need help that is less readily available from the peer group.

Provide explicit instruction in tenses, pronoun references, and connectives.

Children who need help with academic English will profit from explicit instruction tailored to their needs. For example, these children benefit from instruction in connectives. When English language learners learn to read as well as to write, connectives can become a source of confusion. Many readers assume that sentences are always arranged in chronological order, regardless of the connective used. That assumption may be incorrect, however, in a sentence such as "I went to the office because the principal called for me over the PA system." In small-group instruction, then, you will want to provide English language learners with explicit instruction to help them understand connectives, tenses, pronoun references, and so forth. This might be done with sentence strips and pocket charts, cards that get put in order or using mini-transcripts of student conversations that are corrected to show a before and after.

Support students in building vocabulary using their own reading as the context.

Of course, English language learners also need support in developing a rich vocabulary, and again, these children benefit from explicit instruction. If a child overuses a word such as *nice* or *kind*, you will want to help him learn that there are many different, more precise words he could use. Is the character lovely? Impressive? Unusual? Dignified? Compassionate? Some teachers help children to develop word files, with the overused word at the center of a card and five variations of that word around the edges. Remind children to keep these cards on hand throughout the day and look for opportunities to use specific words orally. Some teachers even ask children to place a checkmark beside a word each time they use it orally. Illustrated charts, such as those showing feelings or traits, can be supportive. It can be extra engaging when the students pose for the pictures. You will find it useful to limit the number of new words introduced each week and to provide opportunities across the week for students to use the new words.

Similarly, if children are reading about a particular subject, the teacher or an English-speaking buddy may want to help the child build a domain-specific vocabulary to draw upon as she talks and writes about that reading. If the child is reading about the American Revolution, she would benefit from having lots of conversations about this topic, using terms such as *loyalist*, *patriot*, *British*, and *King George*, but also *revolution*, *unfair*, *furious*. Of course, this sort of vocabulary work is essential for any English language learner, but it can

provide extra language support to the English language learner who is ready to learn precise vocabulary.

Provide small-group instruction for students to learn figurative language.

Children learning academic English will also need support as they come to understand and use figurative language. Of course, literature is filled with metaphors and similes, as are the minilessons in this series. Children who are just on the brink of learning academic English will profit from some small-group instruction that gives them access to literary devices. Again, shared reading can be a wonderful method to support students in studying, reading, and discussing figurative language. Word sorts where students read an idiom or phrase and determine whether it is positive or negative give students exposure to new phrases in a fun way. You might even decide to introduce students to a new phrase each week, challenging them to use that phrase whenever they can across the week and then to add it to their bank of figurative phrases as the year continues.

Tailor your teaching to support reading goals—and language goals.

When you approach a unit of study, you need to think about the language needs of children acquiring English and ask yourself, "What are the language skills that children need to have to understand the work they are being asked to do?" You need to think not only about the reading skills and strategies that will be developed in a unit, but also about the language skills the unit will support. You need to think about the vocabulary, idiomatic expressions, connectives, conjunctions, and grammar you want children to develop in a unit. There has to be a plan for content and a plan for language, side by side.

When approaching a unit on nonfiction reading, for example, you can anticipate that you'll be teaching children how to explain, describe, compare, categorize, and question. It's likely that they'll benefit from learning connectives such as *if*, *when*, *because*, *for example*, *another example*, and so forth. You can plan that you might provide scaffolds such as a chart of phrases, and you can know in advance that children may need help with instructional terms such as *fact*, *example*, *type*, *reason*, and *description*. You know you may teach the language of comparison, including, for example, the use of the *-er* and *-est* word endings, as in *big*, *bigger*, *biggest*.

The power of written curriculum is that you and a group of colleagues can hold your hopes for teaching in your hands and talk and think together about how you can take your own best ideas and make them better. One of the most important ways to make your teaching stronger is to think, "How can we give all children access to this teaching?" The wonderful thing about a workshop is that it is incredibly supportive for English language learners, but if you bring your best ideas to the table, you can make the reading workshop even more supportive.

We have come to realize one thing above all in our work—that assessments of our students' learning say as much about our teaching as they do about our students' skills. Perhaps more. We cannot simply look at low scores, at students reading far below grade level, and say, "Well, these students don't have the background," or "Hmm, . . . these students don't have the brains or the ethic for success." What we must say is "What can we do to teach these students more effectively?" And we must ask, "Have we granted each student in our care every possible opportunity to grow? Every possible support?" Adjusting and differentiating your teaching across all realms of your reading workshop (full class, individual, and small group) will provide your students with everything they need to have success in their writing lives, both inside and outside your classroom walls.

Chapter 15

Authoring Curriculum

THIS SERIES will have done its job well if it not only helps you to teach the units described herein but also helps you and your colleagues author your own units of study. In this chapter, I'll help you do that curriculum development work.

As I do this, I'll be drawing on my experience teaching a graduate course every year designed to help people author upper-grade reading units of study and my experience working in schools where it is commonplace for the teachers on a grade level to develop one or sometimes two brand-new units of study each year while also returning to other familiar units. Another way to prepare for authoring your own lessons and units is to work with the letters to teachers that appear two or three times in each unit. These letters suggest sequences, strategies, and tools to help you begin developing your own lessons.

SUGGESTIONS FOR BEGINNING TO PLAN YOUR OWN UNITS OF STUDY

Before reading this chapter, it will help if you have studied some of the alternative units of study in this series. You'll see plans for units of study on all sorts of topics—critical reading, humor, tackling complex perspectives, content-area reading, social issues, and mystery. The unit plans are elaborated upon within the Online Resources. Those units are not entirely fleshed out, so one possibility for your curriculum development work will be to start by taking one of those units as a starting place. You can borrow the parts of the unit that work for you, develop other parts that seem to you to be missing, and in general use the work that has already been done as training wheels to help you and your colleagues gather momentum as developers of reading units of study.

Alternatively, you can take a topic that has not been addressed and aim to produce a plan for a unit that resembles the plans we've included in *If . . . Then . . . Curriculum: Assessment-Based Instruction, Grades 3–5*. Notice that these plans aren't fleshed out yet. Yours probably won't be either until you and your children actually live your way into those plans. Even then, they'll be revised multiple times as you cycle through the units in subsequent years, learning ways to anticipate challenges your students encounter, to tuck in more tips, and to differentiate more thoughtfully.

Before you embark on this curriculum development work, I should point out to you that the process is a recursive project, requiring enormous amounts of revision. You will not be able to progress through one step, the next, and the next in sequence, finishing one step once and for all before continuing to the next step. Realize, too, that if you spend five days on this effort, you probably won't write your first minilesson until day three, because there are many decisions to make and work to accomplish before writing even the first minilesson.

DECIDE ON YOUR CONTENT AND GOALS

Of course, the first thing you will need to do is decide what you will teach. This is no easy decision, especially because you'll need to decide both what the kids will *think* you are teaching and what you are actually teaching. For example, the children will think of the fourth unit as one on historical fiction; to us, it is really a unit on tackling complex books, interpreting reading critically, and on cross-text synthesis. We could just as easily have taught historical fiction in a way that highlighted the skills of close reading and envisioning. (After all, readers need to be able to create a whole other world as they read, and to do this, readers need to read extremely closely.) So when thinking about what you are teaching, keep in mind that although kids may think that the unit of study teaches them to read a certain kind of *book*, you know that this is actually a unit on a certain kind of *skill*, or on several skills.

There are lots of wonderful units of study that are begging to be written. For example, I think it would be wonderful to develop a unit of study on the following, among other topics:

- Reading with an awareness of multiple perspectives

- Nonfiction author studies

- Intratextuality (finding connections within texts)

- Using writing as a tool for thinking as readers

If you and your colleagues author one of these units or any other one, please consider sharing what you do with the community by sending it to me to be included on the Teachers College Reading and Writing Project's website.

WHAT CAN YOUR STUDENTS DO AND ALMOST DO?

In thinking about what you will teach, think about what your students can do and can almost do. You'll no doubt recoil from the question, thinking, "My students are all different. I can't talk about what 'they' can do as if there is some amalgamated 'they.'" Of course, I understand that, but students are very amenable to instruction, and most of the readers in a class will learn to do roughly similar work—some with a bit more finesse, some with less. Of course, they'll do that work with the level of text complexity they can read. The fact of the matter is, you can probably generalize about the sorts of predicting work that most of your readers do or the sorts of theories that most of your readers grow about characters.

In other words, the kind of thinking work that students can and cannot yet do with texts is often a function of prior instruction and history. For example, as a class, many of your readers may have grown accustomed to reading the dutiful half hour a night at home, and many may not yet carry books everywhere, finding stolen moments throughout their days when they can catch ten minutes for reading. Some of your students may be accustomed to jotting Post-its as they read, but for most of them, those Post-its might capture what they saw in the text that was significant, but not yet what they thought in response to what they saw.

To think about lines of development or about skills and strategies that might pertain to your unit, it helps to think about reading skills. Here is one (of many) possible list of reading skills:

- Decoding

- Monitoring for sense

- Predicting

- Envisioning or building a mental model

- Using a knowledge of story structure or text structure to construct meaning

- Making meaning through personal response
- Inferring
- Synthesizing
- Asking questions
- Interpreting
- Reading critically
- Making meaning through inter- and intratextuality

Remember, you will also need to teach life habits to your readers. You'll want to teach habits such as these:

- Reading with stamina
- Developing relationships that support their reading
- Talking and thinking in response to reading
- Developing and revising theories as they read
- Talking and writing about their theories in persuasive ways
- Learning about a subject through reading
- Developing an understanding of literary terms and concepts
- Noticing and learning from an author's craftsmanship

WHICH TEXTS WILL YOUR STUDENTS NEED, AND AT WHICH LEVELS?

As you think about your students and what they can and can't quite do, think also about the texts that you have available related to the area in which you are designing a unit. For example, if you are considering writing a unit of study in which you channel students to read nonfiction texts pertaining to a particular topic, such as the Civil War, then you will want to think about the texts you have available in that genre, on that topic, with the text levels that your kids can handle. Remember Richard Gentry's research that suggests that if a student is reading a book such as *Stone Fox*, the student needs to read three of those books a week, twelve in a month. For readers who are reading level S texts, it is somewhat unlikely that you have twelve nonfiction books on the Civil War (let alone more than that so that readers can make choices from among them).

One solution might be for students to do lots of work with texts that are easy for them, thereby spending some of the month reading the books you have for less proficient readers. Then, too, perhaps over the month, as students' expertise develops, they can progress to reading texts a notch harder. Another solution might be for students to read relevant historical fiction as well as a nonfiction book. A third solution might be for the unit to channel students to read nonfiction texts that are related in peripheral ways to the Civil War, such as books on race or war or American geography. Then again, you may simply decide your resources can't sustain a unit that is focused in that way.

You will also need to make some decisions about specific kinds of texts. For example, if you are teaching a unit on interpretation and believe that interpretation is best done when a reader is reading the second half of a text, then you start the unit by asking readers to reread the final portion of books that they already know well.

You will also need to decide on the read-aloud texts you will use to demonstrate throughout the unit. Typically, you will select two short texts and a chapter book to use in the unit. You'll need to read aloud parts of the chapter book outside of reading workshop time. You might, for example, read Chapter 1 and Chapter 2 of the novel outside the reading workshop in read-aloud time, and then use the start of Chapter 3 in the reading workshop minilesson. Next, you might read the rest of Chapter 3 and Chapter 4 outside the reading workshop and then bring the book back in, relying on reading Chapter 5 in the unit's next minilesson. Typically about half of a unit's minilessons will be built around the chapter book that threads through the unit.

HOW WILL YOU SUPPORT KIDS' ONGOING READING?

No matter how important your unit will be, children's ongoing reading is even more important. Above all, you need to be sure your teaching doesn't *hurt* students' reading. If you were thinking of designing a monthlong unit involving poetry, for example, you probably need to angle the unit to teach students that reading poetry can alter how they read any well-written piece of literature—or you'll need some other way to make sure that your unit doesn't constrain the volume of reading that children do. This same issue comes up if you consider a unit of study on reading fairy tales (see *If . . . Then . . . Curriculum: Assessment-Based Instruction, Grades 3–5*) or reading the newspaper.

Keep in mind also the research from Gentry that suggests kids need at least ninety minutes of actual eyes-on-print reading every day; make sure that your unit doesn't channel your students to read such short texts that the volume of their reading takes a giant hit. Usually you can get around this problem by angling the unit to show students that intensive work reading the shorter texts can affect the way they read longer texts.

The larger point is this: you must have humility and common sense enough to keep in mind that your teaching is not as important as your kids' reading work. Your teaching needs to support your students doing the reading and thinking and talking about texts that they need to do. Start planning your unit by focusing less on the question "What will I say in my first minilesson?" and more on the question "What will my students be reading and doing across this stretch of time?"

More specifically, this means focusing first and most urgently on designing structures that enable your kids to read up a storm, reading tons and tons of texts they can and want to read—and to read as thoughtfully as possible.

HOW WILL YOU STRUCTURE THE READING WORKSHOP?

As you continue planning your unit, think about the ways you will structure the entire reading workshop.

- Will the workshop end with ten minutes for sharing, and will that time include partnership work?

- Will that final time for talking about reading need to be longer?

- Will you want to give your students five minutes to reread and jot in preparation for their clubs?

- Will the clubs meet daily? Twice a week?

- Will every club meet on the same day, or will they be on different days?

- Will your minilessons support reading and your mid-workshop teaching points support clubs, or will club days be structured so that minilessons support clubs and students go from minilessons to clubs, reading afterward?

- Will kids be reading the same books at home and at school, as is usually the case, or are there reasons to alter that?

- Will your partnerships be same-book partnerships, or will it only be your students who struggle with reading who are in same-book partnerships?

- Will the other partnerships be swap-book partnerships?

- What sort of writing about reading do you envision kids doing, and how will you make this work as thoughtful as possible without letting it overwhelm reading?

- How will you differentiate instruction, and especially, how will you provide your below grade level readers with the regular support they need?

- How will you make use of extra adults if you have access to them?

- How will after-school work or interventions support the unit?

As you think about the structures that you'll provide your students, you'll be thinking about ways structures can evolve over time to support increasing rigor and also about ways structures can be differentiated to support diverse learners. So, for example, children might read books at home and in school for three days without discussing them and then meet for a twenty- to thirty-minute discussion. Then again, you might worry that children won't make good use of a twenty- to thirty-minute time block for conversation. It is much easier to read books for twenty minutes, meet to talk for five minutes, resume reading for another twenty minutes, and then talk for another five minutes and do that every day. Work that encompasses more time, more texts, more people, and more independence tends to be more difficult to do well.

DRAFT AND REVISE MULTIPLE PLANS FOR THE PROGRESSION OF YOUR UNIT

After thinking through the content and goals of your unit, you'll be ready to think about the sequence of instruction you'll provide. You definitely will not want to begin by writing a minilesson! Instead, think about the specific goals your teaching will aim to accomplish and the journey of work and study that the unit will support. To do this work, focus on the learning progression for the skills you hope to teach. Be sure that you keep in mind that teaching involves inviting kids to do the same important work, then helping them ratchet the level of that work up over time. It is important to have the trajectory along which your students will develop in mind.

For example, if this is a unit on asking questions and thinking deeply about texts, you need to decide if you want to begin by showing kids the sorts of questions they might ask as they read. Will you approach this by showing them the questions they could ask at the beginning, the middle, and the end of stories? Or will you move them from asking questions that allow them to grasp the surface level of the story toward asking more provocative and deeper questions? Will you plan your unit so that readers work at first to ask and carry questions on the run as they read, and progress toward them learning to ask questions that support sustained rereading and cross-text comparisons?

It is almost inevitable that when you approach a topic, one progression of study will spring to mind fairly quickly. Delay deciding on that pathway to allow yourself time to entertain other options. In the end, many of the possibilities that you consider and reject will end up giving you ways to enrich your strongest readers, support your most struggling ones, and give nuance and depth to whatever route you select.

CHALLENGE YOUR OWN PLANS

The process of weighing and rejecting options requires that you challenge your own ideas for your teaching. I encourage you to learn to be hard on your wonderful ideas:

- **Are you reteaching?** For example, oftentimes you'll find that you invent teaching plans that essentially reteach what many students can already do, instead of finding a way to tap those capacities and then extend them. Be willing to see that your plan doesn't take your students beyond what they already know how to do.

- **Are you telling, not teaching?** On the other hand, if you are really teaching students to do something that many of them cannot yet do, remember that telling is not teaching. Telling students to ask deep questions will not mean that suddenly they can do it! Whereas you may have imagined that work requiring a few days, it may in fact require a few weeks, and planning for this teaching may require you to think much more deeply about the smaller steps that you'll need to help your students take.

- **Do students have enough time to read?** You'll also want to guard against your fancy unit doing students harm as readers. That is apt to happen if your good ideas crowd out their time for reading. If you are asking students to devote a lot of their reading time to something other than reading—even if it is something related to reading such as writing about reading or dancing about reading or painting about reading—be sure you check yourself. Is this truly what your kids most need?

- **Are you assigning work on teaching readers to know how to do things now and always?** One of the most common problems teachers encounter is that they often realize in retrospect that their minilessons are actually attempts to assign work, asking readers to jump through the hoop of the day, instead of teaching readers a skill that they will draw on repeatedly.

DECIDE ON THE PARTS OF YOUR UNIT, AND BEGIN DRAFTING TEACHING POINTS

Once you've begun to think about a progression for your unit, I'd suggest you study the way other units of study progress. Look over multiple units, including those in *If . . . Then . . . Curriculum: Assessment-Based Instruction, Grades 3–5*. Try to get a sense for the parts in the units of study that others have designed so that you can internalize the text structure for this unique sort of text. When you study other people's units of study, you will probably see that there is a certain way that units tend to go.

The next thing you will probably do is begin to plan your own parts of the unit and start the long process of generating possible teaching points. I'd plan a good deal of this before starting to write a single minilesson, although once I do start writing minilessons, I'm generally back at work on the sequence of teaching points.

When you begin to hone in on what your teaching points might be and how those teaching points might fit into the parts in the unit, you'll quickly find that the first lesson or two in a unit poses special challenges. These first lessons need to rally kids to the new work. This is sometimes tricky because the unit may actually require students to recall some stuff they already know and can do, but asking readers to recall previous work isn't necessarily the most exciting way to create a drumroll for new work. I try to find ways for the first minilessons to invite kids into the exciting work of the new unit. Often the first minilesson involves a short text—a picture book, a short story, a poem, a book written for much younger kids, a snippet of video—so that it can give students an intense overview of the new work.

Then minilessons two and three might be the ones that remind students of relevant work they learned earlier, perhaps bringing old charts forward and showing students how to use these previous lessons in this new context. The message during the first few days of a new unit tends to be "Give this a go! Try it!" I tend to invite kids to approximate the new work, doing it as best they can with enthusiasm and confidence.

You won't be surprised that after a generous "Give this a go!" the minilessons tend to slow down to ratchet up the level of what students are doing and to address the fine points of how to do this work. At this point, the unit will tend to take a turn toward a second part, suggesting that readers can actually aim toward more and do more. Then, at some point, the unit will start to head down its final stretch.

Often this final stretch involves work that goes across several texts or across larger social configurations, or work that encompasses more of students' time (as in work that extends beyond the reading workshop). There is usually less scaffolding provided and more independence expected. The message is "You can do this work for the rest of your lives, even when this unit is over."

INTEGRATE THE READ-ALOUD TEXT INTO YOUR PLAN

Once you have a general plan for the way the parts in your unit might conceivably go, try reading the read-aloud text and other texts that your kids will be reading, spying on the mind work that you find yourself doing. Note what seems to you to be essential mind work that almost any proficient reader would be apt to do. Try to think of the tiny individual steps that you take to do that mind work. Think, too, about how your students would be apt to do this differently than you. In this way, you are uncovering some of the skills and strategies that you'll probably teach in the unit.

As you imagine the progression of work that might unfold across the unit, remember that kids will not proceed in sync with your progress through the read-aloud book. For example, you may read a mystery aloud over ten days. You can't, on Day Ten, teach the class how to read the end of a mystery as if they're all doing this in their books on that same day. Those who are reading easier mysteries will have reached the end of their first mystery on the second

day of the unit! Usually, remembering that readers will not progress in sync with you will nudge you to teach what readers do at the end of books much sooner than you might otherwise teach this, which often supports the decision to start the unit by reading aloud a short text.

DRAFT TEACHING POINTS, CRAFT ANCHOR CHARTS

Most of us work very hard on our teaching points, hoping to make them memorable and helpful. This work is done concurrently with an effort to think about anchor charts. What are the big skills you'll be helping kids to work toward, and what are the specific strategies you'll suggest they could choose between? What charts might thread through the entire unit?

DRAFT THE MINILESSONS

Now you will be ready to plan your actual sequence of teaching points and to plan the minilessons themselves. Remember as you do this that you can usually teach two or three teaching points in a day—one through the minilesson, another through the mid-workshop teaching point, and a third through the teaching share.

You are ready to write some minilessons. I've described the architecture of a minilesson in the chapter on minilessons, and that chapter will serve you well with this portion of curriculum development. But here are a few general words of advice.

First, plan to actually write your teaching point, working with the wording of it a bit while keeping some exemplar teaching points close at hand. It is extremely easy to forget ourselves and shift from teaching strategies that readers can use across books toward assigning them an activity to do for the day. There's a world of difference between the two.

Second, try composing your minilessons by saying them aloud to a pretend group of kids rather than composing while sitting at the computer. You'll find your teaching is more vital and alive if you plan with your kids foremost in your mind, thinking above all about reaching them, teaching them. If you think of this as a new kind of writing, you may get too writerly. Realize that usually the times when you demonstrate a strategy by thinking aloud need to be kept extremely brief. Kids do not want to sit and listen to you yammer on about whatever free associations come to mind as you read. If you are going to think aloud in front of the kids, usually two or three sentences of this will suffice to make your point; then stop and freeze-frame what you have done.

Finally, plan on discarding whatever you work so hard to plan, because when we teach, we take our cues from kids. You'll approach teaching with your best laid plans, and kids will surprise you. They'll struggle in ways you couldn't have imagined possible, and they'll generate insights that turn your thinking upside down. Expect the unexpected and embrace it.

References

Allen, Debbie. 2000. *Dancing in the Wings*. New York: Penguin.

Allington, Richard. 2002a. *Big Brother and the National Reading Curriculum: How Ideology Trumped Evidence*. Portsmouth, NH: Heinemann.

Allington, Richard. 2002b. "The Six Ts of Effective Elementary Literacy Instruction." Reading Rockets. *Phi Delta Kappan*. Available at http://www.readingrockets.org/article/six-ts-effective-elementary-literacy-instruction.

Allington, Richard L. 2002c. "What I've Learned about Effective Reading Instruction from a Decade of Studying Exemplary Elementary Classroom Teachers." *The Phi Delta Kappan* 83(10):740–47. JSTOR. Web.

Allington, R. L. 2008. "Response to Intervention: How to Make It Work." Speech, Teachers College Reading and Writing Project Principals as Curricular Leaders Conference, New York.

Allington, R. L. 2011. *What Really Matters for Struggling Readers. Designing Research-Based Programs*, 3d ed. Boston: Pearson.

Allington, R. L., and P. Johnston. 2002. "What Do We Know about Exemplary Fourth-Grade Teachers and Their Classrooms?" In C. Roller, ed. *Learning to Teach Reading: Setting the Research Agenda*, pp. 150–65. Newark, DE: International Reading Association.

Applegate, K. A. 2007. *Home of the Brave*. New York: Holtzbrinck.

Barth, Roland. 2006. "Improving Relationships within the Schoolhouse." *Educational Leadership* 63(6):8–13.

Beers, K., and R. E. Probst. 2012. *Notice and Note*. Portsmouth, NH: Heinemann.

Bembry, K., H. Jordan, E. Gomez, M. Anderson, and R. Mendro. 1998. "Policy Implications of Long-Term Teacher Effects on Student Achievement." Paper presented at the Annual Meeting of the American Educational Research Association, San Diego, April 13–17.

Betts, E. A. 1946. *Foundations of Reading Instruction*. New York: American Book Company.

Bomer, Randy. 1995. *Time for Meaning: Crafting Literate Lives in Middle and High School*. Portsmouth, NH: Heinemann.

Calkins, L. 1994. *The Art of Teaching Writing*. Portsmouth, NH: Heinemann.

Calkins, Lucy. 2001. *The Art of Teaching Reading*. Boston: Allyn & Bacon Educational Publishers.

Clay, M. 1987. "Learning to Be Learning Disabled." *New Zealand Journal of Educational Studies* 22(2):155–73. Wellington: New Zealand. Available at http://www.nzcer.org.nz/pdfs/9500.pdf.

Clay, M. 2001. *Change over Time in Children's Literacy Development*. Portsmouth, NH: Heinemann.

Corcoran, T., F. A. Mosher, and A. Rogat. 2009. *Learning Progressions in Science: An Evidence-Based Approach to Reform* (CPRE Research Report #RR-63). Philadelphia: Consortium for Policy Research in Education.

Covey, Stephen. 2004. *The 7 Habits of Highly Effective People* (rev. ed.). New York: Free Press.

Creech, Sharon. 2003. *Love That Dog*. New York: HarperCollins.

Cunningham, A. E., and K. E. Stanovich. 1991. "Tracking the Unique Effects of Print Exposure in Children: Associations with Vocabulary, General Knowledge, and Spelling." *Journal of Educational Psychology* 83(2):264–74.

Curtis, Christopher Paul. 1999. *Bud, Not Buddy*. New York: Random House.

Darling-Hammond, L., B. Barron, P. D. Pearson, and A. Schoenfeld. 2008. *Powerful Learning: What We Know about Teaching for Understanding*. San Francisco: Jossey-Bass.

Darling-Hammond, L., and G. Sykes. 2003. "Wanted: A National Teacher Supply Policy for Education: The Right Way to Meet the 'Highly Qualified Teacher' Challenge." *Education Policy Analysis Archives*, Vol. 11.

Daro, P., F. A. Mosher, and T. Corcoran. 2011. *Learning Trajectories in Mathematics: A Foundation for Standards, Curriculum, Assessment, and*

Instruction (CPRE Research Report #68). Philadelphia, PA: Consortium for Policy Research in Education.

DiCamillo, Kate. 2001. *The Tiger Rising*. Somerville, MA: Candlewick.

Dillard, Annie. 1989. *The Writing Life*. New York: HarperCollins.

Dole, Janice A., Kathleen J. Brown, and Woodrow Trathen. 1996. "The Effects of Strategy Instruction on the Comprehension Performance of At-Risk Students." *Reading Research Quarterly* 31(1):62–88.

Duke, N. K., and D. Pearson. 2002. "Effective Practices for Developing Reading Comprehension." In A. E. Farstrup and S. J. Samuels, eds. *What Research Has to Say about Reading Instruction*, 3d ed. pp. 205–42. Newark, DE: International Reading Association.

Ehri, Linnea, Lois Dreyer, Bert Flugman, and Alan Gross. 2007. "Reading Rescue: An Effective Tutoring Intervention Model for Language-Minority Students Who Are Struggling Readers in First Grade." *American Educational Research Journal* 44(2):414–48.

Elley, W. B. 1989. "Vocabulary Acquisition from Listening to Stories." *Reading Research Quarterly* 24:174–87.

Flor Ada, Alma. 1993. *My Name Is Maria Isabel*. New York: Simon & Schuster.

Fountas, I. C., and G. S. Pinnell. 2012. *Genre Study: Teaching with Fiction and Nonfiction Books*. Portsmouth, NH: Heinemann.

Fullan, Michael, P. Hill, and C. Crévola. 2006. *Breakthrough*. Thousand Oaks, CA: Corwin.

Gardiner, John Reynolds. 1980. *Stone Fox*. New York: HarperCollins.

Gardner, John. 1991. *The Art of Fiction: Notes on Craft for Young Writers*. New York: Vintage.

Gipson, Fred. 1956. *Old Yeller*. New York: HarperCollins.

Gladwell, M. 2005. *Blink: The Power of Thinking without Thinking*. New York: Little, Brown and Company.

Guthrie, J., and N. Humenick. 2004. "Motivating students to read: evidence for classroom practices that increase reading motivation and achievement." In P. McCardle and V. Chhabra, eds. *The Voice of Evidence in Reading Research*, pp. 329–54. Baltimore: Brookes Publishing.

Hattie, J. 2008. *Visible Learning: A Synthesis of over 800 Meta-Analyses Relating to Achievement*. London: T & F Books.

Hayes, D., and M. Ward. 1992. "Learning from Texts: Effects of Similar and Dissimilar Features of Analogies in Study Guides." Paper presented at the 42nd Annual Meeting of the National Reading Conference, Dec. 2–5. San Antonio: Education Trust.

Hawthorne, Nathaniel. 1994. *The Scarlet Letter*. New York: Dover Publications.

Hesse, Karen. 1992. *Letters from Rifka*. New York: Macmillan.

Howe, James, and Melissa Sweet (illustrator). The Pinky and Rex series. New York: Simon & Schuster.

Johnston, Peter. 2004. *Choice Words: How Our Language Affects Children's Learning*. Portland, ME: Stenhouse.

Jukes, I., and T. McCain. 2002. "Living on the Future Edge." InfoSavvy Group and Cyster.

Kamil, M., and D. Lane. 1998. "Researching the Relation between Technology and Literacy: An Agenda for the 21st Century." In D. Reinking, M. C. McKenna, L. D. Labbo, and R. D. Kieffer, eds. *Handbook of Literacy and Technology: Transformations in a Post-Typographic World*, pp. 323–41. Mahwah, NJ: Erlbaum.

Krashen, S. D. 2004. *The Power of Reading: Insights from the Research*, 2d ed. Portsmouth, NH: Heinemann.

Lowry, Lois. 1989. *Number the Stars*. New York: Random House.

MacLachlan, Patricia. 1994. *Skylark*. New York: HarperCollins.

Marshall, James. 1972–1988. The George and Martha series. New York: Houghton Mifflin.

Mosher, F. A. 2011. *The Role of Learning Progressions in Standards-Based Education Reform* (CPRE Policy Brief RB-52). Available at http://www.cpre.org/role-learning-progressions-standards-based-education-reform.

National Endowment for the Arts. 2007. "To Read or Not to Read." Washington, DC.

No Child Left Behind Act of 2001, Pub. L. No. 107-110, 115 Stat. 1425.

O'Connor, R. E., K. M. Bell, K. R. Harty, L. K. Larkin, S. M. Sackor, and N. Zigmond. 2002. "Teaching Reading to Poor Readers in the Intermediate Grades: A Comparison of Text Difficulty." *Journal of Educational Psychology* 94:474–85.

Paterson, Katherine. 1987. *The Great Gilly Hopkins*. New York: HarperCollins.

Paterson, Katherine. 1977. *Bridge to Terabithia*. New York: HarperCollins.

Paterson, Katherine, and Jane Clark Brown. 1991. *The Smallest Cow in the World*. New York: HarperCollins.

Paulsen, Gary. 1987. *Hatchet*. New York: Simon & Schuster.

Paulsen, Gary. 1993. *The River*. New York: Random House.

Pearson, P. D., and M. Gallagher. 1983. "The Instruction of Reading Comprehension." *Contemporary Educational Psychology* 8:317–44.

Pearson, P. D., and L. Fielding. 1991. "Comprehension Instruction." In R. Barr, M. Kamil, P. Mosenthal, and P. D. Pearson, eds. *Handbook of Reading Research*, vol. II. White Plains, NY: Longman.

Peterson, R. 1992. *Life in a Crowded Place: Making a Learning Community*. Portsmouth, NH: Heinemann.

Pressley, M., A. Roehrig, L. Raphael, S. Dolezal, C. Bohn, L. Mohan, et al. 2003. "Teaching Processes in Elementary and Secondary Education." In W. M. Reynolds and G. E. Miller, eds. *Handbook of Psychology*, vol. 7: *Educational Psychology*, pp. 153–75. New York: John Wiley.

Pressley, Michael, and Peter Afflerbach. 1995. *Verbal Protocols of Reading: The Nature of Constructively Responsive Reading*. Hillsdale, NJ: Lawrence Erlbaum Associates.

Rebell, M., and J. Wolff. 2008. *Moving Every Child Ahead: From NCLB Hype to Meaningful Educational Opportunity*. New York: Teachers College Press.

Rivkin, Steven G., Eric A. Hanushek, and John F. Kain. 2005. "Teachers, Schools, and Academic Achievement." *Econometrica* 73(2):417–58.

Rosenshine, Barak. 2012. "Principles of Instruction: Research-Based Strategies that All Teachers Should Know." *American Educator* Spring:12–39.

Rylant, Cynthia, and S. D. Schindler (illustrator). 1998. *Every Living Thing*. New York: Simon & Schuster.

Rylant, Cynthia, and Mark Teague (illustrator). 1997. *Poppleton*. New York: Scholastic.

Sarason, Seymour. 1996. *Revisiting "The Culture of the School and the Problem of Change."* New York: Teachers College Press.

Shanahan, Timothy, Douglas Fisher, and Nancy Frey. 2012. "The Challenge of Challenging Texts." *Educational Leadership* 69(6):58–62.

Silverstein, Shel. 1974. "Invitation." In *Where the Sidewalk Ends*. New York: HarperCollins.

Smith, Doris Buchanan. 1973. *A Taste of Blackberries*. New York: HarperCollins.

Smith, M. C. 2000. "The Real-World Reading Practices of Adults." *Journal of Literacy Research* 32(1):25–52. doi:10.1080/10862960009548063.

Swanson, H., M. Hoskyn, and C. Lee. 1999. *Interventions for Students with Learning Disabilities: A Meta-Analysis of Treatment Outcomes*. New York: Guilford Press.

Teale, W. H. 1984. "Reading to Young Children: Its Significance for Literacy Development." In H. Goelman, A. A. Oberg, F. Smith, eds. *Awakening to Literacy*. Portsmouth, NH: Heinemann.

U.S. Department of Education. 1999. *NAEP Reading Report Card for the Nation*.

Venezky, R. L. 1982. "The Origins of the Present-Day Chasm between Adult Literacy Needs and School Literacy Instruction." *Visible Language* 16:112–27.

Vygotsky, L. 1978. "Interaction between Learning and Development." In *Mind in Society* (trans. M. Cole), pp. 79–91. Cambridge, MA: Harvard University Press.

White, E. B. 1952. *Charlotte's Web*. New York: HarperCollins.

Wood, George H., Linda Darling-Hammond, Monty Neill, and Pat Roschewski. 2007. "Refocusing Accountability: Using Local Performance Assessments to Enhance Teaching and Learning for Higher Order Skills." *FairTest*. The National Center for Fair and Open Testing.

Wood, D., J. Bruner, and G. Ross. 1976. "The Role of Tutoring in Problem Solving." *Journal of Child Psychology and Psychiatry* 17: 89–100.

Index

research phase (research-decide-compliment-teach conferences), 50–51, 59, 60–63
research teams, 28
research terms, 51–52
resources for enlivening conferences and small-group work
    building on evidence from reading logs, 87–88
    knowledge of different genres, 85–86
    and monitoring shared conversations, 90
    seeing patterns in running records, 86–87
    understanding work needed to read at different levels, 87
    using evidence from Post-its and notebook entries, 89
    using records of previous conferences and small-group work, 85
responsive teaching, 70–73, 141–42
revision, encouraging, 94–95
Rosenshine, Barak, 23
RTI (response to intervention) model, 142–43
rubrics, performance comparisons, 13
running records, 86–87, 142
Rylant, Cynthia, 97–98, 113

sad stories, reading aloud, 114
same-book partnerships, 33
Sarason, Seymour, 5, 42, 126
scaffolding
    approaches to, 144
    difficult texts, 129
    for emergent readers, 4–5
    for English language learners, 159
    gearing to individual needs, 78, 148–49
    for informational texts, 132
    prioritizing supports, 151–52
    and responsive teaching, 142
    during small-group work, 73, 78
    using visual texts/videos, 146–47
The Scarlet Letter (Hawthorne), 83
self-assessments, 13–14
self-concept, as readers, 4
setting, identifying during read-alouds, 116–17
Shanahan, T., 21
shared reading

for English language learners, 156
and love for reading, 2
share session, workshop closure, managing, 56–57
shared activities/collaborations, 32–33
Simon, Seymour, 135
small-group instruction
    for English language learners, 160
    enlivening, 70–71, 73, 84–90
    flexible approaches, 69–70
    guided reading, 72, 76–77
    and individual student's needs, 143
    managing, 55–56
    overview, 31–32
    planning, approaches to, 77–78
    responsive, 70–71, 78–81
    resources that support, 152
    RTI approach, 148–49
    strategy sessions, 78
    value of, 29
Smarter Balanced Assessment Consortium (SBAC), 3
standardized testing scores, 9
standards, high. See expectations of excellence
Stanovich, K. E., 24, 133–34
Stewart, Melissa, 138–40
Stone Fox (Gardiner)
    rereading at several time points, 42, 79
    time needed to read, 19, 164
strategy instruction
    applying to different genres and skill levels, 9
    explicit, importance, 22–23
    importance, 5
    during minilessons, 28, 42–44
    for reading informational texts, 132–33
    sharing strategies, 9
struggling readers
    and assessment-based instruction, 25
    high-success reading materials for, 20–21, 26, 150
    maintaining within regular classrooms, 25–26
    reading time, 149
    scaffolding, 4
student achievement
    and addressing individual needs, 78
    and assessment-based instruction, 24–25
    basic needs of readers, 17

book clubs, 105–106
and capacity to judge difficulty of texts, 129
and choice of reading material, 21, 29, 150
encouraging analytic approaches, 96
focusing on individual needs and goals, 144–46, 152, 160–61
fostering, 158–59
and identifying place along learning pathways, 89–90
and increasing complexity, 21–22
and life-long learning, 126
making compliments useful, 65–66
promoting excellence, high standards, 3–4, 126, 138
and reading logs, 87–88
and recognizing individual talents, 1, 4–5, 20–21, 141
and responsive teaching, 141–42
and self-assessments, 13–14
and structuring reading workshop, 49
and supporting all learners, 151–52
and time for reading, 18–19
Summer's Bloodiest Days: The Battle of Gettysburg as Told From All Sides (Weber), 101
Swanson, H., 20
swap-book partnerships, 28, 33

Tackling Complexity: Moving Up Levels of Nonfiction, 128
talking about books
    during book clubs, 108–10
    as evidence of fluency, 88
    informational texts, 130
    as key to literacy acquisition, 23
    during one-to-one conferences, 61–62
teachers, effective
    and assessment-based instruction, 24–25
    authoritarian approaches, 5
    and authoring units of study, 162–68
    and communities of practice, 9
    and effective classroom management, 49
    and finding artistry in teaching reading, 2
    and fostering love for reading, 1
    and knowing about available resources, 152–53
    and literacy acquisition, 17–18
    minimizing non-reading, non-writing activities, 19